Chandani Lokuge and Chris Ringrose (eds.)

Creative Lives

Interviews with Contemporary South Asian Diaspora Writers

With a foreword by Janet Wilson

STUDIES IN WORLD LITERATURE

Editors:
Prof Janet Wilson, University of Northampton, UK
Dr Chris Ringrose, Monash University, Australia

Advisory Board:
Dr Gerd Bayer, University of Erlangen, Germany
Dr Fiona Tolan, Liverpool John Moores University, UK

The book series STUDIES IN WORLD LITERATURE is devoted to the analysis of global literature, and the multiple, sometimes contradictory, tendencies it accommodates. Its field of enquiry is the 'new' world literature, a category currently emerging through multiple changes from the old Romantic concept of *Weltliteratur*, attuned to the challenges posed by postcolonialism and multiculturalism, the increasing globalisation of literature (but also its reverse trend, regionalisation), and the diversification of the market place. STUDIES IN WORLD LITERATURE encourages research which celebrates and critically assesses a phenomenon that can be understood, as Pheng Cheah points out, as the 'literature of the world—imaginings and stories [...] that track and account for contemporary globalization as well as older historical narratives of worldhood'.

World literature can be brought into dialogue with postcolonial writing through scrutiny of how it is written, read, circulated, and received transnationally within the contemporary circuit of global cultural capital. The series also responds to the need to examine the inherent contradictions in the concept of a world literature and dependence on a hegemonic (often English-centred) literary and critical discourse.

The series seeks to address these tensions, and consequently welcomes:
1) volumes which debate such matters theoretically (including definitions of what counts as 'world literature' and the place of postcolonial literary production within this larger category);
2) comparative studies of texts and genres from different countries and cultures under common headings or concepts such as memory, ethics, and human rights.

Volumes on national literatures, when these are set in a world/comparative or generic context, will also be considered, and the series will include discussions of other complementary aspects of discourse, narratology, and media. While writing by 'canonical' authors will be covered, the series will additionally propose wider cultural and intellectual genealogies for 'minor' or occluded writers. A key aim of this series is to redeploy the familiar rhetoric of postcolonial theory and discourse in relation to concepts relevant to world literature by introducing arguments that will be integrated with the evidence of individual literary practice. This emphasis on contesting definitions of 'diasporic' or 'postcolonial' writing, 'transnational' or 'transcultural' literatures and 'world' literature as used by writers, critics and thinkers may lead to a reconsideration of the boundaries that divide and intersections that link these related fields.

Recent volumes:

5   Johanna Emeney
    The Rise of Autobiographical Medical
    Poetry and the Medical Humanities
    ISBN 978-3-8382-0938-8

6   Gerri Kimber, Janet Wilson (Eds.)
    Re-forming World Literature
    Katherine Mansfield and the Modernist Short Story
    ISBN 978-3-8382-1163-3

7   Flair Donglai Shi, Gareth Guanming Tan (Eds.)
    World Literature in Motion
    Institution, Recognition, Location
    ISBN 978-3-8382-1163-3

8   Patricia Neville
    Janet Frame's World of Books
    ISBN 978-3-8382-1242-5

Chandani Lokuge and Chris Ringrose (eds.)

CREATIVE LIVES
Interviews with Contemporary South Asian Diaspora Writers

With a foreword by Janet Wilson

Bibliografische Information der Deutschen Nationalbibliothek
Die Deutsche Nationalbibliothek verzeichnet diese Publikation in der Deutschen Nationalbibliografie; detaillierte bibliografische Daten sind im Internet über http://dnb.d-nb.de abrufbar.

Bibliographic information published by the Deutsche Nationalbibliothek
Die Deutsche Nationalbibliothek lists this publication in the Deutsche Nationalbibliografie; detailed bibliographic data are available in the Internet at http://dnb.d-nb.de.

ISBN-13: 978-3-8382-1544-0
© *ibidem*-Verlag, Stuttgart 2021
Alle Rechte vorbehalten

Das Werk einschließlich aller seiner Teile ist urheberrechtlich geschützt. Jede Verwertung außerhalb der engen Grenzen des Urheberrechtsgesetzes ist ohne Zustimmung des Verlages unzulässig und strafbar. Dies gilt insbesondere für Vervielfältigungen, Übersetzungen, Mikroverfilmungen und elektronische Speicherformen sowie die Einspeicherung und Verarbeitung in elektronischen Systemen.

All rights reserved. No part of this publication may be reproduced, stored in or introduced into a retrieval system, or transmitted, in any form, or by any means (electronic, mechanical, photocopying, recording or otherwise) without the prior written permission of the publisher. Any person who does any unauthorized act in relation to this publication may be liable to criminal prosecution and civil claims for damages.

Printed in the EU

Contents

Foreword *by Janet Wilson* 7

Chandani Lokuge and Chris Ringrose
Introduction: The Act of Inter-viewing: A Network of Creative
Lives in the South Asian Diaspora..9

Genres, Languages, Voices:
Rukhsana Ahmad in Conversation with Maryam Mirza.............................21

The Aesthetics of Fragmentation:
Michelle Cahill in Conversation with Chris Ringrose................................29

Writing One Reality, Returning to Another:
Shankari Chandran in Conversation with Birte Heidemann....................44

In a State of Indifference:
Amit Chaudhuri in Conversation with Pavan Kumar Malreddy.............56

Poetry as Radical Resistance:
R. Cheran in Conversation with Aparna Halpé......................................74

An Infinity of Traces:
Suneeta Peres da Costa in Conversation with Reshmi Lahiri-Roy.........92

The Delicious Indulgences of Writing:
Sulari Gentill in Conversation with Angela Savage 105

"An Island Is a World":
Romesh Gunesekera in Conversation with Susheila Nasta 119

A Highbrow "Hijra":
Kaiser Haq in Conversation with Mohammad A. Quayum....................136

Nomadic Thinking:
Tabish Khair in Conversation with Pavan Kumar Malreddy 154

Reading, Writing and the Contours of Power:
Mridula Koshy in Conversation with Maryam Mirza 171

"To Want to Know the World, to Look Outward":
Neel Mukherjee in Conversation with Anjali Joseph 180

Before the Battle:
Karthika Naïr in Conversation with Laetitia Zecchini 192

Remapping Canada:
Mariam Pirbhai in Conversation with Maryam Mirza 212

"I Ground Myself in Multiple Spaces":
Sehba Sarwar in Conversation with Maryam Mirza 221

The Processes of Fiction, Theatre and Life:
Rajith Savanadasa in Conversation with Alexandra Watkins 235

Where Politics and Climate Meet:
Sungchuk Kyi in Conversation with Ruth Gamble 247

Places and Proximities:
Samrat Upadhyay in Conversation with Prakash Subedi 262

About the Editors 275

Foreword

Janet Wilson

The pleasure of reading these fascinating interviews with writers and artists cannot be underestimated. The interview is a way to hear their voices in dialogue with empathetic, discerning readers and interpreters of their work. It offers a snapshot of the writers' world view as it has determined their writing and life moves, and the particular choices they have made. Such motivations towards developing a hybrid narrative voice on the part of the 18 South Asian diasporic writers who appear in this volume hinge on their decision to migrate from their homelands. Since they are exiles and migrants, their journeys are constitutive of the multidirectional trajectories comprising the many South Asian diasporas that extend across the globe: collectively the world's largest diaspora today.

This collection represents a shop-front for the work of the South Asian Diaspora Researchers' Network (SADIRN) established at Monash University, Australia in 2016. It stems from an ongoing project that involved network members and affiliates in discussion with transnational, global writers, both in Australia and beyond, and reflects the oversight and commitment of its Director Chandani Lokuge, and her co-editor of this volume, Chris Ringrose. Its range of interviews reflects SADIRN's international relations with European research groups such as that run by Frank Schulze-Engler at the University of Frankfurt and the European Association for Australian Studies (EASA). There is also its fruitful liaison with the journal *Wasafiri*, through its founding-editor Susheila Nasta, which over the last 35 years has pioneered landmark interviews with writers from "other" cultures.

Creative Lives is an illustrious extension of *Wasafiri's* tradition of fostering these literatures: it features writers who have relocated in diverse European, Australian and US centres yet retain ties with their homelands in Bangladesh, India, Nepal, Pakistan, Sri Lanka and Tibet. Alongside interviews with writers shortlisted for the Man Booker Prize are conversations with writers who are national and international prize-winners, or have been shortlisted for prestigious grants and awards.

In their excellent, wide-ranging introduction, Lokuge and Ringrose, who like many of the interviewees are creative writers as well as essayists, critics and scholars, draw attention to the liminality implicit in the act of interviewing. The interviews themselves demonstrate the contrapuntal diasporic subjectivity that arises from living in two or more cultures, which is refracted in narrative practices of hybrid, transcultural, transnational writing, and the shaping discourses of movement and resettlement. The dual focus on movement to new countries like Australia, Canada, France, the UK and USA, alongside the ongoing pull of homeland issues and cultures, suggests their work may be read according to some mix of postcolonial and world literature writing categories, as proposed by Stephan Helgesson (2014), insofar as they are concerned with "local conflictual histories" and their transcultural production belongs to a "circulational phenomenon that moves across languages and literary fields" (484).

The challenges faced by these writers converge on the crux for all migrants, whether voluntary, exiled, refugee or asylum seeker: national borders, visas, entry permits, and policies of exclusion, as well as the related question of whether cultures' "others" are perceived as located within the nation or as aliens threatening from outside. As a liminal act each one of these 18 interviews is constructed from the writer's re-experience and recreation in words of a material reality—the vicissitudes of migration and dislocation due to political and cultural pressures, and the struggle between familial, national ties and affiliative urges—and each depends for its animation and direction on the synchronicities and affinities between interviewer and interviewee.

Creative Lives reinforces the special value of the interview at a time of devastation wrought by the COVID-19 pandemic, and by political upheavals across the globe. In this era of fake news, shrinking borders, and global uncertainty, our minds are being rewired, our antennae of curiosity and enquiry activated differently. Such reconfiguring processes and increased connectivity between people due to mobile technology— video teleconferencing services like Zoom, TV and video streaming services, and social media networking—have been reinforced by social isolation and national lockdowns. The interview format contributes to this greatly enhanced access to information that enables us, as readers, consumers, and co-producers of knowledge, to choose how to think more critically.

Bibliography

Helgesson, Stephan. 2014. "Postcolonialism and World Literature: Rethinking the Boundaries." *Interventions* 16 (4): 483–500.

Introduction

The Act of Inter-viewing: A Network of Creative Lives in the South Asian Diaspora

Chandani Lokuge and Chris Ringrose

> *What is more important in a network than the interstitial relations? What Hannah Arendt called human "inter-est", that which is between people and brings them together.*
> (Bhabha 2015)

An "interview" is a pragmatic way into new knowledge but is also suggestive of subtle undertones and interpretations of what is already known and familiar. On the one hand, it is an interrogation or conversation that brings together one individual, the interviewee, and an other, the interviewer, who shares their world. In the act of the interview, the individual sees themselves in relation to and separate from the other—who represents the public beyond their own world. When split with a hyphen, as we have chosen to do here, "inter-view" suggests something more introspective and liminal: looking inward or in-between. The effect then could be of something unpredicted, a frisson, perhaps, created between what is said and not said, what is felt and not thought—an inward reaction that resists articulation but is important to our notions of who we are in our continual negotiations with the world.

Through the fascinating and provocative medium of the interview, *Creative Lives* brings together a cross-section of South Asian diasporic[1] Anglophone novelists, poets, playwrights and translators. Their travel lines originate from South Asia—Bangladesh, India, Pakistan, Nepal, Sri Lanka and Tibet. They are interwoven by their geographical positioning, as well as by aspects of pre- and postcolonial histories, cultures, religions, languages and literatures. The majority of our interviewees share

---

1   In the Creative Lives project, the term "diasporic" includes those who are settled outside their homeland as well those who have returned to the homeland after spending a substantial period abroad.

the legacies of British colonization; consequently, inherited local and acquired British cultures blend in them. However, they are also distinguished and differentiated by disparate features that are unique to each home culture. Their voyages out, meanwhile, extend across the globe to many different destinations in the west, ranging from Australia and Canada to France, Denmark, the UK and US. In this Introduction, we seek to situate their reflections on their creative work in the light of: the relationship between "homeland" and "hostland"; the idea of "world literature"; the resources and problematics of "Anglophone writing"; and the meaning and politics of "diaspora" itself in relation to writing.

In a classic study of diaspora, James Clifford (1994) describes diaspora as "jostling and conversing [with] terms such as border, travel, creolization, transculturation, hybridity". All of Clifford's terms are significant for diasporic writers and artists, since diaspora opens up new impulses and topics as they imagine their journey and dis-location. In the interviews gathered in this volume, such "jostling and conversation" is evident in the interviewees' reaction to, and reformulation of, the terms that might define their place "in the world" as they consider, adopt or decline concepts such as transnationalism, globalization and the postcolonial.

Some commentators have expressed misgivings about diasporic writing's capacity to deal adequately with "homelands"; usually they invoke the idea of a lack of authentic belonging. One notorious example occurred in 1996, when the Australian writer Germaine Greer attacked Rohinton Mistry's *A Fine Balance* on British TV. "I hate this book", she said. "It's a Canadian book about India. What could be worse? What could be more terrible?" Mistry's response was to call her comments "asinine" and "brainless". This was five years after Salman Rushdie's (1991) classic essay "Imaginary Homelands", and two years after Homi Bhabha's (1994) *The Location of Culture* had explored the active, dynamic process of interaction between cultural and national identities. Greer seemed to offer instead an ideal of uncontaminated purity in literary responses to a nation, which diaspora theory dissociates from as it suggests xenophobia and exclusiveness.

Today one hardly needs recourse to Homi Bhabha's reflections on "hybridity" to celebrate the brilliant possibilities for literary production offered by intersecting realms of experience, idiom and cultural hybridity offered by migration. And of course, those literary intersections can be set in the homeland, as in Amit Chaudhuri's recent *Friend of My Youth*, or in the hostland, as in his earlier *Odysseus Abroad*, whose very title plays with the idea of antecedents, travel and being "abroad". Nevertheless, Chaudhuri himself is one of those most impatient with the terminology of homelands, hostlands and diaspora. Prompted by Pavan Kumar Malreddy during his interview in this volume to reflect directly on such concepts, he responds that terms like diaspora, exile, nation and identity make his mind "fog over".

Sehba Sarwar, born and brought up in Pakistan, and a US resident for more than three decades, is equally uncomfortable with certain kinds of familiar terminology, and relates her misgivings to the content of her work and her fascination with cross-cultural encounters. "Relationships", she says here, "don't need to be limited by national borders that are, in the end, temporary". She goes on to say that the word "diaspora" itself feels remote to her: "Most people I meet and work with have a history of displacement. Ultimately, I prefer the term 'transnational'—because I ground myself in multiple spaces, and I don't feel the need to select only one as my 'home'". Michelle Cahill, an Australian-based writer who engages with a dazzling variety of locales, genres and literary affinities, takes a similar view. While acknowledging her affiliation with "those of us who have been colonized and have suffered the loss of family, of language, of community, of culture", she is prepared to entertain the idea of having "a global voice", having spent her formative years living in three countries and valuing a family environment that was aware of the world, through its communities, "through coloniality, through trade, through art, through different cultures and languages". Interviewee Mridula Koshy, now residing in New Delhi after a 20-year sojourn in the US, is committed to representing the resilience of her subaltern characters: "I am interested in literature as one space in which power difference and corruption can be addressed. Good literature has always been committed to examining how we structure our lives and the ideas to which we subscribe".

As Yoon Sun Lee (2015) emphasizes, "the diasporic imaginary rests on space: space travelled, experienced and registered as distance" (133). This spatial geography gains depth from the distinctive and idiosyncratic perceptions of the writers as they reflect on their creative worlds—their way of life, artistic concerns, core beliefs, cultural practices and importantly, their literatures—within the context of their diasporic, "returned diasporic" or "nomadic" experiences. As Turkish US diaspora cultural theorist Azade Seyhan (2000) argues, originating at border crossings, and driven by mobile subjects, diaspora narratives cannot be bound by "national borders, language, and literary and critical traditions" (4). Rather, their creativity is inspired by the interrogation of home and belonging, transcultural connectivity, hybridity and diversity, settlement and location (xviii).

Klaus Stierstorfer and Janet Wilson (2018) note that the word "diaspora" has its "etymological origins in the Greek verb *diaspeirein*, comprising the elements *dia-*, 'through, across', and *-speirein*, 'to sow or scatter seeds'" (xix). It was originally used to refer to the dispersion of the Jews after the Babylonian exile; for this reason, it carried overtones of punishment. In broader and later usage, it refers to human dissemination and scattering, and to communities dislocated from their place of origin through migration or exile, and relocated elsewhere. *Creative Lives* shines a light on the earliest and most familiar of diasporas—the forced diaspora—which, commencing from the Jewish exodus from their homelands and inability to return to them, continues to grow within the more recent, entirely new historical period of our times: in the global mass migration of people from all over the world, persecuted in their homelands, who seek asylum in new lands. In his exclusive inter-view for this book, Tamil Canadian poet Cheran gives a searing insight into his exilic suffering consciousness haunted by both his motherland being lost to him through race-persecution and his precarious position in his new home in the diaspora, where racism is rife. With his severed past informing his uncertain present, Cheran's powerful poem "On This Street Anytime – 4" with which he ends his inter-view, is inspired by today's "Black Lives Matter" uprising, in which he sees the image of his son transfer to that of black youths shot by armed police. With this poem, Cheran continues the inter-cultural dialogue of the forced diaspora into our time, exploring losses that can never be repaired, that instead swell mutinously in new soil:

> Both of them looked exactly
> like my son
> Height. Beauty. Black. Brave.

Alongside the forced diaspora and the desperation implicit in much South–North movement, a massive voluntary diaspora has expanded in myriad directions in the new millennium. With intensified globalization, in which transnational and transglobal mobility has been facilitated by affordable air travel and advanced information technologies and the vast international social networks spawned by them,[2] the voluntary diaspora has branched out in diversity over the last 30 to 40 years. This is generally a feature of corporate neoliberalism and the import / export of labour, often for low wages. However, some beneficiaries of these new developments now have the freedom not only to return frequently to the homeland but seek third and fourth new homes outside of it. Taking these new developments in migration into account, Avtar Brah (1996) notes that today, the diasporic dream is built on "a homing desire", the wish to construct home in the hostland, in contrast to the "desire for a homeland" left behind, a model of exile associated with the Jewish diaspora (192–93). Alongside these changes, upheavals of our time such as terrorist attacks and the Coronavirus global pandemic, and also political and socio-cultural phenomena such as "Black Lives Matter" (to which we have referred above), women's rights, "Me Too", and the post-truth Trump fiasco in the US, dubbed the end of democracy as we know it (Fisher 2020), have led to the proliferation of new challenges and frontiers that are already inspiring the contemporary diasporic literary consciousness into new and diverse reflections and articulations. These affiliations can be a complex matter. Shankari Chandran speaks in her inter-view of how

> writing the novel [*Song of the Sun God*, set in Sri Lanka] was developmental and cathartic for me in that it helped me understand and accept so much: where I have come from (ancestrally); what I cannot have, reclaim or be; and who I am now. All of that is evolving, dynamic and imperfect but it's mine.

Part of the complexity here comes from the fact that Chandran was born in the UK, grew up in Australia and set her first novel in Sri Lanka. Of her return to Australia after ten years' residence in Britain ("London made me feel like my South Asian-ness was normal"), she says: "When I returned home, I felt homeless".

Most, but not all, of the authors in *Creative Lives* write in English. The global reach and status of Anglophone writing has recently come under attack, notably by Aamir Mufti (2016) in his *Forget English!* manifesto for vernacular languages as he surveys the theorization of "world literature" and scrutinizes the continuing dominance of *English* as both a

---

2   Vietnamese Australian scholar Anh Nguyen (2019) has shown how diasporic communication has been transformed by social media, which have "brought new possibilities for creating and sharing histories, memories, identities, and diasporic communities, both on and offline".

literary language and the undisputed cultural system of global capitalism. But perhaps the choice between the two is not so stark. Several writers interviewed here have been searching for ways in which to introduce other languages that may co-exist and engage with English. In her interview, the Pakistani Canadian writer Mariam Pirbhai recognizes that "multilingualism is a natural aspect of our multicultural cities, our hybrid cultures—our world. Monolingualism seems like the enforced and unnatural condition". Her 2017 short story collection *Outside People* not only involves a diverse cast of characters (Caribbean, Maghrebi, South Asian, South-East Asian and others), but draws upon a range of languages whose interconnections and interactions are important to the fiction. In this way she hopes "to break with the implied hegemony of English as our default *lingua franca*, and focus on inter-ethnic encounters that bring to view other levels of interlingualism and multilingualism". The celebrated translator and poet Kaiser Haq speaks from a lifetime's experience of writing and translation at the interface of English and Bengali in Bangladesh, noting the paradox that English has gained popularity as a literary medium at the same time that "there is no officially recognized place for English in the country".

A scrutiny of the 18 interviews included in this book shows the continued affiliation of the writers to their homelands and desire to re-engage with them from diaspora. Neel Mukherjee gives powerful expression to this impulse in his conversation with Anjali Joseph:

> The only thing I can say about my continuing interest in India is that I find the country intellectually fascinating. [...] India is so plural, so shifting, so one thing and its opposite simultaneously. [...] To be an Indian [writer] is to be [supplied with] material all your life.

Samrat Upadhyay notes that despite being employed for over 20 years as an academic in the US, he continues to set all his creative work in his original homeland, Nepal. Conversely, Amit Chaudhuri, a self-proclaimed roamer and "nomad", currently simultaneously employed in universities in India and Britain, discusses here how he returns to his homeland India from his travels, intellectually and imaginatively provoked into new ways of seeing both home and the world, writing in a mode similar to what Marcel Duchamp (1999) characterized as "infrathin".

Thus, the original homeland thrives within the diasporic creative world and is the source of much of its energy. As one might expect, current and past military and political conflicts feature in many of the inter-views and the associated texts. Romesh Gunesekera describes how he is drawn to write about "the beautiful but fragile world" of mid-to-late 20th-century Sri Lanka while

> thinking about issues we all still talk about: moving places, dislocation, migration, racism—all pressing in the 1970s and 1980s and now. But then, in 1983, Sri Lanka erupted into a violent maelstrom while I was writing a story—this changed my priorities.

Gunesekera also discusses the way his 1980 short story "The Storm Petrel" plays off nostalgic and romantic yearnings for Sri Lanka against brutality and violence. Such unease is characteristic of much Sri Lankan diasporic fiction, and informs the depiction of a "mixed" Sinhala-Tamil marriage in Rajith Savanadasa's *Ruins*. It was, says Savanadasa, "a way for me to explore the fault lines, the divides in class, generation, ethnicity, religion, gender and sexual orientation, and the tensions caused by those divides".

Political and revolutionary undertones also characterize the most recent work of Suneeta Peres da Costa, who was born in Sydney to parents of Goan origin. She reaches back imaginatively to the sense of melancholy, or *saudade*, in the final years of Portuguese colonialism in Angola, and the experiences of the Goan diaspora there, as one of the country's various groups: native Angolan, Goan, Portuguese and European. She explains here that by making the protagonist's family, who are Catholic Brahmin, "complicit in the native indentured labour economy in Angola, which itself evolved out of the Portuguese slave trade", she was able to reveal networks of power and exploitation.

Potent, too, is the yearning of diasporic authors to immerse themselves actively in their home culture and disseminate it within the hostland and beyond. Pioneering ventures in this respect include Pakistani British novelist Rukshana Ahmed's founding of the South Asian Diaspora Arts Archive (SADAA) and the Kali Theatre Company in London, and Sri Lankan Australian novelist Rajith Savanadasa's introduction of the beloved ancient Sri Lankan (Sinhala) Kolam theatre tradition to Australia through his latest writing.

Of particular interest here is the impressive revisioning of the Indian classic epic *Mahabharata* entitled *Until the Lions: Echoes from the Mahabharata*, by Indian French poet, dance producer and librettist, Karthika Naïr. Predicated by the changing socio-political environment of South Asia and Europe in the new millennium, Naïr contemporizes the *Mahabharata* by re-visioning its context, themes and characters. Published and performed internationally to great global acclaim, *Until the Lions* makes relevant to the here and now an ancient South Asian literary tradition that is revered by Asians. In another project of east-west connection, Naïr's collaborative work *Over and Underground in Paris & Mumbai* connects the French and Indian cities through vivid streetscapes and subterranean travel on their respective metros. Naïr, like Sehba Sarwar, embraces her sense of double (or even multiple) locatedness. In her interview in this volume, she says:

> You know I relate to both of my countries, France and India, in the same way. I am fiercely critical of them, and of the directions they are taking, but also really grateful for the person they've made me, because both have, and also very defensive of the founding principles of both countries, principles that are laudable and vital, and were, for long, successful against all odds.

What could be the germ of inspiration behind this diasporic yearning to give such prominence to the dissemination of the homeland culture, its history, and literature? A creative work is often inspired by conflictual scenarios that the writer / creator develops in a rising narrative arc. As Samrat Upadhyay points out, his starting point for a novel is "a character in a pickle"! We could hypothesize from this that their diaporic creators are also inspired by the uneasy space or frisson that may open up through an inner awareness of (un)belonging to the majority culture, and the tensions caused by such dissonance. Can we detect this claim in the in-between spaces of the interviews? And how does it feature in the context of contemporary multi-cultures in which the minority diasporic culture might be struggling, possibly burdened with an idealized past, to adapt to the majority culture? In a relatively recent interview, Homi Bhabha (2015) provides a theoretical lens through which to interrogate this view and enhance our understanding of a complex sensibility that lies unidentified in the voluntary diasporic who seems overtly adaptable and accommodating. Bhabha contests the idea that a contemporary culture anywhere is a "seamless whole", arguing instead that it is a "misfitting apparatus" in which minority cultures with their multiple differences piece into the majority culture. Using the metaphor of the broken vessel introduced by Walter Benjamin ([1923] 2000) in his essay "The Task of the Translator", Bhabha argues this point with particular reference to the minoritized (diasporic) Parsi community in India that he sees as a vessel patched up of "misfitted" fragments:

> [T]he pieces of a broken vessel fit together not because they are the same as each other but they fit into each other in all their differences. [...] So culture is a translational reality, and to that extent it depends upon its moving parts, its often contradictory, asymmetrical moving parts, its tensile strength. [...] the question 'What is your cultural identity?' is unanswerable. (2015, n.p.)

However, as our group of writers demonstrates, the result is not a "paralysing condition" for a minority diasporic community but one that offers a deeply cosmopolitan space open to "varied contingencies and interventions". Stierstorfer and Wilson's observation that *hope* is an essential element of the original meaning of the word "diaspora" as "the scattering of seeds" (2018, xix), applies to Bhabha's stance that contemporary multicultures open up interstitial spaces from which diasporic creativity may be born and within which it may grow and bear fruit. In moments of interviewing his "nomadic" transnational roaming and its effect on his creative production, Tabish Khair offers insights into the complex and non-linear effects of travelling. Khair admits to inhabiting a kind of "intellectual exile" which can be a creative "impetus":

> [a] paradoxical state of being *in* the world and *not in* the world at the same time. I think intellectual exile enables this necessary (dis)junction of being more or less visible, and one uses it creatively in a form that can be seen as being rooted in a degree of dissatisfaction about what exists in the world.

Khair also acknowledges the ways in which a creative tradition may gain by contrapuntally borrowing from other cultures and writing across national borders.

Diasporic voices share common ground in issues relating to connectedness to the homeland. However, they also draw inspiration from world literature, which, as David Damrosch (2003) theorizes, stems from "widely disparate societies, with very different histories, frames of cultural reference and poetics" (4). It is not surprising, then, that the writers interviewed here are reinventing, appropriating, recycling and translating stories and languages as new points of contact generate cross-cultural fertilisation and result in surprising transformations. A notable example of this is Sulari Gentill ("I'm Australian. I was born in Sri Lanka, learned to speak English in Zambia and grew up in Brisbane"), who adapts the detective fiction genre to produce a highly successful series of nine politically and historically acute crime novels set in the 1930s in Sydney, Shanghai and elsewhere. Anyone interested in the circulation, reading and rewriting of texts as part of "world literature" will find acknowledgement in these interviews of a rich and complex network of writers and material that undergirds South Asian diasporic writing. Here, forms such as the bhakti poetry of Mira Bai are cited by Suneeta Peres da Costa alongside an inspiring series of later writers from Marguerite Yourcenar to Shashi Deshpande and Perumal Murugan, as well as Ingeborg Bachmann, William H. Gass, W.G. Sebald and Eunice de Souza. Lydia Davis is discussed here, as are Roberto Bolaño, and Antonio Tabucchi. Michelle Cahill talks about her inventive "Letter to [Fernando] Pessoa". Unexpected and creative collisions occur, such as Kaiser Haq's homage to Lawrence Ferlinghetti and Walt Whitman—just one of the fruits of his residence in the US. Or Amit Chaudhuri's recollections of the profound effect of his first reading of D.H. Lawrence's *Sons and Lovers*. One comes away from these conversations wondering if Franco Moretti's (2000) notion of world literature as "one and unequal" (56), where he highlights the engagements between "cultures that belong to the periphery of the literary system" and the European (and Eurocentric) literary canon (58) really takes account of South Asian creativity and eclecticism, and its challenge to western canons.

The writers' nuanced observations deepen our understanding of the interstitial diasporic creative space as being neither linear nor simple. In the interview referenced above, Bhabha reflects that diaspora is about "misfits", and that in political terms, the "misfit" is often the minority, leading a peripheral existence, subject to the processes and practices of minoritization. Bearing testimony to this, while clichéd slogans of multiculturalism and cosmopolitanism celebrate equality, overt or subtle forms of racism continue unabated in our time. The diasporic literary culture of today is charged with such realities and we each deal with them in our own way.

For instance, the British-born Indian essayist and novelist Pico Iyer (2019), one of the most celebrated citizens of the world, tells in *Autumn Light: Season of Fire and Farewells* how he is nicknamed "Isoro" or "Parasite" by the "neighborhood kids" of the village of Shikanodai in Osaka, which is currently his home (27). We may assume, that in all probability, the nickname originated in careless adult gossip. If so, one can think of no positive synonym that could even remotely excuse this label that smacks of all things abject, such as bloodsuckers and killers of trees. In relation to the diasporic, it could only describe someone obsessively sucking up nourishment from the nurturing source and destroying it in the process. Iyer, however, laughs it off with gentle irony, and seeks to soothe reader-response by arguing that the nickname may have arisen from his difference from the Japanese cultural norm: his lack of "suit and tie employment" and the role reversal in his marital relationship, by which he assumed the more domesticated role. And yet, that Iyer considered it important enough to register the nickname so early in a book that is replete with observations of and engagement with cross-cultural pollinations, seems to suggest a deliberate if subtle form of literary activism that encourages tolerance and bridge-building—the suturing of diasporic minority-majority collisions; a form of "radical resistance", to use Cheran's words here. For Amit Chaudhuri, literary activism is a significant creative impetus. Chaudhuri's inspiring idea is that however difficult, the creative process must be a "state of argument [...] a dialogue not just internal, but with existing cultures [...] with your past" which then carries the potential of new perspectives that will lead us forward.

In such a dialogue, the work of South Asian diasporic writers is read in at least three contexts. As well as being part of world literature and the literature of their homelands, they are rightly seen as contributing to (as well creatively unsettling) "national" literatures in the US, UK, Canada, France and Australia.

In conclusion, *Creative Lives* projects multiple conversations between the writers, facilitating productive collaborations, augmenting communal, national and inter-national tensions and debates, but also fomenting wellbeing and harmony. They are part of a larger dialogue, too, representing minorities in conversation with the centre. It is for us as readers to pursue the somewhat under-researched form of diaspora interviews, in which writers in dialogue with critics and academics enrich our reading with brilliant new insights.

Finally, a sincere thank you to Professor Susheila Nasta for inspiring the Creative Lives interviews project at a memorable meeting of the core partners of the South Asian Diaspora International Research Network at Goethe University Frankfurt in 2017 that also included Professors Frank Schultz-Engler, Avtar Brah, Klaus Stierstorfer, Janet Wilson and Annalisa Oboe. We are grateful to Alexandra Watkins, the first Project Manager of the Creative Lives initiative, and one of its first interviewers. Thank you also to Susheila Nasta for assisting with the permission process to include her interview with Romesh Gunesekera in this book. Last but not least, we are very grateful to all our interviewees and interviewers for accepting our invitation to contribute.

A note on the introductions

The introductions to each of the interviews have been written by the editors in collaboration with the interviewers. Two exceptions are the interviews with Romesh Gunesekera and Neel Mukherjee, which were originally published in the journal *Wasafiri*. Here, the editors' introductions precede the original prefatory notes by the respective interviewers, Susheila Nasta and Anjali Joseph. The third is the interview with Sungchuk Kyi, for which the interviewer, Ruth Gamble, has written the introduction.

Bibliography

Benjamin, Walter. [1923] 2000. "The Task of the Translator." In *The Translation Studies Reader*, edited by Lawrence Venuti, 75–85. Abingdon: Routledge.
Bhabha, Homi K. 2015. "Diaspora and Home: An Interview with Homi K. Bhabha [with Klaus Stierstorfer]." In *Diasporic Constructions of Home and Belonging*, edited by Klaus Stierstorfer and Florian Kläger. Berlin: De Gruyter. https://blog.degruyter.com/diaspora-and-home-interview-homi-k-bhabha/.
Brah, Avtar. 1996. *Cartographies of Diaspora: Contesting Identities*. Abingdon: Routledge.
Clifford, James. 1994. "Diasporas." *Cultural Anthropology* 9 (3): 302–38.
Damrosch, David. 2003. *What Is World Literature?* Princeton, NJ: Princeton University Press.
Duchamp, Marcel. 1999. "Inframince." In *Notes*, edited by Paul Matisse, 20–47. Paris: Flammarion.
Fisher, Mark. 2020. "The End of Democracy?" *The Washington Post*, Oct. 26. https://www.washingtonpost.com/politics/end-of-democracy-election/2020/10/25/3b8c0940-13d0-11eb-ba42-ec6a580836ed_story.html.
Iyer, Pico. 2019. *Autumn Light: Season of Fire and Farewells*. New York: Vintage.
Lee, Yoon Sun. 2015 "The Postcolonial Novel and Diaspora." In *The Cambridge Companion to the Postcolonial Novel*, edited by Ato Quayson, 133–51. Cambridge: Cambridge University Press.
Moretti, Franco. 2000. "Conjectures on World Literature." *New Left Review* 1 (Jan./Feb.): 54–68.
Mufti, Aamir. 2016. *Forget English! Orientalisms and World Literatures*. Cambridge, MA: Harvard University Press.
Nguyen, Anh. 2019. "Refugees, Museums and the Digital Diaspora." University of Melbourne Forum, Sept. 16. https://blogs.unimelb.edu.au/shaps-research/2019/09/16/refugees-museums-and-the-digital-diaspora/.
Rushdie, Salman. 1991. "Imaginary Homelands." In *Imaginary Homelands: Essays and Criticism, 1981–1991*, by Salman Rushdie, 9–21. London: Granta.
Seyhan, Azade. 2000. *Writing Outside the Nation*. Princeton, NJ: Princeton University Press.
Stierstorfer, Klaus, and Janet Wilson, eds. 2018. *The Diaspora Studies Reader*. Abingdon: Routledge.

Genres, Languages, Voices:
Rukhsana Ahmad in Conversation with Maryam Mirza

Photograph of Rukhsana Ahmad copyright 2021 by Anna Morrison

Born and raised in Karachi, the highly regarded playwright, fiction writer and translator Rukhsana Ahmad moved to London in the early 1970s. In 1991, with Rita Wolf, she co-founded Kali Theatre Company which specializes in presenting plays by women of South Asian descent. She was also a founding chair and trustee of the South Asian Diaspora Arts Archive (SADAA). A collection of short stories, *The Gatekeeper's Wife and Other Stories* (2014), features the experiences of the British Pakistani community as well as those of characters living in Pakistan; the range of backgrounds is diverse—the title story, for example focuses on Annette, the British wife of a Pakistani man in Lahore. A somewhat similar pattern had characterized the novel *The Hope Chest* (Ahmad 1996), with its interactions between upper middle-class Rani, Ruth who meets and supports Rani in a London hospital, and Reshma, the daughter of Rani's family's gardener—instances of Rukhsana Ahmad's interest in those bridges that "transcend family, class and faith", which she discusses in her interview.

Rukhsana Ahmad has written numerous plays, including the Susan Smith Blackburn Prize nominee *Song for a Sanctuary* (1990), the Susan Smith Blackburn International Prize finalist *River on Fire* (2000–01) and *Mistaken ...: Annie Besant in India* (2007–08), which toured the UK and India. She has also adapted several novels and short stories into plays, such as Nawal El Saadawi's *Woman at Point Zero* and Sa'adat Hasan Manto's "Kali Shalwar". Her original screenplays include *Cassandra and the Viaduct* (1996) and *The Errant Gene* (2002). *We Sinful Women,* Rukhsana Ahmad's ground-breaking translation of Urdu poetry by Pakistani women, was published in 1991; she has also translated *Dastak Naa Do,* an Urdu novel by Fatima Altaf (1927–2018), published under the title *The One Who Did Not Ask* (1993), thus making available in English this fine novel about the way the protagonist Gaythi, from an extensive, wealthy, Muslim upper-class family in pre-partition India, has to come to terms with change.

Here she discusses her prolific and multifaceted creative life with Maryam Mirza, in an interview conducted by email in January–March 2018.

The interviewer Maryam Mirza is Assistant Professor in World Literatures in English at Durham University, UK. She received her PhD from Aix-Marseille University, and her first monograph *Intimate Class Acts* (2016) was published by Oxford University Press. She is currently working on her second monograph, provisionally entitled *Resistance and Its Discontents in South Asian Women's Fiction* (under contract with Manchester University Press).

Maryam Mirza (MM): *Ms. Ahmad, who / what would you say are your main literary influences?*

Rukhsana Ahmad (RA): I'm afraid it's difficult to be precise about what these might be. I started reading fiction at a very young age in both English and Urdu without much supervision and have loved innumerable books at different stages of my development. Some were great, some mediocre and some forgettable. I read more fiction than non-fiction until I became a full-time student of English literature at Karachi University. At that point, my reading in Urdu began to slip but I had, by then, learnt to love Manto, Krishen Chander and Ismat Chughtai's work; I discovered Intizar Hussain, Rajinder Singh Bedi, Altaf Fatima and Ghulam Abbas; I was charmed by

Flaubert and Maupassant and totally in awe of Dostoyevsky. Favourites amongst English authors were George Eliot, Jane Austen, Henry James, Jean Rhys and Virginia Woolf. I still love George Eliot and Henry James though, in recent years, contemporaries have held me in thrall. One fears imitation, but I'd like to think I've learnt a little from all the disparate but accomplished writers whose work I've admired and loved over the years: Toni Morrison, Marilynne Robinson, Michael Ondaatje, J.M. Coetzee and the inimitable Gabriel García Márquez.

MM: Your extensive body of work is a testament to the ease with which you move from one genre to another: you have written numerous short stories, a novel as well as plays (both original and adaptations) for the stage and radio. How would you describe your experience of working in multiple genres? Do you have a preference?

RA: It has been a privilege to be able to move between various genres and I've loved the shape-shifting that it enables. Each has its own particular challenges and rewards. I love the immediacy of theatre and its collaborative nature, the total freedom of working on a piece of fiction and the generous canvas a film script or a radio production offers. The constraints of each discipline require a different kind of creative energy and I do enjoy the tension induced by the effort to observe its formal strictures and maximize its strengths. I suspect I am happiest working on fiction but most confident with theatre writing. I also find film scripts an exciting area of work at the moment as they demand a stronger visual awareness and a careful commitment to movement/action alongside the reliance on sound and the use of words. As a writer you are always learning and growing with your work, which keeps it all fresh and exciting.

MM: I was wondering about your relationship with Urdu literature as a diasporic writer and translator based in the UK.

RA: I always loved Urdu literature and read a number of books at a precocious age since I hung out with older cousins and siblings. Bait-baazi was a favourite pastime (this parlour game requires you to quote a couplet starting with the last letter of the last line recited by your preceding competitor). It drew us into poetry reading and a devotion to rhyme and rhythm long before we understood much of the verse itself. It was all traditional poetry. Without TVs, mobiles and social media to distract us, we read extensively ... literally, whatever we could find. However, I never understood the importance of one's first language and of translations until I came to live in England and realized that our second and future generations would have very little access to our literature without them. There was hardly any provision for mother-tongue teaching and no space for our literature within what was then (and probably remains?) a deeply Eurocentric curriculum. I felt it was important to do what I could to rectify that, so I organized Urdu classes for Pakistani children (including my own) at our local state school, got my children to watch Hindi films and set about working on translations. I love translating and regret the fact that I now have too little time to expend on that, or even on attending Urdu mushairas [social gatherings where Urdu poetry is read] and literary events, which I seldom missed when I first came to the UK.

MM: *In the introduction to* We Sinful Women, *your collection of translated Urdu poems by Pakistani women (Ahmad 1991), you argued that "the most innovative, the most radical and the most interesting Urdu poetry of our time is being produced by women and not by male poets". To what extent do you still believe this to be true?*

RA: When you're younger you do make bold generalisations more blithely than you would in your "wiser" middle years. I suspect this claim was gravely unpopular with the Pakistani literary establishment of the day, but when I reconsider it, even today, I feel there is some justification for it. The poets I chose, barring one or two, were almost all political at a visceral level. A bold strand of radicalism informs the DNA of the poems that were written to protest against General Zia's Islamization programme; a couple of them were written at the behest of the Women's Action Forum.[1] The poets addressed the burning issues of the day, speaking out bravely when several of their male counterparts had maintained a stony silence. Choosing to resist meant they had to be innovative both in terms of content and form. The work speaks for itself and the impact of the collection was remarkable.

---

1   The Women's Action Forum (WAF) was formed by a group of 15 women in Karachi in September 1981. It was initially established to respond to the Hudood Ordinances (part of military ruler Zia-ul-Haq's "Islamization" process), and to promote women's interests in Pakistan.

MM: *You have adapted several novels into radio plays, including Kiran Desai's* The Inheritance of Loss, *Nadeem Aslam's* Maps for Lost Lovers *and Salman Rushdie's* Midnight's Children. *What did you find to be the main challenge when adapting a novel such as* Midnight's Children *into a play?*

RA: Adapting any novel into a dramatic form is a challenge. Novels have a sprawling overpopulated world that throbs with energy, emotions and ideas, often expressed with considerable nuance and subtlety. Swathes of it are lost when you're confined to a fraction of the original number of words and are expected to reshape the most coherent dramatic aspects of the story in a manner likely to draw the listener into that world instantly. Ideally, what you hope to do is distil the essence of the novel's meaning through its most powerful moments / scenes and to preserve the tone of the original. My producer and I felt we realized both of those goals but we had to make some tough choices and brutal cuts along the way. The first half of the novel is more vivid and has the immediacy of a family saga, whilst the second morphs into a war fantasy and political melodrama that chugs along a different plane as Saleem is hurled overseas and loses his natal moorings. To connect those two halves of the novel in a meaningful way was perhaps the hardest trick.

MM: *In several of your works of fiction, including* The Hope Chest, *and short stories such as "The Gatekeeper's Wife" and "Through the Rose-Tinted Window", you present the reader with fascinating and unexpected examples of cross-cultural, interracial encounters between women. Could you talk about your interest in meetings and interactions between women belonging to different cultures?*

RA: I find those encounters absolutely fascinating. Subconsciously perhaps, they are at the core of my experience as a woman who came to live in London as an adult and understood, for the first time, in a very direct and personal sense the meaning of the term "the Other". That sense of exposure as the Other has not changed. Though I am reasonably integrated into mainstream culture here, I am sensitive to the grating reality of a growing deep-seated hostility to Muslims or people of Muslim heritage settled here, which has supplanted the racism of the Enoch Powell days. In *The Second Sex*, Simone de Beauvoir [(1949) 2015] argues that women are so divided by class, nation, faith and race that it is hard for them to find common cause with each other. Her insight, perhaps inaccurately recalled here, seeped into my awareness early on and has lingered, I must admit. Sadly, it holds true even today. It probably explains this recurring trope in my work. The encounters work as a vehicle for exploring the contrasts in women's lives but also delineate their inability to identify the commonalties in their experience and their often ineffectual support for each other. Occasionally, as in real life, a bridge is built and crossed and women succeed in creating bonds that transcend family, class and faith. Those rare moments bring hope and light into the stories.

MM: *In your writings you often also explore the tenuousness and fragility of women's relationships with each other. I'm thinking of your play* Song for a Sanctuary, *which is set in a shelter for battered women, but also of your portrayal of Reshma and Shehzadi's cross-class friendship in the novel* The Hope Chest. *How do you conceive of female solidarity?*

RA: Female solidarity is possible, but it does require a degree of self-awareness and political understanding of what divides us as women. It comes often too late. Cultural conflict is at the heart of the breach that erupts in violence in *Song for a Sanctuary,* where the residents in the refuge clash with the refuge workers, who are more powerful than them; one of them is definitely hostile to any perceived weakness in the victims. In *River on Fire*, both sisters, raised in different faith cultures by their liberal atheist mother, fight over the death ritual appropriate for her. Here again, the relatively powerful position of the older sister becomes an underlying trap that prevents the possibility of a dialogue, until it is too late.

MM: *In the Author's Note accompanying your play* Mistaken ...: Annie Besant in India *(Ahmad 2008), you mention that you are not "a documentarist by nature" and "have, at times, grated against the constraints that a 'true' historical play requires". Would you like to expand upon this?*

RA: This is a tricky question to answer. It's easier to explain if I begin with the fact that I did try my hand at journalism when I started writing but found reporting quite hard. It requires meticulous research and a dogged adherence to facts that often lead to a tedious and ultimately inconclusive story. With fiction and drama, you tell stories that excite you, that create an illusion of pattern or a meaning that makes sense of our time on earth. You can invent a character; even one based on a historical personage gives you the space to explore all its potentialities through invented moments of doubt and irresolution, of regrets and joy, passion and hesitation that constitute the fundamentals of his or her journey/lived experience. When I am researching a story or a play, I need simple nuggets of information; the bare facts that will help me build a credible framework for the situation I am recreating and will spark off the trajectory of that character in my imagination. Just to be able to exercise that freedom, I would rather work on a play or a novel that is "based on a historical incident": a mixture of facts and fiction, rather than one that claims all the weightiness of a "purely" historical document.

MM: *The narrator of your short story "Confessions and Lullabies" is an inanimate object, a lace doily. Why did you decide to use this technique?*

RA: It was an experiment in the creation of a narrative voice that appears to have the objectivity of an omniscient narrator without all the knowledge you would associate with a true omniscient narrator. It only knows the world it inhabits. Both my characters in the story were too unselfconscious to function well as first person narrators. The lace doily served them both well, I think ... as the link between the hard-pressed creator and the fragile consumer. Adi's character and her story were inspired by a book entitled *The Lace Makers of Narsapur* by Maria Mies (2012), which I was invited to review a few months earlier. The statistics on labour and wages had left me utterly enraged.

MM: *You have spoken about how, when writing radio plays, it is important for you to read the dialogue aloud to yourself. Is there any difference in your approach to writing dialogue when working on a novel or a short story?*

RA: In fact, I do read my work aloud to myself quite often, whatever the genre. It helps me focus on the material itself, to hear the voices of my characters more clearly and to catch any superfluous words and repetition. One of the dangers of hovering over a text is that you can write the same thought in more ways than one. (A habit in which Urdu literature often indulges.) Hearing the dialogue is, of course, doubly important as you do not want all your characters to have the same vocabulary, inflections and patterns of speech. It does need to express who they are.

MM: *Please tell us about your current project(s).*

RA: At the moment, I am working on a play commissioned by Kali Theatre Company, entitled *From Kabul to Kunduz*, and am developing a screenplay treatment of the same story for myself, with the help of a lovely mentor. Fiction is very much on the back burner at present as I am also reading scores of novels for the HWA Endeavour Ink Gold Crown 2018.[2]

MM: Ms. Ahmad, thank you very much.

Acknowledgements

This publication is supported by the Alexander von Humboldt Foundation.

Bibliography

Ahmad, Rukhsana, ed. and trans. 1991. *We Sinful Women: Contemporary Urdu Feminist Poetry*. London: Women's Press.
---. 1996. *The Hope Chest*. London: Virago.
---. 2008. *Mistaken …: Annie Besant in India*. London and New York: Aurora Metro Books.
---. 2014. *The Gatekeeper's Wife and Other Stories*. Lahore: ILQA Publications.
Altaf, Fatima. 1993. *The One Who Did Not Ask [Dastak Naa Do]*. Translated by Rukhsana Ahmad. Oxford and Portsmouth, NH: Heinemann.
De Beauvoir, Simone. [1949] 2015. *The Second Sex*. Translated by Constance Borde and Sheila Malovaney-Chevallier. London and New York: Vintage Classics.
Mies, Maria. 2012. *The Lace Makers of Narsapur*. Melbourne and Geelong: Spinifex Press.

---

2   The Historical Writers' Association's (HWA) Gold Crown for best historical novel was won in 2018 by Ralf Rothmann for *To Die in Spring*, translated by Shaun Whiteside, and published by Picador.

The Aesthetics of Fragmentation:
Michelle Cahill in Conversation with Chris Ringrose

Photograph of Michelle Cahill by Nicola Bailey

Michelle Cahill has lived in the UK and Australia. Her collection of short stories, *Letter to Pessoa* (Cahill 2016b), won the University of Technology, Sydney (UTS) Glenda Adams Award for New Writing in the NSW Premier's Literary Awards. Her interest in the Portuguese writer Fernando Pessoa (1885–1935) derives in part from his use of a series of masks, or "heteronyms", to write via other selves with different lives. He is one of a number of "companion" writers, including Coetzee, Woolf and Borges, who are woven into her own work. Her novel *Woolf* is soon to be published with Hachette.

Michelle Cahill has received prizes and fellowships in poetry and fiction, notably the Red Room Poetry Fellowship, the Val Vallis Award, the Kingston Writing School (KWS) Hilary Mantel Short Story Prize and the *Australian Book Review* (ABR) Elizabeth Jolley shortlist for the story "Borges and I". *Vishvarupa* (Cahill 2011) was shortlisted in the Victorian Premier's Literary Awards. She co-edited *Contemporary Asian Australian Poets* and Vagabond's deciBels3 series of poets and is the founding editor of *Mascara Literary Review*. She is also a stimulating critic and theorist, whose essay "The Poetics of Subalternity" appeared in *Mascara* (Cahill 2012). In it, she undertakes a critique of contemporary Australian literature, which she sees "in its orientation and its networks of power and interest [...] a subject [that ignores] the divisions of cultural capital and labour".

Her poetry collection, *The Herring Lass* (Cahill 2016a), takes an original approach to the topic of migration, reflecting on the way animals and birds are able to survive extreme climates and resist assailants, using this to consider human global engagements and the exodus of refugees. As elsewhere in her work, women's experience of fragmentation, exile, divorce and motherhood provides an undercurrent of meaning. In his review, the Australian poet John Kinsella saw it as "a superb and complex book, deeply intelligent, pluralistic, linguistically rich, political with a sophisticated way of seeing place and space, intense in its convictions".

Michelle Cahill and Chris Ringrose talked in August 2018; at the time she was writing a novel as part of her Doctor of Creative Arts at the University of Wollongong. A few responses have been revised in 2021, to reflect on her developing craft as a writer.

The Interviewer, Chris Ringrose, is a poet and fiction writer from Melbourne, Australia, who has lectured in literature at universities in Canada, the US and UK. He is currently Adjunct Associate Professor at Monash University. With Chandani Lokuge, he is the co-editor of this volume; his biographical notes can be found in "About the Editors" on page 275.

Chris Ringrose (CR): Michelle, I'm struck by the global "reach" and settings of your poetry and fiction, as well as your travel and research. A number of reviewers have remarked on this as a strength of your poetry collection The Herring Lass. *How significant is the notion of "South Asian Diaspora" for you and your writing?*

Michelle Cahill (MC): I don't know if it is for me to say. Perhaps that is a question best left for critics. I don't think of myself in terms of an identity when I am writing creatively because writing is a process of becoming, a postponement of my "self" in the material and functional sense. In many ways it is depletion, really, of those parts of myself, and who the author is, or who she becomes in that process, feels remote from me. Perhaps that is why I enjoy it; because it is liberating to be free of oneself. However, when I write an essay about race and literature, that involves performing arguments about, or against, notions such as "authenticity" and "identity".

I can say that at least two of my published books explore the South Asian Diaspora: I'm thinking of *Vishvarupa* and the novel that I am currently writing, but there are also several stories in *Letter to Pessoa* that explore the world of the South Asian diaspora and its travel narratives through the lens of Sarita, Hemani, and Nabina. And in *The Herring Lass*, a book about migrations from the Global North, there are poems conversing with the South Asian diaspora, "*Youth*, by Josephine Jayshree Conrady" and "Mumbai by Night". My sense of home is located in language and is contingent. I am cautious of committing myself intellectually to defined categories. Whether this is symptomatic of Buddhist conditioning or whether my thinking is sympathetic to post-structuralism, or an inherent scepticism, who knows? Does it matter? If you read "Letter to Derrida" you may find a trace of Derrida there, and perhaps a trace of his translator, Spivak. She was a young French-speaking Bengali scholar forging a singular career in the United States on a regimen of European philosophy and social theory. So, there you have another iteration of the South Asian diaspora. Actually, Spivak has inspired me quite a lot; from an early essay I wrote on "The Poetics of Subalternity" to what she describes as the "irretrievably heterogeneous" in "Can the Subaltern Speak?" and my theorization of interceptionality. I don't think of myself as a scholar but conceptual language can be useful in one's praxis. I don't want to have to answer to categories. My evidence has been in language and what it can do.

CR: *You're also diverse in that you write successfully in so many genres and modes—short fiction, essays, poetry, a blog and (I think) a novel. Do you see this versatility and variety as essential to your creativity? Is any one genre the most congenial to you?*

MC: That's an interesting question. Supposing that the whole notion of genre is imposed on the text; suppose it is a contrivance? Our relationship to language certainly tethers us to the world and to each other; partly it's through language that we begin to know the real and the abstract. Of course, there are different genres: the novel can be thought of as quite distinct from a collection of short stories, or from a collection of poems. My process relies on concentration, being attentive to what each piece of work requires: whether a poem, a short story, a novel, or whether it is an essay. I like to enter the process fluidly, without excessive preparation; I like to improvise. But with a novel, it helps to have a sure sense of what you want to do. There was a time when I believed that anything is possible in language. Writing enables possibility and the more one writes, the more skilful one becomes. I think of writing in a technical way; when I write I am like a gymnast; over time my language develops strength, flexibility, balance, so that it can perform with grace, with speed and precision so that it can fly, dance and jump. Poetry is a powerful form but the reception afforded to some poetry is problematic; deeply so; there are distortions. This matters because we draw from the world of poetry to write new poems. Fiction is the most technically demanding genre and, I think, also the most satisfying because of its craft and scope. I've always loved prose writing but that is different to a novel. I think a novel can be transformative in a way that a book of poems can't be; even though poetry can be very striking, and necessary.

CR: *In your essay "The Colour of the Dream", you are severely critical of aspects of Australian literary culture and its stultifying "whiteness". Do you see yourself as an Australian writer? or as a global one, or as something else that won't be reduced to that kind of labelling?*

MC: Thank you for reading the essay. I think there is insufficient analysis of trauma, and what that does to our writing; how it morphs for better or worse. Some degree of trauma deepens our understanding, but too much can mutilate our work or silence us. That's why self-care matters. That essay was written during a stage of my career, having spent ten years waiting for and working towards a break through with my fiction. It was only after that break though that I realized the extent to which writers of colour are being filtered, curated and mediated. Very few of us can even find a good literary publisher or agent. We have to achieve something extraordinary. The late Candy Royalle wrote in one of her performance poems: "We search for truth but we're forced to jump through mainstream hoops and loops, daily". I think the process of fighting those systems can have adverse effects.

Critics please themselves and sometimes exploit the hermeneutic privilege. Some have no qualms about overwriting me, but when you look at the history of how the western canon sustains its authority you understand that it is not simply individual critics who are positioning us, it is the "his-story" of erasures, reductions, that goes back centuries, how those marginalized by hybridity or class are written over by those with more agency. This can happen at the administrative level of the industry or the editorial level. How minority narratives are framed by the canon-makers mediates those stories and becomes equally, sometimes more powerful than the stories themselves. So, agency is very much located in theoretical and industry frames.

Ultimately, however, this is not my problem. I usually work on more than one project and I have found that writing criticism, for the present, is a necessary part of my work. Fiction is demanding and also immensely pleasurable. I try to just focus on my work, on my writing. It's very demanding to give oneself to writing and to develop a manuscript. I am not receiving much of an income these days so that is also a challenge.

CR: *I wondered whether, in that essay "The Colour of the Dream", you are a bit hard on a review of Maxine Beneba Clarke's collection of stories* Foreign Soil? *You say that "Wright's verdict [on the book] hinges on a single word. She pegs* Foreign Soil *as 'flawed'". It's just that I remember thinking that was a perceptive and enthusiastic review, even though it expressed certain reservations.*

MC: "Flawed" is a conspicuous description for *Foreign Soil* given the anti-immigration rhetoric and the White Australia Policy. Also, to be fair to the context of my essay, "The Colour of the Dream" is about gatekeeping and policing Australia's cultural borders, the stereotyping of the refugee narrative contrasted with a personal experience of travelling to Indonesia in 2012 and visiting the Belawan Detention Centre. I had spent several days visiting refugees from Afghanistan and Sri Lanka who were being housed outside detention.

Underpinning all racism is the notion that others are "flawed". Structural racism is not simply an abstract jargon. It is about restricted rates of inclusion in immigration, in industry, within the literary workplace, and in academia. At a micro level it is transacted through seemingly neutral discourse: conversations, reviews, articles, reports. There is an accumulation of archival and administrative subtexts, paratexts, errata and erasures that accrue to devalue the narrative legitimacy of those who are marginalized and to delimit how they can move across narrative subjects and genres.

What is difficult to appreciate is that filters are not always intentional; the filters are an inherent part of mainstream frames.

How do we recognize the voice of structural racism? We have to record these things: the reductions, the erasures, the absences, which are often minor and anecdotal but which are sufficient to position us hierarchically and to disqualify us. Colonialism did not simply end with independence or with equal rights to citizenship. These spaces are being negotiated through a range of discourses, formal and informal, macro and micro. They are deeply rooted in our legal frameworks which are inherently racist and do not acknowledge the sovereignty of First Nations people in Australia. Our immigration laws enforced racial aspects until 1973. Now we are witnessing a revival of racist rhetoric concerning immigration and Islamophobia with Malcolm Turnbull's paranoia about African gangs, with Fraser Anning's "Final Solution" Senate speech, with the treatment of refugees on Manus Island and Nauru, and with Pauline Hanson's One Nation party.

Analysing literary criticism may require us to adjust our focus to consider historical and legal frameworks, but master narratives and mainstream frames are less flexible.

CR: *"Mumbai by Night" is an interesting example of your treatment of South Asia, because the title suggests a tourist trip, and there is that sense of the exotic in the "miasma of smog over the Dharavi slums, the marsh / redevelopment, the Indiabulls and Oberoi towers". You even say you "catch [your] flight all the way back to oblivion until the next stop-over" and that your friend Sharlene to whom the poem is dedicated might just see you as a "foreigner [she's] obliged to entertain". Yet you're not really (or quite) a "foreigner" in that environment ...*

MC: It's a poem that expresses the disconnection that happens with diaspora. The poem is dedicated to my cousin, Sharlene, and it mourns the loss of family and time. The meeting of poet and cousin; or as you have read it, poet and friend, is so transitional and fragmented that it can be misread, and must be contained in the economy of verse, something the speaker regrets and resists by the telling of an ordinary experience: sharing a meal, going out to a club and dancing, having fun, packing, unpacking, falling short on what she can offer and how little she can take away. These are the conditions of diaspora; it doesn't explore the reasons for leaving, but it tries to embody a way of not forgetting.

CR: *I like the way in which you refrain from being "authoritative" about the city, while still giving a vivid impression of it that is more than that of a tourist. As with some of the stories in* Letter to Pessoa, *it conjures the experience of visiting, belonging, and not belonging ... you are drawn to the way Pessoa used a series of masks, or "heteronyms", to write via other selves with different lives. You write as Sarita (who also appears elsewhere), Jo, Nabina and Luke, as well as a number of others. Can you reflect on that writing process?*

MC: Well, my heteronyms are not typical, but writing is an act of masking. The diaspora life splices narrative time and place, bumping my personas one into the other. Unlike Ricardo Reiss or Alvaro de Campo they do not have accompanying biographies or signatures and they are often narrated in the third person. And some of the authors whom I address become another aspect of themselves: Pessoa, Coetzee, Woolf, Nabokov, Borges, with resonances with the real persona. Do they become heteronyms (or homonyms) of themselves? I like the expansiveness of fiction and its suppleness, but no two writing processes are the same. It is organic for me: contradictory, fluid and broken, as time is. It is only structure that creates the appearance of being whole. That kind of architecturally stable narrative can be beautiful to read, particularly when done masterfully, and I deeply enjoy reading those stories; but is that my story? Is that my task?

I think that the diaspora narrative is interrupted and the minority narrative is fragmented. How can it be represented as a whole, without losing its contingencies, without being absorbed into larger stories that flatten its vulnerability, its gaps? Why are we so focussed on positive representations? Why are we afraid of the erasures in history, in coloniality, the silences? How can we find a language and a structure for the experiences that we, those of us who have been colonized and have suffered the loss of family, of language, of community, of culture, know best?

CR: *Can we talk about your latest poetry collection,* The Herring Lass? *Tell us about the striking Winslow Homer painting of the same title that features on the cover—and provides the subject for one of the 48 poems.*

MC: I didn't want to use the Scottish images, as they are stereotyped. I admire Homer's conjuring of the weather, the woman's stubby hands and muscular arms in the painting, the way the net is draped over her shoulder. She is wearing ordinary working shoes, yet she is gazing outwards.

CR: *"The Herring Lass" poem itself refers to "shoals of migrant herring" that provide the woman's tough livelihood. Would it be fair to say that the collection as a whole is a meditation on the important and worldwide phenomenon of migration—forced as in "Harbour", or occupational as in the title poem? Did you always have that overall design in mind, or is it the cumulative outcome of your artistic and political interests?*

MC: I had the idea to write from the experience of northern migrations as I spent ten years living in the northern hemisphere. I thought this might be something of interest also for Australian readers, since as a nation, European invasion and settlement began with these migrations. I wanted to explore the brutality of territory and frontiers.

It seems to me that exploitation of labour and environmental impacts of migration are disturbing contemporary problems that remain unresolved. So, the fishing and sealing industry poems in "The Herring Lass", "Bear", "Day of a Seal", "Pirogue", and the refugee experience in "Interlude" cast historical shadows on situations like extinctions, corporate piracy, and the warehousing of refugees.

CR: *I admire the way you blend different animal voices into the collection: the seal and the thylacine, for example. There is also the example of the journeying cat in the story "Biscuit" from* Letter to Pessoa. *Do those personae allow you to try out new things?*

MC: In many of the animal poems, I wanted to write about violence. I was going through divorce at the time and I went through an intense, almost hallucinatory period of writing during which memories came harrowingly back to me, of male violence, sexual violence, domestic violence and the human exploitation of animals and their homelands; how it has endangered them.

To experiment with form in fiction is enjoyable and it can extend my skills. When I wrote "Biscuit" it was thrilling; I couldn't wait to get back to the story when I was interrupted by housework or having coffee with a friend. It was also exhausting. Of course, sometimes it doesn't work; at other times the result seems to exceed what I expect of myself. I don't like to address subjectivity directly. I am not confessional as a poet. In fiction, I suppose I integrate figurative elements with plot structure and I am interested in prose writing that does this. I like to texture the writing; but it's not really intentional.

CR: *That's interesting. I did feel, as I read "Biscuit", that the story had a special significance for you. Do you want to say a little more about it?*

MC: Well, it is partly autofictional, using elements of magic realism, and poetic tropes. The cat's fantastical journey from Africa to England, with its coincidences and exigencies, is a way of telling a complex history of migration, without having to over-explain, digress or politicize the storytelling act of a minority experience. I use a simple, open-ended and sometimes ironic style for the story, allowing the reader to consider and to feel a range of possibilities and outcomes from the migration experience. It extends the limited migrant narrative we hear of through media reports or public talks. Hopefully, the reader can reflect through the cat's perspective more freely about subjects such as home, coloniality, belonging and citizenship. But if I were to write in a realist mode about my early life journeys, the truth might be compromised by memory, the need to protect others, by the demands that conventional storytelling places on gaps, disruptions and conflicted emotions which result from a traumatized landscape. So, for me, it was a process of reinventing that landscape as playful, energetic and imaginatively reconstituted. I do trust fiction to reveal the truth about our lives without restricting it to definitions.

CR: *Can we talk about the stories in* Letter to Pessoa*? In their concerns, settings and the way they play against a range of other writers, they could find an enthusiastic audience anywhere in the world. I know you might be wary of categories like "world literature", but do you find that notion inspiring at all? Or are you happy to leave that kind of assessment to others?*

MC: I probably do have a global voice. I spent my formative years living in three countries which is not very typical. But like many Australians my family background was aware of the world, through our communities, through coloniality, through trade, art, different cultures and languages. The mobility of people across borders, religions and caste was not foreign though it posed difficulties that we didn't anticipate. Now, when I travel overseas, it's primarily for my writing, and somehow, place, travel and writing are connected for me.

I'm glad that *Letter to Pessoa* can be read as "world lit." or "global lit", even though its publication has been limited to Australia. I hope in time it will be published overseas. I am very fond of the opening story because an early draft was written whilst I was traveling in Spain; at that time, it seemed like a failure, a fragment, a futile exercise. But the act of imagining and believing in our fragments holds much promise. The uncertain proximity to meaning is where rich stories can have humble beginnings. When I read the opening story "Letter to Pessoa" I'm reminded of how I wrote it in a hotel, alone, during transitions and how a writer often needs to be stripped of a great deal of routine and security to embark on fictional journeys. That multiplicity matters to me. I did take risks engaging poetic tropes but I was pleased the language was able to cross gaps in migrant time and colonial history, providing structural cohesion and literary complexity for the book as a collection of stories. I was inventing and developing my own structural devices. The book also feels like a progression from my previous work, which is validating for me as a writer. Alexis Wright, in conversation with Melissa Lucashenko and Kim Scott at the First Nations Australia Writers Network (FNAWN) symposium last week, spoke, inspiringly, about always learning and challenging oneself as writer. So yes, I am pleased on a personal level with the book, because it was the product of self-learning and thinking about themes like exile, belonging, difference and the writing process.

CR: *I love the way that in* Letter to Pessoa *you take the work of other writers—sometimes particular works, like Lolita in "Chasing Nabokov" or "Aubade" in "Aubade for Larkin", and at other times the spirit of a whole oeuvre—and use them to create stories which can both stand alone and be read at an angle to the originals. (I'd say they riff on the originals, but I'm not sure that's the right word—though I see you use it in the notes to the collection, in terms of particular phrases and sentences.) How do those stories grow in your imagination?*

MC: The epistolary stories started with an early draft in third person prose which appeared on my blog. It was titled "Derrida's Reinscriptions". This was a few years before "Letter to Derrida" was developed and appeared in the journal, *TEXT*. I had also written a theoretical paper on Derrida's deconstructionism and Buddhism and I am interested in the idea of the fragmentation of the self; and how writing is postponement. (When the book manuscript was edited, I was asked to revise the Derrida story further, which led to allusions to Derrida's life and his work being included.) But the blog post is proof that strong stories can have humble beginnings. *Letter to Pessoa* is a book of stories, but also a book about reading and writing, the writing process.

I began to write more letters to authors which was rather enjoyable. It required me to read their work and to think about my writing as a departure, a variation and a conversation. One of the challenges of poetic language is to make different things seem similar so that we apprehend the world in a new way; we see things with fresh eyes. My technique was to texture the language as a medium, using it like paint or fabric, and to manipulate the layers. I enjoy that aspect of language and how it carries meaning; so that was how the letters in the book were crafted. Another aspect was being able and willing to go deeply into my story so that it wasn't simply a variation. Each has to have its own existential validity, its characters and tensions.

I enjoy reading these stories to an audience because they work best when read with an inner voice trusting of the music, or to an audience. There is a performatory aspect to them because of how they use voice.

CR: *Virginia Woolf clearly has a special place in that set of creative talents. I'm thinking of the story "Letter to Virginia Woolf", which strikes one as deeply personal as well as a poignant tribute to her, as in "maybe I cannot live without words. Each one maddening as a stone thrown into the river, heavy as death ...". Elsewhere you cite Woolf's words: "So long as you write what you wish to write, that is all that matters; and whether it matters for ages or only for hours, nobody can say". Do you see her (and Larkin, Pessoa, Coetzee and others) as allies and companions in your creative journey? Or sometimes as adversaries or counterpoint?*

MC: I see them as companions. Some of the stories are homage pieces. I read Tadeusz Różewicz (2013) at a time in my life when my mother was very ill. His book, *Mother Departs*, helped me understand and cope with the alienation a writer feels and the sacrifices, the losses; also, the indifference of history towards minorities. Who is going to teach us the way forward with compassion and understanding? Not society. Society, after all, does not really value our work as writers. Writing is rewarded in our world based on whether it can be consumed and traded. So, these writers have helped me enormously to model a pathway; I don't mean a career pathway. I mean I've learned how to live as a fragment, and how to decolonize. The Borges story, "Pierre Menard, Author of the Quixote", made me think radically about authorship, about the canon and history; about how we are innovators as much as we are imitators. What Coetzee does with *Robinson Crusoe* in *Foe* can be traced back to what Jean Rhys did with *Jane Eyre* in *Wild Sargasso Sea*; and in *Waiting for the Barbarians* there is a trace of Cavafy. We share in a repository of dreams; we receive the language and the visions of these writers, as other writers in time will receive ours; that's what I mean. That is very real for me.

But you're right. I do feel in a special sense connected to Woolf, no less than many women writers have done, I expect. My novel, *Woolf*, engages more deeply with her work. But also, with her life and her essays. She was extremely privileged and charmingly sociable; an English woman with aristocratic Anglo-Indian forebears. Certainly, she lived in a different world, but she suffered childhood trauma, she was poetic and inventive in her language and she worked as an editor and independent publisher with Hogarth Press. She was somewhat to the side of the canon as a modernist and a feminist; she was an essayist in her own right with strong opinions and a formidable critic; a photographer, a Londoner; she was openly bisexual. As a couple Leonard and Virginia Woolf were anti-imperialists, Leonard having served for seven years in Ceylon. So, there are several aspects of her life which I can relate to. I find her exploration of class distinctions fascinating and almost callously observed. I think what I relate to most, however, is her intensity; the overwhelming way that language absorbed her and was inseparable from her life, determining her destiny. I understand that gravity; it can be harrowing and exhausting but also exhilarating.

CR: *"A Year of Smoking Menthol" from* Letter to Pessoa *is a brief story suffused with tenderness and friendship. Plus some great metaphors (such as "you were my litmus strip"). You end it with powerful abstractions: "decency, morals and society". In its quiet way, does that story throw down a kind of challenge to the reader?*

MC: It's the story of a friendship between two young women who aren't content to use their minds in the way society expects because they see the hypocrisy and fakeness and misogyny of the world and they long for something more; Lulu is becoming unhinged, suffering insomnia, delusions, sharing suicide fantasies, while her friend, the narrator, cannot save or protect her, and things are spiralling out of control, but there is a sense that Lulu's illness is part of what's wrong in society. There is a sense of repressed sexual tension and a betrayal is implied. Sometimes the most ethical people in our lives are considered dysfunctional and pathologized because they subvert or fail to conform to an insensitive system of values.

A gap between the upbeat, vernacular tone and the seriously disturbing themes makes it provoking and poignant. I'm glad that it works because it was risky to write in second person, and in such a brief, poetic form. It could have been a standard-length short story of 4,000–5,000 words, but the brevity and intimate second person address make it an affecting and unique narrative.

CR: *In an article "Interceptionality, or The Ambiguity of the Albatross" (Cahill 2018) published in the Provocations series of the* Sydney Review of Books (SRB), *you develop the concept of "interceptionality" and its special usefulness today—for example in relation to other concepts like "intersectionality", which was broached in a 1989 essay by Kimberlé Crenshaw and has been much used since then. Is it possible to briefly outline the importance of "interceptionality" for you?*

MC: Interceptionality is a communications tool using social media, email, written correspondence also phone conversations. It's about speaking as an equal and reclaiming one's subjectivity as a minority individual or it could equally apply to a minority argument in contentious issues, for example arguments about cultural privilege or even issues on climate. Minority positions and arguments get flattened and homogenized or reduced by mainstream frames and paratexts within the publishing industry, the media and education. Interceptionality ruptures through the frame repeatedly to change the status of the speaker. It is also a decolonizing strategy because when used to question the assessment of merit, the distribution of cultural capital or structural racism it resists the silencing of voices that are already positioned with less agency within discourse. Inspired by narrative theory, it uses narrative to mediate oppression; and it has a spatial appreciation of representation: an understanding that there are master narratives that hierarchically position and validate all the stories we are permitted to tell. Interceptionality enters the methodological gaps of intersectional discussions, which have been powerfully descriptive, but which have failed to address arts policy. An example of interceptionality is the work of the Kurdish author, Behrouz Boochani, detained on Manus Island since 2013. He has used the technology of a smart phone to write stories, articles, interviews in international media to send messages to the world on the atrocities happening there daily, to write a book, *No Friend But the Mountains* and to send videos via Whatsapp to produce a documentary film, *Chauka, Please Tell Us the Time*. Because they are remote it is easy to lose sight of what is happening in the detention camps on the islands; his work intercepts that framing to expose the cruelty of the state, to show from the centre of his subjectivity how fragile and humane the refugee's experience is in detention. This is not without personal risk; but it is more powerful than journalists or refugee advocates speaking on his behalf.

CR: *In that essay you move from a fascinating account of the possible meanings of the albatross in Coleridge's "Rime of the Ancient Mariner", through conceptual bearings and contemporary social commentary, to a powerful statement of your own personal experience in relation to these things. That seems to me one of the strengths of your writing—that you bring together other writers, ideas, creative fictions and personal experience. Is that a fair comment? Or are you thinking "that's just what writers do"?*

MC: I don't have an overarching plan for my work. I work from within my creativity outwards. My strength is from within; focussing on my creative task and working outwards. I don't want to lose that deep connection with my work, and I don't think I possibly can, entirely. Interceptionality teaches us to believe performatively in what is vital: our truth, reclaiming our subjectivity. Even when we are displaced within the master narrative, if we are centred within our own process, it becomes deeply meaningful and it can survive. My preference is to write fiction, but I have learned that discourse is a powerful moderator of fiction and I have used language and theory to intercept the cultural frame that colonizes and reduces myself and others.

Understanding more about the canons and master narratives has really questioned my understanding of what history is and what authorship means.

CR: *In the poem "The Sound of Our Brown Bodies" you address (among other things) Australian border policies and bullying, saying "how hard on the body / being brown is in this white country". In terms of your own writing, you write in the* SRB *essay of the experience of being "marginalized as a literary writer of colour in a culture that seeks to limit its migrant authors to the closed narratives of immigration, assimilation and consumption". This is obviously something you feel strongly about and want to explore ...*

MC: Yes, as a migrant, I came to Australia, studied a profession and was treated as an equal in that industry. Citizenship enables me to become a doctor, a lawyer, a teacher, a dentist, an accountant. But if I enter the arts, if I enter literature, I am immediately disadvantaged by the canon; my voice is not recognized by the literary representations that our culture knows and endorses. I must work several times harder; the measures of appraisal are rarely on a par. This is strenuous physically and psychologically. It is becoming increasingly harder to deny class privilege and Eurocentric privilege; and to this I would add canonical privilege. There is a policing and punitive dynamic if you are critical in a public space. I felt it was my responsibility to share these dynamics. To be able to map our history of erasures, oppressions, to talk about entitlements, and how they work in the arts industry, this will serve our communities as we go forward towards a more inclusive, participatory arts culture.

Bibliography

Cahill, Michelle. 2011. *Vishvarupa*. Perth, WA: UWA Publishing.

---. 2012. "The Poetics of Subalternity." *Mascara Literary Review*, May 23.

---. 2014. "The Colour of the Dream: Unmasking Whiteness." *Southerly* 74 (2): 196–211.

---. 2016a. *The Herring Lass*. Todmorden: Arc Publications.

---. 2016b. *Letter to Pessoa*. Sydney: Giramondo.

---. 2018. "Interceptionality, or The Ambiguity of the Albatross." *Sydney Review of Books*, August 7. https://sydneyreviewofbooks.com/essay/interceptionality-or-the-ambiguity-of-the-albatross/

Clarke, Maxine Beneba. 2014. *Foreign Soil*. Sydney: Hachette Australia.

Rózewicz, Tadeusz. 2013. *Mother Departs*. London: Stork Press.

Wright, Fiona. 2014. "Listen: *Foreign Soil* by Maxine Beneba Clarke." *Sydney Review of Books*, June 25. https://sydneyreviewofbooks.com/review/foreign-soil-maxine-beneba-clarke/

Writing One Reality, Returning to Another: Shankari Chandran in Conversation with Birte Heidemann

Photograph of Shankari Chandran by Clare Lewis Photography

Shankari Chandran is a novelist and a lawyer whose experience in the field of social justice informs much of her creative writing. Born in London to Sri Lankan Tamil parents, her life and work have been shaped by the cultures of three countries in three continents. After growing up in Australia, she spent ten years in London working as a lawyer before returning to Sydney in 2010 where she started her writing career. Her debut novel *Song of the Sun God* (Chandran 2017a)—a family saga chronicling Sri Lanka's war through the history of a Sri Lankan Tamil family—was recently commissioned for television. It was short-listed for Sri Lanka's Fairway National Literary Award in 2017 and long-listed for the Dublin Literary Award in 2019. The story begins in 1932 and its protagonists, Nala and Rajan, are married in 1946, just before Sri Lanka's independence from Britain. With the country's descent into civil war, they are forced to make profound decisions that will affect them, their children and grandchildren, and take their diasporic story across three continents until the narrative ends in Sydney in 2010. The book drew enthusiastic responses from readers and literary critics for its intelligent and well-informed treatment of race, language, migration and Sri Lankan history. Chandran's richly textured writing moves at the outset from the young Rajan's witnessing of the shocking self-immolation of a monk to the homogeneous, warm world of his first home, conveyed through details of cooking and reading:

> Every day, Rajan read until it was dark and then he read by candlelight. He meticulously scraped wax from the bottom of the dish with his footruler. He would reuse it with a new wick tomorrow. Years ago, Lali had shown him how; she was very careful. For his birthdays he never asked for books because they were so expensive—he could borrow books—instead he asked for candles.

As Shankari Chandran reveals in her interview, much of her own family history, life on three continents, historical research, social and legal awareness are explored in her first novel, as well as her own reflections on home and homeliness: "*Song of the Sun God* was a way for me to explore, find or even create, a connection to Sri Lanka—the actual Sri Lanka, the historic one and the Sri Lanka that I had received through my family's memories".

Moving from a historical novel to a dystopian thriller set in the future, her second book *The Barrier* (Chandran 2017b) creates a world devastated by religious war and the Ebola epidemic. Short-listed for the Norma K. Hemming Award for Speculative Fiction (2018), it uses "action-packed, tech-savvy speculative fiction to examine intractable problems of today's world" enthused the reviewer in the *Sydney Morning Herald*. Within three years it was to prove remarkably prophetic in the light of the onset of COVID-19. The book is abuzz with ideas and, with its "faith-inhibiting" side-effects of a vaccine, rogue virologists and debates about faith, freedom and justice, is in some ways closer to the concerns of *Song of the Sun God* than one might initially think.

Shankari Chandran has completed a third novel, which combines the generic elements of her previous two works: a political thriller set in post-war Sri Lanka. A fourth novel, *Chai Time at Cinnamon Gardens*, is forthcoming with Ultimo Press.

The interviewer, Birte Heidemann, is Assistant Professor of English Literature at Dresden University of Technology, Germany. Her most recent publications include *Post-Agreement Northern Irish Literature* (Palgrave,

2016) and the co-edited collection *Violence in South Asia: Contemporary Perspectives* (Routledge, 2019). Her work has appeared in *The Journal of Commonwealth Literature, Journal of Postcolonial Writing, Wasafiri,* and *Postcolonial Text,* among others.

Birte Heidemann (BH): *Shankari, you grew up in Australia and began working as a lawyer in London. Only in 2010, after moving back home and giving birth to your fourth child, did you decide to commit to creative writing. Could you tell me a bit more about what prompted you to switch careers and become a full-time writer?*

Shankari Chandran (SC): We moved back to Australia because I wanted to bring our children back to my home, to the home of my childhood. But when I returned, I felt disillusioned and disappointed, and I felt that home was not home. And through that sense of disappointment, I felt lost, and I turned to writing in order to work through my feelings. I began by just blogging for myself, and it actually attracted a following. After the following grew, the blog was picked up by a lifestyle website that introduced my writing to a much broader audience in Australia. This gave me the confidence to attempt a novel—something that I had always wanted to do but for which I previously lacked the time or confidence. And so, I wanted to give that one great novel a go, a novel I think so many of us feel within us. In 2012, after a year of blogging, I attempted what eventually became *Song of the Sun God*. It was the first time in my life since I was young that I was not working for money, because I had chosen to be the stay-at-home carer for our family. We were having our fourth baby, and it seemed like an opportunity to pursue that ambition.

BH: *You mentioned that when you returned from London to Australia (where you were born and grew up) you were terribly disillusioned and disappointed by the experience. Could you elaborate on why that was? Especially from the point of view of a traveller / diasporic? What in the return to Sydney brought you to this mood? Had London changed you? Had Sydney changed in your absence?*

SC: I lived in London for ten years where I was considered (and where I quickly considered myself) a British Asian. I felt like I had a valued place in Britain, where the distinct impact of my culture on British culture was recognized, and where I felt a part of the society, entitled to claim a more equitable place in the country. Perhaps this has changed in Britain as it is changing elsewhere in the world.

When I went home to Australia in 2010, it was a shock for me. I did not understand the country I was raised in. I did not understand the hatred towards asylum seekers, the public fear-mongering about boat people and the attribution of many of our societal problems to migrants. There was a xenophobic undercurrent hidden in the rhetoric of border security, Australian-ness and patriotism.

When I turned on the TV, I wondered where all the brown people were. All multicultural representations were siloed in the ethnic public broadcaster SBS. It was as though we'd done our bit for multicultural Australia, by funding SBS; TICK. But everything else in the public space was as it has always been, monocultural and essentially white. This was also true of the bookstores—the "Australian fiction" that was making it past the gatekeepers was distinctly white.

The public spaces (the media, TV, the arts and national dialogues) were not reflecting or representing what I was seeing on the streets. They were not accepting of the Australia that I was living in and the Australia that I had brought my children back to. The disconnect was upsetting. And it was more than that—the disconnect felt like a manifestation of a deeper refusal to fully acknowledge the presence, position and value of non-white Australians. This was really troubling for me because I had actually felt at home in London, a place I had only lived in for ten years. On my return to the "home" of my childhood, I felt like Australian society did not want to accept me on my terms.

London made me feel like my South Asian-ness was normal. I had forgotten in those ten years that Australia often made me feel like an outsider, generously allowed in but only if my voice did not challenge its own.

I think my kind of normal should be recognized within the multiplicities and complexities of a rapidly evolving, dynamic and spacious Australian identity. I want my children's kind of normal to be recognized not because they are the quiet, grateful, hardworking grandchildren of quiet, grateful, hardworking immigrants, but because they are who they are. When I returned home, I felt homeless. Writing was a way of trying to understand myself, and then write myself back into the "Australian narrative" by creating my own.

BH: *For how long had you been contemplating the idea of writing?*

SC: I think it was only in 2012 when *Song of the Sun God* took form and substance that I realized how much I loved doing it and that I really wanted to keep doing it. I wanted to create a career out of it, and I wanted to be published. There is a certain point when you are writing where you realize that you do not want to just write but you want to be published.

BH: *You want to share it, your story.*

SC: Yes, you want to share it with a wider audience, and you also want the validation of being published. With this particular novel, it's from my heart and it's for my people, so the motivation to share it with a wider audience became very powerful. You know, there is something that seeks that external validation. In terms of how long I had wanted to be a writer, I knew that I loved writing from the time I was a child. I could sense that I enjoyed it. "Enjoy" is such an empty word—I loved it. When I was in fifth grade, my teacher gave me a diary and she literally said to me: "just keep writing". And so, I used to journal on and off from then, and I would write short stories but never consistently and never critically. I would write something but never go back to it and try to make it better. But writing has always been a way of comfort for me, a form of therapy and also one of affection. I loved it since I was young.

BH: *You wrote your first novel,* Song of the Sun God, *on a Sri Lankan Tamil family's history and lineage. Could I ask an additional question about why you returned to Sri Lanka and not to Sydney for your first novel? Were you returning further back into your roots from the disappointment of Sydney? Were you reaching back to ancestral roots—a diaspora tendency of course, as evidenced in several of the interviews in this book of* Creative Lives— *springing from lack of roots in the process of your (three-continent) routes?*

SC: In *Song of the Sun God,* I returned to Sri Lanka and eventually settled in Australia. This narrative follows the course of my family's life and mine— geographically but also spiritually I suppose. At university, I read T.S. Eliot's "Little Gidding". The following lines have stayed with me:

> We shall not cease from exploration
> And the end of all our exploring
> Will be to arrive where we started
> And know the place for the first time.

I sound so tragic, but these lines still move me and I often find myself thinking about them. As a member of a diasporic generation born outside of our ancestral homeland, I have often felt without roots. I have often felt untethered and have longed for that deeper sense of belonging that my parents take so deeply for granted that they do not even know they have it.

Growing up in Australia, I did not feel I "fitted", nor did I have a relationship with or lived connection to Sri Lanka. *Song of the Sun God* was a way for me to explore, find or even create, a connection to Sri Lanka—the actual Sri Lanka, the historic one and the Sri Lanka that I had received through my family's memories. The family in the book, like me, loses home (in the different ways we define home) and must create a new one. Writing the book was developmental and cathartic for me in that it helped me understand and accept so much: where I have come from (ancestrally); what I cannot have, reclaim or be; and who I am now. All of that is evolving, dynamic and imperfect but it's mine.

BH: *It is interesting that you are using words like "comfort" and "therapy". I wonder whether it was the very act of writing that helped you navigate all these shifts in your life at that time?*

SC: Absolutely.

BH: *So, writing is an escape, a comfort and an energising force; you write from the nest of the family. But are you also escaping the wider diaspora of Sydney in which you live, into a Sri Lanka that might have been more positive and inclusive of you, perhaps? An original homeland—even if you were not born there?*

SC: No, because it is very hard to see Sri Lanka, given its recent history, as a place that could be more inclusive of the Tamil people. For that, I would need to re-write history, and I wanted to create a novel that was as historically accurate as I could.

BH: *The process of writing and sharing your story with a wider audience can be unsettling. Does the act of writing—developing a story, its characters, a setting—still serve as something settling or comforting for you?*

SC: I think, 100 percent, yes, it does. Overall, I am, as a person, far more grounded and at peace with myself when I am writing. It comforts me, it uplifts me, and it connects me to myself. I feel my most authentic self and very present when I am in the middle of writing. It might seem contradictory that I feel very present when I have deliberately taken myself to another world. When I am writing, I am 100 percent in that world to the point where my husband is concerned that if there was a house fire, I wouldn't be aware of it. So, I don't write and don't even edit on screen when my children are home. I will research when the children are in the house, and I will edit on paper. I can sit with them and do a bit of editing, but I would never work on the first draft of a manuscript or an idea when they are around because I am too deeply absorbed into that world. It's not fair for them, and it's not safe for them. I owe them as their mother the mindfulness and the presence. I need to give that to them when they are with me.

The other part of that answer though is that I often write about very traumatic things and *that* is unsettling for me. It is traumatic for me. When you write, you really are inside your mind, the picture is very clear, and you are with those people. You are as close to them as you could possibly be, without being them, and that is traumatic. At the end of the day, depending on what I have been writing about, I find that I really need to take some time to pull myself out of that world and re-set my mind for reality and my children. On those days, I need to just hold them for a while to be reassured that reality is safe and secure, and that my children are OK.

BH: *You write about the Sri Lankan civil war in both your first and (I gather) third novel-in-progress. What is your angle? How do you see it, as someone in some senses* outside—*a diasporic—returning to the land of her ancestors, one that is not immediately "yours"? Also, did you feel welcome in Sri Lanka? How did Sri Lanka receive you?*

SC: For both *Song of the Sun God* and *The Phantom Limb* (my third novel), I spent a lot of time researching and interviewing insiders—Sri Lankans with lived experience of the events and places I write about. However, my writing will always be from the outsider's perspective. I am a diasporic outsider, someone with an ancestral connection and love for the place, but still an outsider. At times, this gives me an ability to see things that are best seen from the outside. And at other times, it means that I am not seeing as much as I should. My lens is obscured and distorted.

My angle is Tamil and I can't apologise for that—I can only tell the reader who I am. I can declare my conflict of interest as it were, whilst also reiterating that I tried to write as historically accurately as I could, interrogating the motivations, actions and failures of all of the stakeholders in both the micro (family) and macro (political) story I told. I felt that bias and inaccuracies would undermine the veracity and credibility of the whole piece, and I wanted people to read this perspective of Sri Lanka rather than dismiss it. The lawyer in me also wants detail, facts and testimony—in a sense, the truth.

I felt so welcome in Sri Lanka—all people welcomed me and supported my research. People wanted to talk and share their stories, even the ugly, hard ones. All people are storytellers, not just writers. We are unburdened by telling stories. We bind ourselves to each other by telling stories. I felt truly welcomed. The response to *Song of the Sun God* in Sri Lanka has been really humbling. People read it and reach out to me. It has been an honour to write something that seems to resonate with Tamils and Sinhalese people.

BH: *In fact, I was wondering how you would manage to switch between the often-violent worlds of your writing and the all-encompassing world of motherhood. I can imagine that moving from writing a war scene onto making dinner or helping with homework can be quite exhausting. And even if the process of writing is mostly comforting for you, the task of traversing both worlds—the real and the imagined, the one around you and the one inside of you—might drain energy from you as well.*

SC: I think one of the contradictions of writing is that it is really energizing and exhilarating to write. I am very uplifted when I write and if I don't write, I can feel a heaviness within myself. If I don't write, I am difficult to be with. I am uncomfortable with myself, and I am slightly agitated and unsettled. At the same time, though it is energising and exhilarating, it is also meditative and prayerful. And it is traumatic and draining. It is all of those things.

BH: *But fulfilling in that way?*

SC: Yes, ultimately, it is incredibly fulfilling. I feel extremely fortunate that I had a job in the law that I loved. I would wake up every morning with a rush of adrenaline and march into the office determined to do something useful today. And I feel so fortunate to have had that for more than ten years, and I loved it. I thought I would never love a job as much as I loved that. But when I began to write, I realized I had found something that I loved more.

BH: *Judging from the two novels that came out in one year, and the third one already in the works, you are undoubtedly a prolific writer. This makes me all the more curious about your writing routines, especially being a mother of four. You've already shared some of your routines but how exactly do you find the time and space to work on your manuscripts? And do you have a fixed workspace from where you write at more or less fixed times, or do you squeeze in time for writing whenever and wherever you can?*

SC: That is a great question, because I love to hear how other authors do it. I am fascinated, because every author always thinks of other authors doing it so much better. I work in a very small study, which is about the size of a closet and has no windows or natural lighting. My husband finds this hilarious and a little unhealthy, too. He worries that it is just not natural to sit in a small windowless room for hours on end with the doors shut. When he tries to work an hour in the shared study, he finds it very difficult. For me, the reason I am fine with that space is because I am not there. It is because I will be inside my mind, I will be in Sri Lanka in 1932 or in 2014 and, most recently, I've been in Sri Lanka in 2009. So, I am not in the room, the physical room, but mostly in the past.

From 2013 to 2016, I had a very good routine. Whenever the children were not in the house, I would sit down to write. When my youngest child started school, I was able to do this more effectively because I had no children in my house then. I used to walk the children to school, with the dog, and run back to start my day of writing. I am quite organized and disciplined and try to ignore everything else during the middle of the day. Chances are I did the laundry at ten o'clock the night before, because I yearn for my time to write. There are a number of things that eat into my writing time but on a "writing day" I will sit down at 9:15 to write and at 2:30 a really loud alarm will go off to give me 15 minutes to pull myself out of wartime Sri Lanka and allow myself to re-enter the leafy streets of our neighbourhood. And then I will be with my children in the way they deserve it. So, I have a really compressed writing schedule, which can be very stressful because there is so much to say in so little time. All the things that parents do, I will try and do late in the evening, like cooking dinner for the following night, bulk producing spaghetti bolognese and chicken curry, answering the endless notes from the PTA. This is how my day used to be structured in the past.

BH: *So how has your routine changed, and what prompted you to change it?*

SC: With my third novel, I tried out something different. It was very deliberate because that year of my life was a very unsettled one. We had a lot of sickness in the family, and I returned to work as a lawyer. So, I had things that pulled me away from writing, and I was becoming increasingly stressed and anxious that I was not writing my third novel. I had an idea, but I was not able to create or protect the time to write. I remembered Stephen King's book *On Writing* where he says: "just put superglue on your bum and bash it out". It's easy for Stephen King to say this because he is a full-time, successful and well-paid writer, but I thought, OK, let me try this. He sets himself aggressive targets, like 3,000 words a day in six hours of writing. I was at a stage where I just could not give it six hours of writing a day. But I could put superglue on my bum, and I could set some targets for myself. I am very target orientated, perhaps because I am a lawyer. If you set me a target, like a robot, I feel the need to achieve that target. So, I would say 500 words a day or 1,000, and I would secretly be aiming for 2,000. I wrote the first draft of that third novel in eight weeks because in every spare moment, I would try to channel Stephen King. Even if it were only for ten minutes, I would sit down and just bash it out. I didn't look at it again. I didn't read it. I didn't ask myself if it's any good because those questions are the death knell. I just tried to bash it out. And then I had to stop when my first and second novel came out, so I didn't look at the draft until some four months later. I was terrified to open the document, to look at what I had actually produced. I went back to it very anxiously but, for a first draft, it was okay. It needs a lot more work and it needs energy and it needs time. I have been doing that this year, but I need to do more. As a first draft, it wasn't terrible though, and I was relieved to realize this.

BH: *Indeed, it must have been very reassuring to realize that you were able to pull this together despite your disrupted and unpredictable schedule. How would you describe the next stage of writing a novel, that is, your process of editing a first draft?*

SC: It is different, but a big job. For the next round of edits, I really feel that I need a lot of time because I actually need to restructure it. I can edit language while I am in the car waiting to pick up a child from their guitar class but, for a structural edit, you need to step back and look at the whole novel. Then, you need to step in and look at individual scenes. You constantly step out and step in, and this process requires time. I do not have much time any more because I've returned to running a social justice program. Given that writing is not necessarily a way to create a sustainable income for a family of six, I have focused back on being a lawyer at this stage in my life. I feel fortunate to return to the law after a few years of not working in the paid economy, and I am very fortunate that it's a job that I love.

But I do hope that I will be able to write at least a minimum amount that nourishes my soul. Time and fatigue are my worst enemies. I need to think, once again, about Stephen King and work out how to make time my friend. And I do have an hour or two in the evening if I can overcome my fatigue. Of course, we also need to allow ourselves to not write. We have to recognize that all the other things that we're doing are valid and necessary because, as writers, all we want to do is write. That is all I want to do. I want to be with my children and my husband, occasionally hang out with friends and then write some more. I would very happily have a completely binary life where I am either with my family or writing, either writing or with my family.

BH: *Maybe one day ...*

SC: One day, one day.

BH: *I gather that that* Song of the Sun God *has been accepted as the basis of a TV series. Could you give an update on the progress of that project?*

SC: I'm excited about the proposed TV series. Olivia Hetreed, BAFTA-winning writer of Oscar-nominated film *Girl with A Pearl Earring,* will adapt the novel for Synchronicity Films, producer of the recent ABC / BBC drama *The Cry*, and Australia's Dragonet Films. Olivia is working on a six-part series based on the novel, and the adaptation will focus on the youngest generation through Smrithi, a young woman living in London, who is disconnected from her culture and long-held family secrets. I have been working with the team over email and was fortunate to go to London in January 2020 with Karen Radzyner from Dragonet, to work with Olivia and Claire Mundell from Synchronicity in developing the adaptation. The team has created a compelling overview of the series which is now being pitched for development funding.

BH: *A final question about the process of your writing. I was wondering how you gather and develop ideas. Do you simply type them into your computer? Or do you prefer to keep a notebook where you can jot down notes or map out more complex ideas like the intricate web of family relations in* Song of the Sun God*?*

SC: I make notes of interesting ideas or scenes—sometimes a scene will just flash into my mind—or words. I love words. I have a notebook where all of this just gets dumped but sometimes I will put up a file on my computer where I collect ideas for future books. I keep this document secret somewhere in my computer because I think my husband would be terrified to see it—"What? You haven't finished with the third book?" But when I write, I write directly into the computer. For *Song of the Sun God*, I did do some writing on a notepad because my children were much younger then, and I often needed to sit in a doctor's waiting room or one would have speech therapy, and for an hour or so, I would just handwrite scenes. But nowadays I write directly into a computer and I actually prefer it because it is very fast, and it allows me to check my word count. A good day of writing, though, is a day when I forget about the targets because I am absorbed into my world. And when I emerge from that world, I realize that in those few hours, I wrote 2,000 words. You know, that is a beautiful day. And there are days like that. They are a real joy, and I feel that they are good for me.

Bibliography

Chandran, Shankari. 2017a. *Song of the Sun God*. Colombo: Perera-Hussein Publishing House.
---. 2017b. *The Barrier*. Sydney: Pan Macmillan Australia.

In a State of Indifference:
Amit Chaudhuri in Conversation with Pavan Kumar Malreddy

Photograph of Amit Chaudhuri by Geoff Pugh

Amit Chaudhuri is the author of seven novels, three collections of poetry. a collection of short stories, three books of essays, two works of non fiction and numerous edited collections. *Finding the Raga*, about his relationship to North Indian classical music, will appear in 2021. He is also a composer, singer, and a concert performer of Indian classical music. His musical creations are known for their eclecticism, improvisation, and experimental quality across genres: jazz, blues, and classical Hindustani. Born in Calcutta and raised in Bombay, Chaudhuri spent his formative years between London, Bombay, and Oxford before choosing Calcutta as his home. Chaudhuri's artistic oeuvre is at once expansive and elusive. It is hard to pin down his work to a specific genre, tradition, or movement in the catalogue of literary criticism. He is a diasporic South Asian writer in the sense that his geographical location spans Europe and India, yet as he says in this interview, the terms diaspora, exile, nation and identity make his mind "fog over" and are not at the forefront of his artistic practice. Modernists, postmodernists, and postcolonial critics have all grappled with his work, and at times, struggled to place him amongst canonical literati.

Chaudhuri is one of the great stylists of modern fiction. The difficulty of defining his output can be gauged by the fact that while the novelist Sumana Roy (2017), in an engaging essay, recalls her delighted laughter on first reading Chaudhuri's first novel, *A Strange and Sublime Address* (Chaudhuri 1991), critic Ian Almond (2010) has written of "melancholy, fantasy and economy in Amit Chaudhuri's short fiction". Both responses are valid. The delicate, poetic richness of his writing, and his avowed debt to the great Bombay poets Nissim Ezekiel, Adil Jussawalla, Arvind Krishna Mehrotra and Arun Kolatkar (Chaudhuri 2017a) give his novels a particular sense of intimacy. This is the case with the walks through London of 22-year-old Ananda and his uncle Radhesh in *Odysseus Abroad* (Chaudhuri 2014), where the attention to relations between the generations is characteristic. It features, too, in the vivid detail of the return to Bombay of a novelist named "Amit Chaudhuri" in *Friend of my Youth* (Chaudhuri 2017b). In the opening pages of latter novel, the narrator finds himself in a taxi, registering unfamiliar aspects of the city:

> the new flyovers, the disappearance of certain things which weren't quite landmarks but which helped you orient yourself—furniture showrooms, fisherfolk's settlements. I would be surprised—maybe even disappointed—if these large-scale changes did *not* occur. On the right-hand side at the end of the road from the airport towards Mahim is, I know, the mosque with loudspeakers, hemmed in by traffic on the left; further up, past the brief stink of the sea, will be the church where I once went to attend an NA meeting. I was keeping Ramu company.

The details carry the mood, the sense of connection and detachment, the significance of the narrator's friend Ramu who is his remaining human connection to the city. It is not surprising that Amit Chaudhuri, in his interview here with Pavan Kumar Malreddy, expresses his admiration for D.H. Lawrence, recalling his first reading of *Sons and Lovers* and his sense of Lawrence's desire to convey "the incandescence of living in the here and now". Postcolonial criticism, as Sumana Roy says, often tends to focus on the nation, the race, the marginalized. Chaudhuri's writing, while it does not ignore these elements, is, in Roy's words, "grounded in explorations of the sensuous, the emotional, the affective" (2017, n.p.). Cristina Sandru

(2010), writing in the volume *Rerouting the Postcolonial*, has noticed a similar development in postcolonial writing.

In his review of *Odysseus Abroad*, the writer Neel Mukherjee (himself interviewed elsewhere in this volume by Anjali Joseph) remarks that Chaudhuri's "signature sentences" are "elegant and classical, rich in parentheses, subclauses and digressions; unexpected, surprising spaces open up within them to accommodate the ever-present past and the infinite branching of thought" (Mukherjee 2015). Throughout the novels, there are piquant observations concerning social and intellectual life. The taxi journey of "Chaudhuri" on his arrival in Bombay soon leads him to reflect mischievously on his early years and to the comment that "Lacan says our subjectivity takes form at the 'mirror stage'. The term and notion are so well worn they might make you laugh—the fate of most revolutionary ideas in psychoanalysis". This piquant observation does not prevent the narrator from exploring his early years and impressions in intriguing ways. In similar fashion, Chaudhuri can turn the usual advice to aspiring writers on its head: "For me, the protagonist is only one element in a story: evening, room, wall, smoke, car, are other possible ones" (Chaudhuri 2016), or mount trenchant social and political commentary on contemporary India: "India has not, outside of Indira Gandhi's declaration of emergency, been in this place before, and certainly not with the degree of popular support we see now, which can only be characterized as a form of inebriation" (Chaudhuri 2019).

In this interview, which took place at Amangalla Hotel on 25 January 2018 in Galle, Sri Lanka—"against the piano tinkles of a guest performer in the lobby, and the distant echo of Tamil vocals from the wall-mounted radio", recalls interviewer Pavan Malreddy—Chaudhuri discusses his literary influences, musical inspirations, and what it means to produce art in an age of "market activism".

The interviewer, Pavan Kumar Malreddy, teaches English literature at Goethe University Frankfurt. His recent publications include a monograph, *Orientalism, Terrorism, Indigenism: South Asian Readings in Postcolonialism* (2015), the co-edited collections *Reworking Postcolonialism: Globalization, Labour and Rights* (2015), and *Violence in South Asia: Contemporary Perspectives* (2019). He has co-edited special issues of *Journal of Postcolonial Writing* (2012), *ZAA: Journal of English and American Studies* (2014), *Kairos* (2018), and *European Journal of English Studies* (2018) and has authored over 30 essays and chapters on terrorism, political violence, and postcolonial theory in journals such as *The European Legacy, Third World Quarterly, Journal of Postcolonial Writing, Intertexts,* and *AlterNative*, among others. He is currently working on a monograph titled *Insurgent Cultures*.

Pavan Kumar Malreddy (PKM): *Let me start with a quote from the Somali writer Nuruddin Farah: "Being away has helped me to write with a clear vision. Distance distils and makes ideas worth pursuing. [...] One needs to extricate oneself from the daily needs and demands of living at home" (quoted in Jonas 1988, 74–75). I am aware of the fact that you are neither a diasporic nor an exile writer but you do spend a considerable amount of time away from home; you hold a professorship in England, and you have a second home in Oxford. But unlike what Farah is saying—that one needs to extricate oneself from the grind of domesticity, you seem to make an art out of domesticity. Much of your fiction is, in my reading, about the aesthetics of domesticity, the slow and slumbering lives of the urban Indian middle classes, where nothing moves. How do you look at this rather enabling tension with domesticity in your work?*

Amit Chaudhuri (AC): Firstly, I think what Nuruddin Farah says must be true, but for me, my mind fogs over when I hear terms like exile, diaspora, nation, and identity, just as my mind fogs over when I see terms like description, character, or setting.

PKM: *That's the reason you once said you don't like 19th-century novels?*

AC: Right. So, categories like those are very difficult for me to comprehend. My mind won't get around them. I think, yes, distance can produce a renewal of perception and perspective. It certainly happened to me when I was in London [in the early 1980s] without my being aware of it, because I was in such agony at that time, of homesickness. So being away not only influenced the way I'd look at home, but also the language—in terms of the way I use words, and the way those words change in their resonances in other locations.

PKM: *And their effects?*

AC: That too. But I also know that it is possible to have that kind of renewal and that sense of movement even if one has not travelled very far, and you might be living in a city whose landmarks you've never seen. In fact, we do not visit the landmarks of our own city, or certain places in one's own city that may be 45 minutes away by car. One might find these places not only strange, but almost unreachable because one hardly registers their existence. I think it is important to understand those experiences as to why a place that is just 45 minutes away is so seldom visited by you. Why, when you go there, you feel a reconstitution of what you know about your city. I think those things are of great interest to me.

PKM: *The difference between Farah and you is that you talk about a certain variation and the creation of these affects rather than having a clear vision, or an objective vision. But thinking about movement—at least the way you talk about it—that is, moving without having travelled afar—reminds me of Yann Martell, who told me that he writes while moving. He has a treadmill in his garage with a writing desk mounted on it, and he writes while strolling on the machine.*

AC: That's fantastic.

PKM: *Like I said, I don't consider you as a diasporic writer who is on the move, but you do move quite a bit between Mumbai, Calcutta, and Oxford.*

AC: But I also move between rooms in my house because I don't have a fixed writing desk or spot. People do ask me about it, especially when they come to photograph me after an interview: "where do you write?" I don't have one place. I move between bed, sofa, bedroom, and drawing room. And I often write, because I write longhand, in my notebook while walking from one place to another. So, what you're saying with Yann Martell surprises me because I didn't realize there were other people like that. But I do write and revise often while walking.

PKM: *In movement.*

AC: Yes, while walking.

PKM: *Yes, that's one of the arguments made in performance arts, that artists think better when they're on the move. On that note, I wanted to ask you about another kind of movement, that is, movement between different kinds of thinking or, say, imaginary worlds. You are one of those rare people who have a foot both in fiction and academia. In the academic world, there is this idea of dialogue and public engagement. But in fiction, there is a romantic* *notion that writers do everything in private; they are under no obligation to reveal their notes or sources of inspiration or imagination. How does this tension play out with you as a fiction writer? Do you collect some sort of ethnographic notes, and is there any kind of dialogue in your fiction in the process of its making?*

AC: Of course, yes, but firstly, I don't see myself really as part of academia. I see myself, throughout my life, as having used academia to further my interests as a writer. I make use of certain fringe spaces in academia to have discussions which involve not only academics, but also artists, publishers, and thinkers. I want a space which is unlike an academic conference or a literary festival. I feel it's important to have that space. And to get back to your question: yes, writers are always in a state of argument. Writing itself is a form of argumentation. When you write something, you reject a whole range of things as part of a dialogue with yourself and your traditions. On some level, it would have been easier to go in a direction which is familiar; the direction that the time or age is going in. And yet, there are writers who step out of their time and reject that direction. So, there is always a process of dialogue and argumentation in the moment a writer takes a decision about the direction of his or her work. But it's not even a decision; it's not even a choice to do something that their innocence compelled them to do because it would be much easier to go with the flow. Once you go against the current, you're in a more difficult position. But you do this because you have to do it. And in that, you're engaging in an argument. Your writing is an argument.

PKM: *So there is a dialogue, an internal dialogue.*

AC: Yes, there's a dialogue not just internal, but with existing structures, conventions, your past, your inheritance and more importantly, with what you are supposed to be as a writer, and what is expected of you as a writer; as an Indian writer, or as a writer of novels—all the things that are expected of you, you are in dialogue with that.

PKM: *This is very avant-gardist, in my view, though I am not sure if that is a term used to describe your work, as it is typically associated with European art. Your response reminds me of G.V. Desani's (1948)* All About H. Hatterr, *and now I think of it, there are parallels between Desani's classic and your* Odysseus Abroad *(Chaudhuri 2014). It also reminds me of Borges's famous* quote on Kafka that "every writer creates his own precursors" (1964, 177), in the sense that a writer's work sheds a renewed perspective on other (established) writers. Odysseus Abroad *does exactly the same: it casts a new angle on Joyce, Homer, or G.V. Desani. I know this is a question that should be reserved for critics, but I wonder if you've ever thought about your work in this way.*

AC: You know, it is very interesting you should say this and I hesitate to make this reference because it's a reference that both touched me and also it's one, as you said, others should be talking about. The other person who said this, oddly enough, was the novelist Will Self. When introducing me at a particular event, he made the same comparison, invoking Borges's essay on Kafka. I feel very embarrassed because I don't deserve …

PKM: *But I have a specific example in mind that prompted this comparison, from your novel* The Immortals. *The protagonist Shyamji says: "you cannot practice art on an empty stomach". Now, in his famous story "The Hunger Artist", Kafka turns this empty stomach into a form of art. But my question is more general: why is it that in the Indian literary tradition, writing against set conventions, or bourgeois conventions of art, or doing "art for art's sake" has not been very fashionable?*

AC: If you look at Indian vernacular literatures in the past, they have astonishing avant-garde traditions, some of which have also been translated into other domains such as cinema and art. We only know of a few of these great avant-garde figures like Satyajit Ray, Ritwik Ghatak, and Mani Kaul.

PKM: *Adoor Gopalakrishnan, O.V. Vijayan …*

AC: U.R. Ananthamurthy, and Urdu writers like Saadat Hasan Manto, where you often see not just a testing of extreme experience but also a sense of drift, and a sense of pausing over inconsequential things with an absurd amount of attention to them as well. You see these avant-garde preoccupations by which I mean, slightly irresponsible traditions, very robustly forming in Indian vernacular writings. I wouldn't even call this an "art for art's sake" avant-garde tradition, but a particular kind of exploration of consciousness.

PKM: *On that note, it is also quite refreshing to see your work not being labelled as "postcolonial literature", though it's not a term you completely disassociate from, and you do use it very carefully and selectively, especially in* *your essay collection* Clearing a Space *(Chaudhuri 2008) where you make a case for "lowbrow" modernities. But you do not talk about middlebrow modernities as such, although most of your stories are about urban middle classes who, in your own way, fall under the subaltern category. I find this curious because much of the postcolonial discourse takes the middle classes for granted, as though they do not deserve the same kind of security or attention as the rural or peasant subalterns.*

AC: I don't like the middlebrow as a category because the middlebrow is a mainstream category where the parameters have to do with conventional realism, all of the things I don't like. I'm very interested in, as you've said, the avant-garde and modernist element. But the history of the middle class does interest me and it's a very rich history in India. We are all products of that history. So, to suppress the ways in which we are products of that history is to suppress our own everyday. Indian Anglophone writing and thinking is often about suppressing ourselves and inhabiting some kind of transcendental, neutral tone. Even the postcolonialists do not speak as themselves, but within a kind of neutral tone of an objective academic discourse ...

PKM: *Speaking for others?*

AC: ... and speaking in a way where, somehow, they are not enmeshed directly, the persons who have seen those things or are writing those things are not enmeshed directly with what they're saying. This reproduces a sort of enlightened objectivity of speaking from above, where the self's existence in the world and its memory don't come into play. All those things are suppressed.

PKM: *It's very interesting you say this because in your piece in* Literary Activism *(2017c), you invoke this very intimacy and memory you say is missing in postcolonial Anglophone discourse. You start with a peculiar encounter in a car park and suddenly drift into involuntary memory, delving into insignificant yet intimate details. This is quite formulaic of your literary essays, most of which begin with your own personal encounters. Even when you are addressing serious discursive themes such as modernity, intertextuality, or deconstruction, you tend to refrain from an overtly scholarly or value-neutral tone.*

AC: Because these things, in my case, are always emerging from a life encounter. It's an encounter in life that produces the thought process. So, the encounter with life has to be a part, in my essays, of the thought process.

PKM: *I find this approach all the more remarkable in your book on D.H. Lawrence's poetry, in which you propose a major theoretical intervention between canonical and communal poetry. But I have always wondered why you were so drawn to the poetry of Lawrence? I mean he has enough prose to inspire, or was your book* D.H. Lawrence and 'Difference' *(2003) completely an academic exercise?*

AC: I was transformed by my reading of *Sons and Lovers* (Lawrence 1913). As I've said many times before, *Sons and Lovers*, to me, was the first text I read that was contemporaneous with the modernists, which seemed to reject the metaphysical, by which I mean an extraneous source of value—whether that source of value is religion or heaven, or whether it's a lost religion, or a lost civilization—as was the case with a certain kind of modernism. That civilization once existed and it had been fragmented, and, it was those fragments that animated a kind of sense of value that was receding. With Lawrence, there is no sense of civilizational crisis in *Sons and Lovers*. There's a rejection of that idea and a kind of affirmation of being in the present, the incandescence of living in the here and now. And he was saying something in *Sons and Lovers*, without using so many words—and I've said this before—which he would say again closer to the time of his death in a book called *Apocalypse* (Lawrence 1931): "whatever the dead and unborn might know, they cannot know the marvel of being alive in the flesh". This seemed to me a rejection of metaphysics on behalf of the fact of existence. I realized when reading *Sons and Lovers* that this was very important to me—the affirmation of the fact of existence. So that directed me in the ways I was to think about writing.

PKM: *Your fiction writing?*

AC: And that transformed into my fiction writing, beginning with *A Strange and Sublime Address* (Chaudhuri 1991), which I wanted to be a narrative about the present moment: what it means to inhabit the present moment. I could have made it a narrative about childhood or the past because I was basing it on precisely those things, or my visits to Calcutta from Bombay. But I decided in some subconscious kind of capacity that I would make it about living in the here and now, and thereby reject this narrative to be grounded in the past, of what has occurred. Roland Barthes says the "unreal time of novels, cosmogonies, and histories" depends on the simple past tense. And it begins with, in the case of the novel, a sentence in the simple past tense like "The marchioness went out at five o'clock". So, I wanted to reject that sense of time, where the narrative represents something that's over and perfect and available for reproduction in a novel. I wanted to reject all of that. It's not that I didn't write in the past tense. But you can use that tense to somehow still give a sense of the present moment.

PKM: *But besides Lawrence, one also sees the influences of the likes of Joyce and Borges in your work. These are canonical writers now, but were avant-garde figures in their own times. Writers likes Borges are also fabulists, and fabulists, as William Golding (1989) argues, are moralists who "cannot make a story without a human lesson tucked away in it" (77). So, do all your influences—be they modernist, avant-gardist, or fabulist—reject metaphysis in the way you just described, or do they also inculcate moral lessons? Or do they have their own kind of politics?*

AC: I think they comprise their own kind of politics, and their own kind of argumentation. I don't like moralism, again moralism depends so much on the suppression of the self and its encounter with life. And I don't like that.

PKM: *But coming to the music part of your work, there is a lot of improvisation which is again a sign of being in the present, or performing in the moment. Is there some sort of interaction between your writing and your music? I remember you telling us in Chemnitz at the 2013 Association for the Study of New Literatures in English conference that you were practising your vocals in the hotel minutes before you came down to deliver a lecture on art and literature.*

AC: I neither think of them as existing separately, nor do I think of them as separate selves co-existing with an overseer looking upon them, where that overseer is somebody who exists in my brain. They are discontinuous but related.

PKM: *They feed off each other?*

AC: They must do so, because of their existing neighbourliness. But they're not aware of existing in relation to each other any more than when you're sitting in one lane, you're aware of what is going on in the next one. There must be some kind of give and take going on between that lane and this one.

PKM: *But you don't do it consciously.*

AC: Yes, you don't do it consciously.

PKM: *But it's very interesting though because in your music, you work within traditions, there is no rejection of sorts?*

AC: But I also experimented, with jazz and the blues.

PKM: *That's right, your own beginnings were a bit unorthodox; you wanted to become a Canadian singer-songwriter? Could you tell a bit more about how you became interested in Hindustani classical music?*

AC: As I was growing up in Bombay, my creative life, like my musical life, had been very fitful, and I arrived at places without expecting to arrive or wanting to arrive. I never knew I would be a prose writer when I wanted to write poetry. But that's what happened. Similarly, I never knew that I would become a Hindustani classical singer. Once I became a Hindustani classical singer, I completely rejected other kinds of music, like my earlier background in western popular music. So for years, I never listened to western music, especially after I started practising Hindustani music when I was in England. Only after 16 years did I go back to listening to western music again. That eventually led to the experiment I mentioned earlier. One morning, I thought I heard the riff to "Layla" (by Derek and the Dominos) as I was practising *raag todi*. So I decided to do something with the notes I was singing in compositional terms. But if you told me in 1985, when I was in the midst of training myself as an Indian classical singer, that one day I would be listening to Derek and the Dominos again, or that I would be incorporating something that they had written into a composition involving *raag todi*, I wouldn't have believed you. If somebody had told me at the age of 14 when I was listening to The Who and playing the guitar that one day I would be a classical singer, I wouldn't have believed them either. At each place, I've arrived by chance.

PKM: *It's your own odyssey in that sense.*

AC: Perhaps, yes.

PKM: *Talking about experimentation again, my thoughts drift in the direction of your latest novel* Friend of My Youth *(Chaudhuri 2017b), which is, in my reading, a prime example of experimental avant-garde. Fiction, non-fiction, or auto-fiction, however you want to call it. Usually works involving* *autobiographical elements arrive at the end of one's career. I'd like to think that there is a lot of writing left in you. I'm just curious why, at this stage of your writing career, you decided to write a semi-autobiographical work. Is it something you had to do now?*

AC: My writing has always been trying to unshackle itself from the pretence of fictionality. I've been trying to free myself of this dichotomy between fictionality and fact, between fictionality and life, creative writing and non-fiction. I'm only interested in creativity. All the rest of the terms are not relevant to me. And I've been writing from the beginning in a way that ignores those kind of set parameters according to which you represent reality within a novel. I tried to do that in *A Strange and Sublime Address*—to throw those dichotomies out of the window. In *Friend of My Youth*, I address head-on the question as to whether there is a difference between living and writing, or whether writing is also in some ways continuous with living. I don't want to say it is continuous with *life*, because that's a noun, but *writing* is both a noun and a gerund; something in the process of happening.

PKM: *The presence again.*

AC: Yeah.

PKM: *Thinking presence. Your take on creativity is very interesting. I mean the way I look at it, you create things by consciously or unconsciously wanting to move away from set traditions. But when I look at your work more closely, particularly the non-fiction, I get the feeling that you don't want to walk away from traditions altogether, in the sense that you do engage with your influences, your precursors and so on. This brings me to the question, could creativity be cultivated in a vacuum? Or is it something that cannot fully escape the grasp of traditions? Even in your case, there has to be some grounded thing that is the source of your creativity.*

AC: It's not that, I think, we cannot ignore our literary history, but we cannot take it as a given, either. Our history is not just out there, prefabricated with everything in place for us either to reject or to accept. Our rejection and our acceptance of a history, of a literary history, is something that we need to work out at any given point of life. It's not that the solutions have not already been given to us as to "this is unacceptable, that is acceptable", but that at any point of time one has to work these things out because they are not the answers readily available.

PKM: *If I read it correctly, you take a similar position in your collection of essays* Literary Activism *(2017c). Is there a price a writer pays for taking such an unconventional approach?*

AC: [chuckles] What do you have in mind?

PKM: *Oh I have what you call "market activism" in mind, which you discuss in relation to the aggressive mainstreaming and marketing of literature that creates overnight classics and the multitude of "bestseller" rankings while simultaneously burying the old ones. But my sense is that you didn't care about any such rankings or recognitions. I wonder what your advice would be for younger generations of writers who would want to think that way— defying traditions and market forces [I, for one, struggle with this anxiety about writing fiction and not being able to defy the tradition or expectation of an Indian or migrant writer.] What is the price one would have to pay and what would one gain from that?*

AC: Look, Pavan, I don't have a clear answer, and, unfortunately, I don't have a clear answer for any of your questions but I'm ready to think it through. I think I would say that many of us possibly reach this stage in our lives just about everywhere, so I'm not speaking about you. I've seen people who reach this stage of their lives when they're quite young when they open themselves up, and then arrive at a kind of intellectual and creative independence. As we go through our childhoods, we are still absorbing things. When we are adolescents, we become very puritanical and close-minded. And a certain point might come in our lives where we suddenly unshackle ourselves and don't care at that moment what dominant hegemony or our teachers and peers are telling us to do: "How can you not be doing this, we should all be doing that". We might arrive at our own indifference toward the expectants. That indifference is very important. And we open ourselves up then, to our own indifference.

PKM: *And be at peace with that?*

AC: Yes, be at peace with that at that time. When I see people, young people who arrive at that moment, I feel hopeful that a kind of change is coming about in terms of freedom from—to use a specific example, in India—a kind of social science moralism, and all prefabricated ideas of what is important and what is not.

PKM: *What is political?*

AC: Yes, what can be discussed and what can't be discussed. What happens, however, is that as people get into new jobs and new roles, they begin to suppress that part of themselves, and start speaking the language that their predecessors have spoken. All I would say is that it is important to not do that. If one has arrived at some kind of opening-up at a certain point in one's life, one should find ways of allowing that to continue and survive. Even if one has to make certain compromises, in fitting in with the existing structure of things, one must still find a way of allowing that kind of unshacklement, which informs what one does in the future. In that way, the disciplines can be taken to new places. But what I see unfortunately is people often being forced to set aside that moment of freedom and speak in the too familiar voice, that of the predecessors.

PKM: *And one is constantly being imposed upon, like you said, by the standards set by the then "greatest writers" or "bestselling writers" as if they're set in stone, but they keep changing. I really enjoyed your sharp critique of the Booker in* Literary Activism.

AC: All right, yes.

PKM: *Let me return to the question of diaspora, which is often defined in relation to the separation or distance—be it physical, cultural, or imaginary—from one's nation or home. In your work, there is always a distancing within the nation, and then, gradually, a distancing away from the nation; from Bombay to Calcutta, and to the UK. I wonder if there is a gradual move towards diaspora—both away from home and within home—in your work?*

AC: Not quite. *Friend of My Youth* is about Bombay. But I don't think just about being in Bombay but also about the idea of return and …

PKM: *Of course, your work has always had this element of being grounded in Calcutta or Bombay and characters coming in and out of the diaspora. Have you been conscious of having your own footing in two different worlds?*

AC: I think I must have been placed in Calcutta with genuine ties to England as well. But I also think of myself as being a reluctant traveller when going to various places. I would rather not go to any of them, but going to them educates me in some way. So, in a way, I'm a product of these kinds of reluctant travels; even being here has educated me in some way. I didn't particularly want to come here, you know, to Galle, but now that I've come here yes, obviously, it educates me about modernity, the history of modernity, which is the thing that most interests me when I encounter cities, their architecture, and ways of life.

PKM: *Colonial history?*

AC: What remains of those ways of life ...

PKM: *That's exactly my reading of* Calcutta: Two Years in the City *(Chaudhuri 2013), which is not hung up with colonialism in a deterministic way as much of postcolonial writing is. I myself grew up in Hyderabad which was never under direct colonial rule, but there is still this pan-colonial aura and you are being constantly reminded that "hey, you were colonized, you should know that". When you come to places such as Galle, do you also look for the remains of colonialism?*

AC: No, I see remains of modernity which I want to distinguish from colonialism.

PKM: *Very interesting. Would you then say the colonial heritage had both an enabling and disabling impact on our current traditions?*

AC: I don't know. Every tradition has an enabling and disabling impact. Colonial traditions definitely had a disabling impact but modernity, of which colonial tradition is a peripheral part, had an extraordinary efflorescence in our country, as it did in other parts of the world. We don't understand it very well because we often confuse it with colonialism.

PKM: *So, it has its own life detached from the sort of modernity you describe?*

AC: I don't think Calcutta would be an interesting city if there were no cultural modernity. If it were only a centre for British colonialism, it would be a marginal city, it would be of very little historical significance. The reason it is of great significance is because of Bengali modernity. You know, of what happened in the period.

PKM: Bhadralok *[Bengali educated middle class]?*

AC: Yeah, of what happened in the period. The *Bhadralok* and the movements against the *Bhadralok*. So over there the colonial institutions are of only a particular kind of interest, but they do not turn Calcutta into the astonishingly compelling city of imagination. So, on the other hand, if you don't want to see that reality of modernity, I don't know what you're looking at when you see those cities.

PKM: *It's interesting you say that this is the kind of conclusion many postcolonial theorists arrive at nowadays.*

AC: It is not that I do not have sharply critical views of the colonial project as in when it impinges upon us. I've made these views clear most recently in the long essay I wrote in *The Guardian* in support of "The Rhodes Must Fall" movement, and in other kinds of shorter essays about the British and their pride about the railways in India. But I write about those things when they impinge on our lives today; for me it's not a professionalized kind of activity.

PKM: *So, this history is not like a threat that continually impinges upon on our lives. The railways contribute to the history of the past, but also become the histories of the present ...*

AC: It may be a threat but also the elites within our own countries are quite stifling and feel entitled [to such pasts].

PKM: *There's an argument Ashis Nandy made in* The Intimate Enemy *(1983) in which, as the title suggests, our elites are bound to replicate these models of hegemony.*

AC: And on top of that we have our own consciousness to deal with in terms of its mastery over us. And finally, there's the market. Now we live in the hegemony of the market.

PKM: *Market, yes, and you mentioned this aspect of local hegemonies. I do not expect you to have an opinion about everything that happens in India, but you did spend a better part of your life in Calcutta ...*

AC: And Bombay ...

PKM: *Could we also make a case, say, for diaspora within the country because, as you say, there are unfamiliar zones within the nation? I return to this question because it is a question that we grapple with as researchers of South Asian writing.*

AC: Yeah, I mean, as I said, not only unfamiliarity within the nation, but unfamiliarity within one's own city, but also familiarity with cities with which one has no seeming historical connection: to find certain neighbourhoods in Geneva seem familiar to me. How does that happen? Berlin seems familiar, Atlanta City doesn't. Dubai doesn't. Why is that? I think I spoke about these things at Chemnitz.

PKM: *It was Dubai you spoke about in Chemnitz.*

AC: Right, culturally, we may be closer to Dubai. But I feel alienated there as I do in Atlanta. Berlin? I feel as if I've seen it before. So, all of that signals the fact that we cannot take who we are or our inheritance as a given, that this question has been sorted out for us already. The question needs to be re-addressed all the time, as to how we interact with the world, and in what ways, and on what terms, do our senses of alienation and homecoming play out? They do not play out in any predictable way.

PKM: *Amit, thank you very much for your time.*

Acknowledgements

This publication is supported by a grant from the German Research Foundation (DFG): MA 7119 / 1-1.

Bibliography

Almond, Ian. 2010. "Melancholy, Ghostliness and Economy in the Short Fiction of Amit Chaudhuri." *Journal of Postcolonial Writing* 46 (2): 164–74.
Borges, Jorge, Luis. 1964. *Labyrinths: Selected Stories and Other Writings*. Edited by Donald A. Yates and James E. Irby and Preface by André Maurois. Cambridge. MA: New Directions Publishing.
Chaudhuri, Amit. 1991. *A Strange and Sublime Address*. London: Minerva.
---. 2003. *D. H. Lawrence and 'Difference': Postcoloniality and the Poetry of the Present*. Oxford: Oxford University Press.
---. 2008. *Clearing a Space: Reflections on India, Literature and Culture*. Oxford: Peter Lang.
---. 2013. *Calcutta: Two Years in the City*. London: Vintage.
---. 2014. *Odysseus Abroad*. London: Oneworld Publications.
---. 2016. "My Best Writing Tip by William Boyd, Jeanette Winterson, Amit Chaudhuri and More." *The Guardian*, Sept. 10. https://www.theguardian.com/books/2016/sep/10/my-best-writing-tip-william-boyd-jeanette-winterson.
---. 2017a. "'I Had to Construct Lineages for Myself': An Interview with Amit Chaudhuri. [With Laetitia Zecchini]." *Journal of Postcolonial Writing* 53 (1–2): 255-63.
---. 2017b. *Friend of My Youth*. London: Faber and Faber.
---. 2017c. *Literary Activism: Perspectives*. New Delhi: Oxford University Press.
---. 2019. "A New India Is Emerging, and It Is a Country Ruled by Fear." *The Guardian*, Oct. 8. https://www.theguardian.com/commentisfree/2019/oct/08/narendra-modi-bjp-india.

Desani, G.V. 1948. *All About H. Hatterr.* New Delhi: Arnold Heinemann.
Golding, William. 1989. "Fable." In *The Hot Gates*, 76–99. London: Faber and Faber.
Jonas, M. 1988. "An Interview with Nuruddin Farah." *Journal of Refugee Studies* 1 (1): 74–77.
Lawrence, D.H. 1913. *Sons and Lovers.* London: Duckworth.
---. 1931. *Apocalypse.* Florence: G. Orioli.
Mukherjee, Neel. 2015. "*Odysseus Abroad* by Amit Chaudhuri: Review." *The Guardian*, February 7.
Nandy, Ashis. 1983. *An Intimate Enemy: Loss and Recovery of Self Under Colonialism.* Oxford: Oxford University Press.
Roy, Sumana. 2017. "The Deeply Unserious, Important Work of Amit Chaudhuri." *Los Angeles Review of Books*, Feb. 19. https://lareviewofbooks.org/article/amit-chaudhuri/.
Sandru, Cristina. 2010. "Introduction." In *Rerouting the Postcolonial: New Directions for the New Millennium*, edited by Janet Wilson, Cristina Sandru, and Sarah Lawson Welsh, 101–05. Abingdon: Routledge.

Poetry as Radical Resistance:
R. Cheran in Conversation with Aparna Halpé

Photograph of Cheran by Sharryn Aiken

Cheran is a Tamil Canadian academic, poet, playwright and journalist, who writes poetry in Tamil using the single name, Cheran, and is regarded as one of the most important poets writing in that language today. Cheran was born in Alaveddy in Jaffna, Sri Lanka, and began writing poetry in the 1970s, when ethnic conflict in Sri Lanka was escalating into civil war. His earliest published poem was "The Sea", which appeared in 1977 (Cheran 2013, 27), and for the majority of his writing career he has been a relentless and vivid documenter of the history of Sri Lanka. Specifically, as he himself says, "anyone that reads my poems from 1980 all the way up until May 2009 can see a history of Tamil people and of National oppression. It's very significantly weaved into my poetry" (Cheran n.d.). While he has also written of love and loss, exile and the diasporic experience, he has come to be seen as the pre-eminent poet of that Tamil experience, as in "A Second Sunrise", his poem on the burning of the Jaffna Public Library by Sinhalese police on June 1, 1981 (Cheran 2013, 35) or the searing opening of his 1999 poem "Apocalypse":

> In our own time we have seen
> the Apocalypse. The earth
> trembled to the dance of the dead;
> bodies burst apart in the wild storm
> (Cheran 2013, 87)

In a 2009 interview with Sascha Ebeling, Cheran stated that "I am a poet as a witness, a witness to history" (Ebeling 2013, 17).

Cheran pursued a perilous career as a journalist in Sri Lanka, which he discusses in this interview with Aparna Halpé. In the 1980s he worked for *Saturday Review*, a Jaffna English language weekly which came under attack from the government for reporting atrocities carried out by Sri Lanka's security forces. "It was not liked by the various Tamil militant groups either", he remarks wryly (Cheran 2015). Cheran came to Toronto in 1993 to pursue his doctoral studies. He is currently a professor at the University of Windsor, Ontario, in Canada, has authored more than 15 books in Tamil, and his work has been translated into 20 languages. Cheran was the recipient of the International Poetry Award from ONV Kurup Foundation in Dubai in 2017. He has performed his poetry at various International Writers' festivals in the UK, US, Singapore, Indonesia, India, Sweden, the Netherlands, Canada, Ramallah, West Bank, Dubai and Mexico. His English language plays have been produced and performed in Toronto, Canada, and New York, Chicago and New Jersey in the US. Singapore's modern dance group Chowk has produced and performed a dance play based on his poems titled *The Second Sunrise*, which was also performed at the Singapore International Dance Festival and Washington's Kennedy Centre for the Arts. In this interview conducted in September 2020, Cheran speaks candidly about his experiences as a radical Tamil poet living in exile, and his extensive work as a poet, journalist, teacher and scholar.

The interviewer, Aparna Halpé, is a Sri Lankan poet, musician, and scholar living in Toronto. She holds a doctorate in postcolonial literature from the Department of English and the Centre for South Asian Studies at the University of Toronto. Dr. Halpé's research focuses on the function of myth in contemporary fiction from South Asia, Southeast Asia, and the Caribbean, and her scholarly work has appeared in *Moving Worlds* (Leeds, 2010), *Mythe Mode d'Emploi* (Interférance Litteraires, 2015), and *Confluences 2: Essays on the New Canadian Literature* (Mawenzi House, 2017).

She is the author of a collection of poems, *Precarious* (2013), and is currently co-editor, with Michael Ondaatje, of *Lakdhas Wikkramasinha: A Selection of Poems* (forthcoming). Dr Halpé is currently Professor of English at Centennial College, Toronto.

Aparna Halpé (AH): *It is September 2020, and most of the world is shut down due to the COVID-19 pandemic. Many artists and poets to whom I speak describe a sense of paralysis stemming from an intuition that the future that approaches is unlike anything we have tried to imagine; others have been furiously productive, resisting through expression, through community and practice. Have you continued to create in this time?*

Cheran (C): I was not expecting to be very productive during the COVID-19 lock down and the subsequent restrictions. I never believed the notion that crisis or duress can make someone more productive and creative although, as you know, some of my most powerful works were my response to the military and political oppression of Tamil people in Sri Lanka.

However, with COVID-19, it is a very strange experience. In the past I have experienced several months of economic blockade, continuous curfews for months, and military lockdowns in Jaffna, Sri Lanka. I still have eerie memories about them. But this Corona lockdown is totally different. The enemy is an unseen one. We created this enemy, and we knew it was coming. We have witnessed the disappearance of millions and millions of birds, bees and what science calls biodiversity. Mindless accumulation and profit-making through dispossession and elimination of nature is one of the reasons for this epidemic.

While preparing for my new course at the University of Windsor titled "Beyond Anthropocene", among other reports and books, I read the report issued by the Trump administration's Department of Transport on climate crisis. It says that the global temperature would rise by four degrees by the end of this century and that would be a disaster. The solution they propose is the most troubling, albeit not surprising: erase all restrictions on emissions by cars and other motor vehicles and, hey presto, go for sales!

I am afraid COVID-19 is the beginning, and more sinister and deadly pandemics could follow if we do not put the environment before economics. I have written several poems on humans "terrorizing" nature in my collections, and the disappearance (see my "Tree Poems") of our social and ecological architecture. Some of the images I came up with 15 years ago have become real in these pandemic times. I am deeply disturbed and scared.

"The Giant Tree in the Rain Forest"

A wondrous landscape
where mountain, rain forest and ocean
merge,
the weather mild,
I stand on
the moist earth.

The imprints of
a swelling ocean draw
patterns on the sand;
even now

a heavy fog
smothers the ocean slowly
where the sea ends and land begins
blurred in this magical moment;
the lighthouse siren blares
intermittently
to guide the confused canoes.

The fog now swallows
the mountains and the forests.

Towering four hundred feet,
having survived the axe of Columbus
having lived a thousand years,
the cedar, now threatened by a fog;
does this presage a battle?

Marked by the wisdom of time
the giant tree smiles,
embraces the fog.
I stand below.

The life of the forest in its roots
the soul of the air in its crown,
the tree,

> no tongue to speak,
> but in its breath
> the tale of history.
>
> Its patience
> having vanquished the earth
> having spurned the hills,
> the giant tree
> now flings a branch
> to appease the enraged wind.
>
> And below
> with chain saws
> petty humans stand.
>
> (2011, 139–40)
>
> *(Translated from Tamil by Chelva Kanaganayakam)*

On a slightly different note, I must admit as an immunocompromised person, I have been self-isolating for several months. I have been writing, delivering numerous lectures via Zoom and Google Meet, reading and performing my poems and participating in various discussions online. I was surprised by the "mediated proximity" that these communicative platforms offer, and I think they have reached multiple times more audience and viewers than my traditional classrooms and seminars.

I have also lost some very good friends to COVID-19. It was very painful not to be with them in their last moments. One of them was cremated against his own religious wish in Sri Lanka, which was very insensitive on the part of the authorities there. Unlike many other countries, in Sri Lanka, it is the military that conducts the "war against COVID-19". Therefore, no surprises here.

So far, I have been very productive—so are many of my creative friends—and I am glad to realize that, at least sometimes, writing under duress is good. One of my poems on the pandemic has been included in a fine literary anthology titled *Singing in the Dark*, edited by K. Satchidanandan and Nishi Chawla, and published by Penguin Random House (2020). And another piece of work appeared in the collection titled *Lock Down: Poetry, Diary, Interview*, edited by Santosh Kalluzhathil (2020).

AH: *What does your writing practice look like these days? Do you find yourself drawn to new preoccupations, or even more haunted by the foundations that brought us here in the first place?*

C: As always, poetry has been my staple and will remain that way. However, two years back I was tempted to write a few chapters of my memoirs. Most of my creative non-fiction is in English. I began writing my memoirs when I was a writer in residence at the Banff Centre for the Arts on a fellowship in Alberta 20 years ago. I wrote a chapter, about 3000 words in total. Then I never had the mindset and inner urge to finish it. But I wrote a few other pieces—one for English PEN, and a few other pieces in Tamil for the Tamil journal *Kalachuvadu*.

I launched a course on genocide at my university in 2017. Preparing for it, organizing visual, social scientific, and literary materials, and teaching it has had an enormous impact on my writing practices and academic work. I have tons of stories to tell and all of them cannot be told or framed in a traditional social scientific manner, or as a typical "journal article". Hence, for a while, I wrote a few papers, kind of auto-ethnographic work, and included my experiences and narratives. There is a complex and competitive, but often underappreciated space in academia for someone like me who combines literary and "research imagination" (in the sense that Arjun Appadurai [2001] uses it in the Introduction to *Globalization*) to grapple with an "ungrabbable" issue such as genocide.

I always use fiction and poetry in my sociology courses. And for the course on genocide using poetry and fiction—including my own work—has been illuminating. While we all, in the field of academia, know and appreciate imagination as a social and research practice, we should cherish the power of literary and poetic imagination in social and other sciences too.

My current writings are focused on literature, my past, trauma, and multiple forms and formats of registering, narrating and witnessing. I must admit it is not an easy task. It is appropriate to say that I am haunted and hunted by the foundations of traditional social sciences. However, this is just another inevitable struggle.

AH: *And what are you reading these days?*

C: I am slowly returning to fiction. There was a time when I would read novels and short stories in Tamil and English non-stop—a kind of marathon reading. I do not know why, but after writing my doctoral dissertation, I could not continue reading fiction. Non-fiction and poetry have been my main sustenance. Then, after the war ended in 2009,[1] several novels and collections of short stories appeared in Tamil, and a few in English translations as well. I began to read them and that was a significant turning point for me. Remarkable works of non-fiction in Tamil had already begun appearing 15 years ago, and the trend continues till today. Some of these works are by former combatants.

The COVID-19 lockdown has actually facilitated my reading of fiction. In addition to re-reading Anna Akhmatova, Osip Mandelstam, bpNichol, W.S. Mervyn, Jean Arasanayagam and Mahmoud Darwish, I read Richard Wagamese, an Ojibwe author and journalist from the Wabaseemoong Independent Nations in northwestern Ontario. There are several Tamil writers whose powerful novels and short stories that came out in the past ten years are part of the reason I have returned to reading fiction.

I have read Sinhalese fiction mostly in Tamil and English translations and Sinhalese poetry in Sinhala. I have also translated a few Sinhala poems directly from Sinhala into Tamil. There is a small but powerful body of Sinhala poetry written about war and genocide, some which I published in Tamil translation in various journals in India and Canada. I am thinking of poets such as Ajith Herath, Manjula Wediwardene, Mahesh Munasinghe, Timran Keerthi, Subhadra, Kalpana Ambrose and fiction writers such as Isuru Chamara. Liyanege Amarakeerthi and Prabhath Jayasinghe are my other favorite Sinhalese writers.

AH: *Before we get into talking about your poetry, I want to touch on your other authorial processes. You are a writer who wears many hats, as scholar, journalist, dramatist and poet. Looking back on your time as a journalist, which you have documented in your piece "Salad Days" (Cheran 2000), your*

---

1   Following 26 years of civil war, Sri Lanka's army declared that it had defeated the separatist Tamil Tiger rebels in May 2009. But as Sascha Ebeling asks in his Introduction to Cheran's collection *In a Time of Burning*, "what does it mean for such a war to be over?" (Ebeling 18).

commitment to writing through the silence of censorship called for a radical kind of creativity that allowed you to report fact through metonymic imagistic systems and references.

For example, you describe the Saturday Review[2] *being dubbed "the only wholly government-censored newspaper", or, when describing some of the more inventive strategies used, you say, "we'd simply leave a chunk of white space where a censorship story should have been and headline it 'Who Killed Cock Robin?'" (2000, 131). This was a creative departure from bare fact in order to speak truth to power.*

We are now living in an age where the notion of truth and fact are under siege, but in many ways, this was terrain with which you were already familiar in the Sri Lanka of the 1980s. The robust presence of a free press seems to be more important than ever, and yet perhaps more precarious than ever. Can you speak to this?

C: It may sound old, but I must confess that I am addicted to print. Censorship has a disproportionate impact on print as opposed to other media. I spent a significant time in the printing presses, and I love the smell of newsprint, fresh off the machine. I used to smell the machine proof page first, before checking and signing off on it. When I began my life as a journalist, first as an editorial assistant, then as an acting editor and finally as a deputy editor, most of the time I had to work with the letter press and occasionally Linotype. For our press, I selected and brought all different kinds of fonts from India. Page design and font selection were my other preferred jobs at the newspaper.

You can imagine what it was like when our press was partially damaged in an aerial bombing by the Sri Lankan Air Force in 1986. Publish and be bombed! The creative ideas we deployed as you mentioned above, were the results of playing with the design, fonts, and perhaps an uncanny ability to hoodwink the authorities. We were unable to publish the details but could at least indicate the enormity of the atrocities and the nature of "bleeding statistics". The censorship and aversion to freedom of expression were also characteristic of the various Tamil militant movements.

---

2   The *Saturday Review* (1982–87) was an English-language weekly newspaper published from Jaffna in Sri Lanka.

There are three other issues I am seriously concerned with in the context of press freedom in Sri Lanka today. The first one is the practice of self-censorship that has evolved as a strategy not to be on the "bad list" of the authorities. In the Tamil media scenario, this has a long and sordid history. Second, there is a great divide in the way Sinhalese and English media report the events and news and the way Tamil media report it. The Muslim-owned Tamil press would take a different perspective. The media in Sri Lanka is "ethnic media". For the past 40 years I have been reading, and to a certain extent monitoring, news media in Sri Lanka, and I have no hesitation in saying this: the mainstream Sinhala and English media—almost all of them based in Colombo—hardly ever truthfully cover the news, developments, and events in the North and East. Their priorities are different. This is part of the reason why there was (and still is) a powerful, regional Tamil press in the North and, for a short while in the 1990s, in the East as well. There are seven daily Tamil newspapers published in Jaffna and a weekly Tamil newspaper published from Batticaloa. There is no Sinhalese or English language press in areas other than Colombo. And third, given the intense militarization and surveillance of the country, more so in the North and East, it is difficult for an independent and free press to operate. Just last week, two Tamil journalists, who went to report on the illegal logging in the Vanni area, were severely assaulted by the loggers, who work very closely with the military and government authorities. And there was hardly any reporting on this in the mainstream media.

As Arundhati Roy notes in the context of the Indian media, racism, anti-minority violence, and majoritarian supremacy are facilitated by important sections of the media. This is the case in Sri Lanka as well, which is neither new nor surprising. The task in front and ahead of us is difficult. The age of "manufacturing" consent is gone. This is the age of fabricating "truths" and re-inventing history and heritage to justify them.

AH: You are teaching a course on genocide. (Full disclosure: your poetry has been on the syllabus since 2011 in my own course on genocide). Teaching genocide literature in Canada's multicultural classrooms can be a tricky thing. I recall a personal example, when I was teaching the Palestinian poet Rafeef Ziadah to a class that had a pro-settler Israeli student. Can you share your experiences of negotiating the conversations that need to happen in such difficult pedagogical spaces?

C: I agree with you that teaching and discussing genocide, ethnic cleansing, and mass atrocities is difficult and sensitive, and could be re-traumatizing for some students and professors. Historical events of genocides and other related atrocities are often tangled up in emotions and contested perspectives, and the repeated failure of the so-called "international community" to act decisively to end genocidal violence is tragic, but not surprising. Understanding genocide remains an important part of prevention and healing. Arguments, controversies, or challenging and emotional situations in a classroom setting are not necessarily a bad thing. They can be transformed into a learning opportunity. Difficult knowledge inevitably offers very effective teachable moments.

Some of the limitations of the study and teaching of genocide come from the fact that we tend to emphasize the international law perspective and try to limit ourselves to a legal lens. In my opinion, sociological and anthropological perspectives and analyses are crucial. Mass rape and sexual violence as a deliberate weapon of war have been recognized as genocide only recently. And, as I said before, literature is indispensable in our attempts to understand and teach genocide. Therefore, I use a mixture of materials—traditional scholarly articles, narratives and testimonies, art, poetry and memoirs—and the teaching and learning process is multidisciplinary.

I would also include political economy perspectives in the context of modern genocides and ethnic cleansing, especially when identifying and exposing the interconnections between global capital, resource extraction, and genocidal violence. I have always included various case studies—from Indigenous genocides to the forgotten "genocides without witnesses"—in my courses. I have also had students from Africa, Asia and the Middle East, who have survived or witnessed genocide, ethnic cleansing, and mass atrocities. It would be very difficult for most of them to present in class, although several of them bravely attempted to do so. I had to find different modes and strategies to evaluate their participation. The difficult situations I faced mainly came from the context of Israeli occupation, the genocide of Bangladesh people, and a few in-class conflicts over the Bosnian genocide. I haven't had any ugly incidents so far. In terms of negotiating controversies and emotion-filled partisan arguments, I found it useful to explain the selective and hypocritical usage of human rights—and definitions of genocide, war crimes, and crimes against humanity—by nation states and international institutions. Often, I ended up insisting that my students read more literature or watch certain films and artworks created by the "other side".

AH: We have recently noted the modest success of bringing the Rohingya genocide to light, most notably through Gambia's decision to launch an altruistic litigation on behalf of the Rohingya. Why do you think that similar efforts—for example, the attempt to persuade the UK to refer Sri Lanka to the International Criminal Court for crimes against humanity and acts of genocide—have failed?

C: A lot of countries, including the UK, are complicit in the genocide of Tamils in Sri Lanka. It is no surprise to me that you should mention the UK. As we all know, even a few days before the beginning of the Rwandan genocide, the UK was selling arms and ammunitions to the Hutu government. In the case of Sri Lanka, way back in the 1980s a UK private militia, with the tacit support of the UK government, assisted and participated in attacks against Tamil civilians. A recent film, *Keenie Meenie: Britain's Private Army* (Miller and Macnamara 2020), based on the book by Phil Miller (2020), *Keenie Meenie: The British Mercenaries Who Got Away with War Crimes*, documents the British government's complicity. India, Pakistan, China, Israel, and the US are a few other countries that were either complicit or tacitly supporting the Sri Lankan government. There is a list of other countries that choose to remain silent. That's part of the reason why it would be difficult to bring Sri Lanka to face justice. Moreover, Sri Lanka is not a signatory to the ICC. Only the Security Council can refer Sri Lanka to the ICC, but Sri Lanka has very powerful allies at the Security Council so it would be unlikely. There may be other ways, which may take a long time.

Reflecting on the role of the UN, it is important to remember that in 2009 the UN withdrew from war zones at the request of the Sri Lankan government, despite pleas from the civilian population and Non-Governmental Organizations. The UN refused to publish the number of civilian casualties during the last stages of the war in order not to jeopardize its relationship with the government. The first UN resolution on the war congratulated the Sri Lankan government for "successfully defeating terrorism". In the intervening years, there have been two other UN resolutions on this issue demanding accountability, but there has been no follow up action. Just a few weeks ago, the UN Country Team in Sri Lanka invited Mahinda Rajapaksa, the current Prime Minister and former President accused of war crimes, as "Chief Guest" to celebrate the 75th anniversary of the signing of the UN Charter! In this context it is difficult to expect a breakthrough.

AH: *You've mentioned in another interview (with Akilesh Udhayabanu in July 2020) that you bring an auto-ethnographical approach to this course on genocide. How difficult is it for you to return to the wound, the trauma, over and over again?*

C: I have included my poems from the collection *In a Time of Burning* (Cheran 2013) in the syllabi, in addition to a part of my memoir detailing my arrest and torture. The piece was titled "Salad Days" and is included in the book, *To Arrive Where You Are* (Cheran 2001). With prior warning, I showed Callum Macrae's documentary *No Fire Zone* (Macrae 2013). I have also included a few short stories by Jean Arasanayagam, and Benjamin Dix and Lindsay Pollock's (2019) graphic novel *Vanni: A Family's Struggle Through the Sri Lankan Conflict*, among other materials. Reading them again and marking the assignments on them is very hard.

In March 2009, my twins were two years old. Every night, after putting them to bed, I would return to my computer to check the situation in Vanni. From March until May, I used to get regular news from my fellow journalists in the war zones, horrific images and messages from them and my friends and family. I had two good friends who worked in the "No Fire Zones" as medics. One day in April, I received a photo and a message from a friend: amputation of right hand and right leg of a two-year-old toddler without anesthesia while her screaming mother was not far from the scene. I turned off my computer, walked into the bedroom, kissed my twins, and cried. That image and returning to the wound are beyond prose. And, a few days later, I wrote a poem that is now part of my series of poems on genocide.

AH: *In Sri Lanka, the politics of progress and so-called "reconciliation" seem to make strange bedfellows; Gotabhaya Rajapaksa and Karuna Amman, for example. What would truth and reconciliation look like if it could be applied to Sri Lanka? I think here about poem 41 in your forthcoming collection,* Land of Melting Sorrows:

> "Grave Hole"
> Don't ask why we don't know.
> Don't ask how we forgot.
> Don't also ask why we didn't write.
> For each his own memory.
>
> A land without witnesses.

C: I am very pessimistic about the prospect for reconciliation between the State and the Tamils in Sri Lanka. Acknowledgement is the first step for reconciliation. The State together with the major part of the Sinhalese public opinion is not willing to acknowledge this. The unprecedented electoral successes of the current President and the Prime Minister—both Rajapaksas—are aided and abetted by the euphoria and institutionalization of the victorious Sinhala Buddhist nation. Reconciliation and healing need closure. There is no closure now. You can burn the forest. It is easy. But you cannot heal it.

Having said that, I must point out that there is a small but active group of Sinhala writers, journalists and activists without whom exposing the genocidal acts by the Sri Lankan state during the last phase of the war would not have been possible. They are symbols of humanity and torch bearers of solidarity who offer us some hope for reconciliation. Tamils have their own reconciliation process too which has not been properly initiated. They need to take responsibility for the atrocities against the Muslims by all major Tamil militant groups, and the ethnic cleansing of Muslims by the Liberation Tigers of Tamil Eelam (LTTE), and begin a sincere process of reconciliation. Tamils know that internecine warfare among various Tamil militant groups in the mid-1980s, and the elimination of other militant groups by the LTTE, resulted in hundreds of young Tamils killed and hundreds disappeared. Several Tamils were killed or disappeared for dissenting. We have a moral and political obligation to initiate truth-telling and to go forward with reconciliation.

AH: *I would like to dwell on this poem in* Land of Melting Sorrows:

> There is no land to light a lamp
> the land has been stolen and sold
> But Chera
> whose land?
> whose place?

The translator, Geetha Sukumaran, powerfully evokes the loss of Nanthikadal in her introduction to the translation, but I want to stretch this idea even further, and ask: Is there an echo here of the fundamental question of whether the island that is now named Sri Lanka was always already-stolen land, a terra nullius (albeit before the 1095 Papal Bull was even articulated), stolen from the Indigenous peoples of a precolonial space for which we have no historical name?

C: All the current inhabitants of Sri Lanka, whether they are Sinhalese, Tamils, Muslims and various mixed and hybrid "ethnic" communities can have a valid claim to the ancestry and heritage of the country. The peopling of Sri Lanka has been a complex and contested issue not because of informed archeological debates, but because of the politicization and militarization of history, historiography and archeology. The Presidential Task Force for Archaeological Heritage Management in the Eastern Province was established on June 2, 2020. A Buddhist monk Ellawala Medhananda Thero, who was described as "Archeological Chakravarthi" (Emperor of Archeology) in the official *Gazette* proclamation, was appointed as the chairperson of the task force. The members were military officers and a few Sinhala academics. This monk says that 99.9 percent of archaeological and heritage sites in Sri Lanka are Buddhist.

What is most important is that the racial / race and racist discourse (I am using the term "race" here as a term under erasure), dominating our battles for identity, domination, nationalism and territory, should be abolished. "Race" as a scientific and biological category was discarded in the dustbin of knowledge a long time ago. Sinhalese and Tamils are not "racial" categories. Even the terms "ethnic" and "ethnicity" are of recent origin. To claim and to implement policies and practices for exclusive ownership and heritage by the Sinhalese Buddhists, as the Sri Lankan state does, is another sinister form of violence.

AH: *Scholars such as Geetha Sukumaran, Chelva Kanaganayakam, Anushiya Ramaswamy, to name a few, all identify you as a poet who writes within and beyond tradition, and one might make the case that your poetry heralds a radical, and perhaps inevitable, departure from tradition due to the context of your life. For those who may not be familiar with your book,* The Sixth Genre: Memory, History and the Tamil Diasporic Imagination *(Cheran 2001), can you explain to us what you conceive of as* Tinai? *Did this radical understanding of convention arise through your own poetic practice?*

C: Yes. I have been thinking and writing about the Tamil concept of *Tinai* for a very long time. I consider the concept of *Tinai* as a unique contribution of the Tamil literary and critical tradition to world civilization. The *Tinai* concept as part of Tamil classical poetics is central to our literary and intellectual tradition as well. The concept is a creative blending of cultural, economic, ecological, musical and emotional attributes in a spatial-temporal system. *Tinai* can be used simultaneously as a taxonomical tool for literary criticism and to encapsulate a creative Tamil eco-poetics of the human / nature relationship and interdependency, while expanding our understanding of Tamil-ness and the notions of Tamil identity and its relationship to landscapes and spaces. What I argued in my previous works is that a critical deployment of the concept of *Tinai* can offer us more nuanced perspectives in the study of literature and its social, historical, and cultural milieu. I have also argued that theoretically, the concept of *Tinai* can be profitably employed to chart new contours for our understanding of Tamil-ness—exile and displacement, the diasporic and transnational, hybridity and fusion—in contemporary Tamil societies.

AH: *We have spoken before about your experience of living through the burning of the Jaffna library in 1981. As Sri Lanka makes token efforts at reconstruction in Jaffna, I still return to what was lost, and a fundamental question about the capacity to rebuild in the face of such loss. If we could think of the Tamil language as a nation, does poetry become a radical resistance to the erasure of genocide?*

C: Poetry can be a radical resistance to any kind of erasure, and epistemic violence too. There is a progression of metaphor, politics, and poetics in my poetry. The titles of collections from 1983 to 2019 would tell you this. *The Second Sunrise* (1983), *Yaman: The Lord of Death* (1984), *We Live Amidst*

Death (edited volume, 1985), *Mirage* (1986), *At the Time of Burning* (1988), *The Procession of Skeletons* (1990), *The River You Step in Now* (2000), *Return to the Sea* (2005), *Healing the Forest* (2010), *Anjar: Trauma and Beyond* (2019), and *Thinai Mayakkam: Overlapping Landscapes* (2019). These are highly symbolic and, in a sense, historical too. Together, the entire collection can be read as our tragic but resistant history—poet as a witness and visionary. My life in exile and travels through various lands, languages and literatures have enriched my poetics. My imagery has changed. As one of the titles of my collection indicates, you will never step twice in the same river.

We want to convert our house that my father built into a museum for Tamil poetry. We are in the process of doing it. But there are still a lot of uncertainties. Do we want to keep all the archival material there? I am not sure. The memories of the burning of the Jaffna public library are still fresh. We do not have any power in that country. The Sri Lanka state is hellbent on Buddhisizing and Sinhalizing the Tamil-speaking regions. So, there is a huge question mark. Of course, I miss living in my home village. All my nighttime dreams are still about my village, and my parents and relatives. At the same time, I know I am a transnational. I am comfortable in simultaneously belonging to more than one space, one history, and one culture.

AH: *At this moment, issues of systemic racism rise to the fore with movements such as Black Lives Matter, the protests and actions of civil disobedience following the report of the National Inquiry into Missing and Murdered Indigenous Women, and Justice for Grassy Narrows (to name a few that preoccupy us in Canada). As a father, how concerned are you that the future of your children in this place might become in some way precarious, as your own youth was? Your words from poem 6 of* Land of Melting Sorrows *come to mind:*

> You say that
> the dream blooming
> from the fingers of
> sleeping children
> reveals a new poem
> to you.
> Chera,
> let the poem be,
> read the child.

C: I can only think about our own embodied vulnerability and would like to suggest it would be best to answer with a poem from a series of poems I wrote titled "On This Street Anytime" while under lockdown.

"On This Street Anytime – 4"

On this street anytime awaits
an unfilled pothole
Rain during the winter season
leaves that fall in the cold
The wind that freezes in the chill
Fill that hole
Near it
A white policeman
Shot.
Two boys.
Multiple times.
That pothole
twice filled up with blood.
Both of them looked exactly
like my son
Height. Beauty. Black. Brave.

Bibliography

Appadurai, Arjun, ed. 2001. *Globalization*. Durham, NC: Duke University Press.
Cheran, R. 2001a. "Salad Days." In *To Arrive Where You Are: Literary Journalism from the Banff Centre for the Arts*, edited by Kim Echlin, Barbara Moon, and Don Obe. Banff: Banff Centre Press.
---. 2001b. *The Sixth Genre: Memory, History and the Tamil Diasporic Imagination*. Colombo: Marga Institute.
—. 2011. *You Cannot Turn Away*. Translated by Chelva Kanaganayakam. Toronto: TSAR Publications.
---. 2013. *In a Time of Burning*. Translated by Laskshmi Holström. Todmorden: Arc Publications.
---. 2015. "Sri Lanka: When Loved Ones are Stolen, Can Poetry Repair the Wound?" Amnesty International, Oct. 6. https://www.amnesty.org/en/latest/campaigns/2015/10/sri-lanka-when-loved-ones-are-stolen-can-poetry-repair-the-wound/
---. n.d. "Cheran: A Brave Tamil Poet [Interview with Laura Dennison]." *DESIblitz* https://www.desiblitz.com/content/rudhramoorthy-cheran-a-brave-tamil-poet
Ebeling, Sascha. 2013. "Introduction." In *In a Time of Burning*, by R. Cheran, translated by Laskshmi Holström, 15–19. Todmorden: Arc Publications.
Macrae, Callum, dir. 2013. *No Fire Zone: The Killing Fields of Sri Lanka*. London: Channel 4, BRITDOC And ITN.

Miller, Phil, and Lou Macnamara, dirs. 2020. *Keenie Meenie: Britain's Private Army*. UK: Yardstick Films.

Miller, Phil. 2020. *Keenie Meenie: The British Mercenaries Who Got Away with War Crimes*. London: Pluto Press.

Pollock, Lindsay and Benjamin Dix. 2019. *Vanni: A Family's Struggle Through the Sri Lankan Conflict*. University Park, PA: University of Pennsylvania Press.

Satchidanandan, K., and Nishi Chawla, eds. 2020. *Singing in the Dark: A Global Anthology of Poetry Under Lockdown*. Delhi: Penguin Random House.

An Infinity of Traces: Suneeta Peres da Costa in Conversation with Reshmi Lahiri-Roy

Photograph of Suneeta Peres da Costa copyright 2021 by Suneeta Peres da Costa

Suneeta Peres da Costa was born in Sydney—on Gadigal Country of the Eora Nation—to parents of Goan origin. In her essay "A Home in Ananda and the World" she comments that:

> My sense of home and belonging has been so enmeshed with the cultural longings and affiliations of my parents, economic migrants to Australia from Indira Gandhi's India in the early 1970s, that untangling the threads and finding the 'I' at the centre of this skein feels knotty indeed. (Peres da Costa 2016a)

Her first novel, *Homework* (Peres da Costa 1999), was shortlisted for the Nita Dobbie Award. It was an assured debut novel that blends a coming-of-age story with elements of magical realism to explore love, family, and diaspora.

Her most recent book, the novella *Saudade* (Peres da Costa 2018), was shortlisted for the Australian Prime Minister's Literary Awards, where the judges noted that "the author's eye for vivid and telling details [...] evokes the African setting in all its colour and richness" (2019, n.p.). *Saudade* was also shortlisted for the 2020 Adelaide Festival of Literature Awards and was a finalist in the 2020 Tournament of Books (USA).

The novella takes its title from a Portuguese word that is often translated as "melancholy", but which also carries overtones of yearning and sorrow. The book received a number of perceptive reviews in Australia (see Woodhead 2018; Rogers 2019; Wikramanayake 2018), several of them observing how a beautifully written novella made up of 11 chapters, which "at times reads like a prose poem" (Fernandes 2019) manages to give a sophisticated and nuanced account of Portuguese colonialism, the history of Angola, and the experiences of the Goan diaspora in Portuguese Africa, where racial distinctions permeated the relations between various groups: native Angolan, Goan, Portuguese and European, among others.

Suneeta Peres da Costa's honours include awards, fellowships and residencies from the Literature Board of the Australia Council, Create NSW, The Copyright Agency, The Bundanon Trust, Varuna—The Writers' House, MacDowell and The Corporation of Yaddo. She has worked with the National Gallery of Victoria, the National Museum of Australia, the Australian Broadcasting Corporation, the University of Technology, Sydney, and other organizations, and been published in *Sydney Review of Books*, *Meanjin*, *Southerly*, *Heat*, *Peril* and *Mascara Literary Review* and elsewhere. A former Fulbright Postgraduate Scholar, she received a Master of Fine Arts in Writing from Sarah Lawrence College, New York.

The interviewer, Reshmi Lahiri-Roy teaches within the Faculty of Arts and Education at Deakin University, Melbourne and is an interdisciplinary social scientist whose research interests meet at the intersection of race, gender and education in Migration and Literary Studies. Reshmi has published in journals of repute including the *Journal of Intercultural Studies, Emotion, Space and Society, Women's Studies International Forum* and *South Asian Popular Culture*. Her work also includes government reports, a monograph and book chapters. She is the co-editor of *Asian Women, Identity and Migration: Experiences of Transnational Women of Indian Origin / Heritage* (Routledge, 2020).

Reshmi Roy (RR): *Who or what do you consider to be the main influences, literary, cultural, personal or other, on your writing?*

Suneeta Peres da Costa (SPdaC): The early events and circumstances of my life seem to have been quite formative as they continue to arise both consciously and unconsciously in my writing. I am reminded of what the Italian philosopher Antonio Gramsci in his *Prison Notebooks* called "an infinity of traces, which do not leave an inventory" (to paraphrase). For me these include family dynamics, coordinates of being such as place (including Goa, India and Australia and the evolution of these places during my lifetime), being female, being a daughter and specific cultural values, both voluntary and involuntary, associated with these identities in the world. My curiosity about, and awareness of, intersections between these personal layers have also deepened in recent years through my interest in, and practice of, Zen and Mahayana Buddhism.

For example, growing up Goan Catholic in Australia in the late 1970s to mid-1990s, the Bible and Church ritual and symbol figured strongly. I could call this a *samskara*?[1] Some of the early stories I wrote, heavily influenced by the Gospels, were retellings of the Flight into Egypt, the Wedding at Cana etc. Language must have played its part too—hearing spoken at home by the extended family, but also feeling cast out from (since I did not know them), Konkani, Portuguese and, on trips to India, Hindi, Marathi and other European languages like German and Dutch. I think this Babel made me conscious of a Blakean sense of a thingness beyond language which tied in with my experience of the numinous.

A very strong intimation of suffering and injustice emerged I believe from stark disparities of value for human (and animal) life I would witness in India; I visited my grandparents in Bombay and Goa every three or four years as a child. In high school, I was fortunate to have had incredibly inspiring English and drama teachers who encouraged whatever early talent I had; they made me feel that art was a gift, could be a vocation and was potentially revolutionary. These teachers were the readers of my early works, bound with hair ribbons, which included earnest, angsty poems and passionate protest plays on topics like Apartheid, female

---

1   From Sanskrit, meaning mental impressions, karmic and/or conditioning mnemonic and psychological impressions or even traces.

infanticide in India, the US Civil Rights Movement and the occupation of East Timor.

The classics, Shakespeare and T.S. Eliot etc., were on the syllabus, but even early on I was interested in world literature and decentring the canon. One of the first books I recall buying was a bilingual edition of Nathanial Tarn's translations of Pablo Neruda's poetry (Neruda 1966; 1970). More than once, called to give a reading in Chapel, I recited with a friend from his Spanish Civil War poems! I remember discovering a Robert Bly translation of Rainer Maria Rilke's (1981) poems in my suburban library in Sydney and feeling transparent, transformed, seen in a profound way, again *beyond* language. For one of my favourite teachers, an Anglo-Australian who taught Hinduism, I produced a textual analysis of the bhakti poetry of Mira Bai.

Later Franz Kafka and Virginia Woolf became very important and still are at least subliminal influences. At university, I read so much magic-realist, post-modern, post-colonial, black and emigré 20th-century writing. Authors whose works were pivotal included Salman Rushdie, Julio Cortázar, Gabriel García Márquez, Italo Calvino, Jean Rhys, Edna O'Brien, James Baldwin, Maxine Hong Kingston, Toni Morrison, Jamaica Kincaid, Derek Walcott, Joseph Brodsky and theorists such as Edward Said, Frantz Fanon, Gayatri Chakravorty Spivak, Homi K. Bhabha, Julia Kristeva, Jacqueline Rose, Juliet Mitchell, Trinh T Minh-ha, Michel Foucault, Hayden White, Roland Barthes, Susan Sontag, Walter Benjamin and Maurice Merleau-Ponty. Later, in the US, I became highly influenced by North American poetry—Elizabeth Bishop, Wallace Stevens, Louise Glück, Li-Young Lee, and Robert Hass, and the work of writers like Anne Carson and Lydia Davis which subverts genre orthodoxies.

At one time Thomas Bernhard was a favourite writer; at another Marguerite Yourcenar; Ingeborg Bachmann; William H. Gass; W.G. Sebald; Roberto Bolaño, and Antonio Tabucchi, an Italian who wrote in Portuguese. I love the work of Shashi Deshpande and Perumal Murugan but admit to coming to reading Indian literature in translation quite late. By contrast, I read and admired the Goan historian Teotónio de Souza's work quite early, as a teenager. Eunice de Souza and Meena Alexander remain touchstones among Indian writers in English. Joyce said, "writing is memory"; I would say that writing draws from the well of memory but also has many other sources, including desire, dreams, our encounters with other beings and the natural world, plus material, psychological and physical—including bodily—states and conditions.

RR: *Do you see yourself as an Australian author or as a South Asian one? How do you think your upbringing in Australia has seeped into your writing?*

SPdaC: In a different historical moment, I might have answered, must I choose? Because I don't really feel comfortable with a claim of being a South Asian author right now, as I enjoy significantly greater freedom of expression than my counterparts in India and a very different level of cultural infrastructure from the state for my writing career. Moreover, being South Asian is for me an idea, perhaps even less unitary than the idea of "being Australian" or "being Portuguese" (as I am a citizen of Portugal too); it's very regionally and linguistically particular and historically quite unstable, subject to change and even rupture, despite what Hindutva ideology may be promulgating.

Further, we writers—diasporic or living in India—are each so different in our outlook and sensibility, and my "India" is certainly not that of Arundhati Roy, Kiran Desai, Jhumpa Lahiri, Rohinton Mistry, Aravind Adiga or Jeet Thayil (however much I admire their work). If I were Goa-based, I would perhaps feel more comfortable claiming a Goan authorial identity but even that feels quite tenuous, for reasons already mentioned, regarding material disparities of citizenship and my relative global class mobility—not to mention recent rapid transformations of Goa's own identity within India. So, I am an Australian writer of Goan origin, a diasporic South Asian writer who loves (and is also frequently dismayed and disillusioned) to spend time in India and who cannot escape the influence of India on my imagination and work.

Beyond citizenship and the comparative freedoms being Australian has afforded, the land and environment have become a living part of my identity, shaping how I belong and invariably contributing to the ecology, texture and sense of place in my writing. Yet being an Australian writer is at this juncture also fraught, for reasons different to being a South Asian writer—in particular the fact that Australia is unceded, Indigenous land that was inhabited continuously for at least 65,000 years before European invasion. At the time of colonization in 1788 there were over 250 and perhaps more like 300–700 Indigenous languages being spoken.² I believe that Australia's present border and refugee politics and the climate crisis are also connected to the foundational wound of Indigenous dispossession. The Waanyi Aboriginal writer Alexis Wright has written eloquently about this.

As an Australian writer, I feel it incumbent on me to write against denial of the violence of the colonial interface and Indigenous sovereignty by centring my particular experience as the daughter of recent immigrants from the subcontinent, caught up in the legacies of British and other colonialisms, to which India was also admittedly, but differently, subject. Drawing on the work of Amitav Ghosh (2016) in *The Great Derangement*, I also feel a duty to write in a way that challenges our realist presumptions about landscape, weather and the environment, one that speaks to the reality of the climate catastrophe we face and without any literary delusions that koalas, kangaroos and quokkas have seeped into or are unproblematic nationalist synecdoche in my work!

RR: *Although you were born in Australia, your latest book Saudade is set in colonial Angola; in what way do you feel Goa's identity and history as a former Portuguese colony shapes your work?*

SPdaC: Certain biographical realities have made the Portuguese aspect of my own identity fairly ineluctable. My parents themselves are descendants of converted Catholics; my father, born in a South Goan village, was schooled in a seminary and even today works as a translator of Portuguese in Australia. That side of the family was very Luso-identified, even Lusophilic. Bombay, my mother's birthplace, was of course also a Portuguese imperial possession, given in 1661 as dowry to the British Crown (and later leased to the British East India Company). Her parents were among Goan Catholic migrants to Bombay who, at the end of the 19th and beginning of the 20th centuries, were favoured by the British Raj for lower civil service jobs. My mother later returned to do university studies in Goa, so learned Portuguese, which was still the medium of instruction.

My parents migrated to Australia, another former British colony, in the early 1970s, about a decade after India's takeover of Goa in 1961. I

---

2 See https://theconversation.com/the-state-of-australias-indigenous-languages-and-how-we-can-help-people-speak-them-more-often-109662.

notice some synchronicity with dates even as I write this. Yet, although I only inherited Goa's Portuguese as a legacy, a memory, it is still very potent. I think this has much to do with cultural change that, anthropologically-speaking is, for better or worse, inexorably indexed to history. When one considers the timespan of Portugal's colonial presence in Goa from 1510 to 1961—just over 450 years—we are talking about a very long swathe of history, by comparison much longer than Goa has been a political part of modern India to date and also longer than the colonial and postcolonial history of Australia.

I do hope that Goa's Portuguese identity and history have conditioned but also augmented the global coordinates of my imagination. In the same way James Joyce's Stephen Dedalus is obsessed with Ireland's identity as a British colony, I admit to being endlessly fascinated by Goa (and India's) identity as a part of the Iberian Empire. Surely Goa's identity as a former Portuguese colony has been crucial to my understanding the culture of colonialism generally and for understanding phenomena like forced and voluntary conversion, the Inquisition, the Iberian slave trade, casteism and even fascism—some of whose impacts I have tried to write about in *Saudade*.

In *Homework* I satirized the political relevance of the takeover of Goa by India, in so far as the Australian-born children in that novel are enlisted by their Goan migrant father to campaign for Goa's sovereignty long after it is a *fait acccompli* and from the unlikely, secondary postcolonial site of suburban Sydney, Australia. The father has a clandestine, under-the-house printing press on which he publishes anti-Indian propaganda and, because of her domestic austerity measures, he likens his wife to Indira Gandhi. Against the backdrop of partition and The Emergency, I was perhaps trying to show how the double and triple yokes of colonialism, such as we find among Goans and Indians of the diaspora(s), can give rise to contradictions and crises of identity, even psychopathologies.

RR: *During our conversations, you touched upon caste identity politics and mentioned your own background as a Catholic Brahmin. This is a notion many of your readers will be unaware of. As a Brahmin woman myself, I would be very interested to understand how your view of caste ties in with* *your South Asian / Goan or even Australian diasporic identity? How do you weave this into your fiction?*

SPdaC: It is undeniable that my being an Australian woman of Goan Catholic heritage is a marker, a trace, a *samskara*, such as I've described above and that in a multitude of ways I am a beneficiary of the caste status of my family of origin and the material conditions, including educational migration capital, they possessed on entering Australia towards the end of the White Australia Policy.

However, I would never call myself a "Catholic Brahmin" in a positivist sense, since I don't identify with Brahminism, which I have come to see as an ideology rooted in patriarchy and, lately, associated with Hindutva ideology. I'm also neither a Hindu nor religiously Catholic and find troublesome any consideration that being a Catholic (or Hindu) Brahmin might be a God-given status even when placed in inverted commas. As a temperamental socialist and someone who subscribes to Mahayana Buddhist precepts, I renounce the feudal and existentially dehumanising basis of the caste system. I do not subscribe to reincarnation or dharma theory in which any single being is exceptionally born "on the favoured side of destiny". Overall, *pace* Foucault, I prefer to talk about casteism ideologically, to emphasize its social and historical constructedness, its discursive element. I look forward to a time of "an insurrection of subjugated knowledges" (to paraphrase Foucault [1980]) about caste.

Despite what it may seem, the term Catholic Brahmin is not an oxymoron! Recognizing it might be expedient for consolidating imperial hegemony, the Portuguese built on the existing caste system when converting the local Goan population; the Hindu and Catholic elites (*Bamons* and *Chardos*) could fight among themselves for political and bureaucratic favour while the situation of the lower castes, *Sudras* and *Dalits*, and aboriginal / tribal groups, such as *Gaudes* and *Kunbis*, particularly those who did not convert, would not alter. The traditional Goan *ganvkar* system of agricultural production and distribution was transformed into the *communidades*, with the caste system remaining largely intact and reproduced through relations of labour and capital, marriage and property ownership, clerical and educational access etc. Divide and conquer, a tried-and-true colonial formula.

Casteism, which I regard as similar to institutionalized racism, is deeply embedded in Goan society, especially in its villages. At a young age, perhaps because of my Australianized consciousness, it was conspicuous to me and I found psychically repugnant the idea that another could be untouchable, or existentially reduced to their *varna*. For example, I questioned why the tea glasses were segregated for labourers who came to my grandmother's house etc.; I was horrified to hear of another person being causally described as "a Sudra" or "a Vaishya", or that a girl "who might otherwise be marriageable" (because of fair skin, good looks etc., rarely, notably, intelligence!) was from *this* or *that* village or had *this* or *that* family name (which are insidious but prevalent caste identifiers in Goan villages).

Eunice de Souza's poem "de Souza Prabhu" encapsulates the hilariously pompous delusions of grandeur, the pretensions to privilege and entitlement, the "wanting to have it both ways" of some types of Catholic Brahmin:

> No I am not going to
> delve down and discover
> I'm really de Souza Prabhu
> even if Prabhu was no fool
> And got the best of both worlds
> (Catholic Brahmin!
> I can hear his fat chuckle still.)
>
> (de Souza 2009, 26)

Although casteism is also a blight on and pervasive in the Goan and Indian diaspora(s), when I am in Goa or India—being both an expatriate and of Catholic Brahmin background—I am aware that I am doubly protected from its violence. The apparently genteel social decorum of segregated tea glasses conceals an existential violence, precisely because there is real-world brutality and punishment for caste transgression and this is overwhelmingly experienced by Dalits, Muslims and those of whom the caste system makes "Others". But ultimately, I feel it's a luxury to speak of caste which, to borrow from Foucault again, disciplines certain bodies, inscribes certain bodies, enslaves certain bodies too.

Personally, I cannot accept that my existential privilege is connected to a cycle of someone else's existential suffering and servitude; that my bodily, ontological capital is literally interdependent with a system that involves someone else's enslavement. I wished to incorporate some of these ideas in *Saudade*. I have done so by making the protagonist's family, who are Catholic Brahmin, complicit in the native indentured labour economy in Angola, which itself evolved out of the Portuguese slave trade.

RR: *In your essay "At Home in Ananda and the World" (Peres da Costa 2016a) you talk of your instincts to free and save all living creatures, especially those considered pests such as lizards, insects etc and you are not sure whether this instinct does not originate from the "latent Hindu in you". Given the stark demarcations of ethnicity and religiosity today, particularly in the Indian subcontinent, could you expand on this comment?*

SPdaC: My comment about being a latent Hindu merely referred to the historical fact that at one time my own ancestors were converted from Hinduism. Arguably, Hinduism itself was not a religion so much as a social system at that time; it was the British Raj and Indian anti-colonial movement that gave rise to notions of "Hinduism" and "Hindustani" as we understand them today. Per my comments about caste identity above, I simply don't subscribe to the idea there are any God-given Indians and certainly no particular religious, ethnic group or caste has a claim to being more or less or really "Indian". Romila Thapar's (1978; [1992] 1999) classic scholarly work, Tony Josephs' *Early Indians*, Wendy Donniger's *The Hindus*, alongside more recent interventions such those of, among others, Divya Dwivedi, Shaj Mohan and J. Reghu (2021), have put paid to that kind of mythologising. According to Indo-Aryan migration theory, archeologically-speaking the *Vedas* could be Central Asian imports that flourished in India post-Harappa. So, we need to question our understanding of the grand narratives—Parashurama as much as "Goa Dourado" (Golden Goa).

India is a relatively recent political entity; like Goa's own statehood, its history consists of millennia of invasions, occupations, and rule by people of a variety of faiths and foreign backgrounds. I have been heartbroken to know about the destruction of mosques and killings of Indian Muslims, arbitrary arrests and the imprisonment of journalists, writers and intellectuals and the repression of peaceful democratic protests in India. It seems freedom of religion, political association and speech are already casualties of the NRC and CAA and that Kashmir's loss of sovereignty is the constitutional collateral of the abrogation of Article 370. Thinking of the women of Shaheen Bagh[3] and, as I write, farmers who have left their fields,[4] homes and families, as well as so many others who have risked their lives resisting, it's sobering to remember that Independence, which came about through sacrifices, *satyagraha* and *ahimsa* of ordinary Indians, also involved the trauma of partition. Seeing what is now happening to Indian democracy, whose original architects and visionaries included Dr Ambedkar and Gandhi, is both a paradox and truly devastating.

RR: *I see in your writing that you describe pain as you do many things with lyricism. For instance, in your essay "Yoga Diary" in* Southern Crossings *(Peres da Costa 2016b) you poignantly describe your courageous battle with endometriosis and* Saudade *is interwoven with the pain of domestic violence and Portuguese slavery. To what do you attribute this lyricism?*

SPdaC: That's very kind of you to say, Reshmi. I do read a lot of poetry so perhaps that has resulted in a lyricism of style / mode of expression. Song and oral poetry were of course the source of storytelling long before writing was invented and I like to recall this in my writing, almost against the many technologically-mediated and disembodied ways we experience narrative nowadays. It seems pain is fairly inevitable in life, but I do believe the human impulse to make art and transform suffering creatively is also universal. In *Saudade* I was drawing on Portuguese folk music traditions like *fado* and *morna* which are soulful and melancholic songs. Indeed, the

---

3   The Shaheen Bagh protest was a response to both the passage of the Citizenship (Amendment) Act (CAA) in both houses of the Parliament of India on December 11, 2019, as well as to the police reaction to protests by students opposing the Amendment. The Shaheen Bagh protesters, mainly Muslim women, blocked a road in New Delhi from December 14, 2019, until 24 March 24, 2020. See: https://en.wikipedia.org/wiki/Shaheen_Bagh_protest.
4   The Indian farmers' protests are a response to three contentious farm acts the Parliament of India passed in September 2020, which relax domestic farm produce sale, pricing and storage rules. At the time of writing, in April 2021, the protests were ongoing with farmers demanding the laws, whose implementation is the subject of a Supreme Court stay order, be repealed. See: https://en.wikipedia.org/wiki/2020%E2%80%932021_Indian_farmers%27_protest.

word *saudade* does not have a literal meaning, is more equivalent to a mood or feeling, a bit like *duende* in Spanish.

Point of view is often called the writer's or narrator's "voice" and a consonance of sound and meaning is something of which I'm quite conscious when writing. Words, language and imagination are extraordinary media; through them one is able to transmit experiences, memories, feelings, observations to a reader / listener who may have no direct knowledge or immediate understanding of them, and to conjure other worlds. In this regard, writing is an act of trust, faith, attention and intimacy similar to love, and I believe that one must be measured and ethical with one's power of suggestion. I try to be sensitive to the inner life of characters, to get "inside their skin". For me the subject gives rise to a certain literary tone and a palette, not vice-versa. I aspire to description that is both precise in its realist detail and rich and painterly in its imagery, language that both reveals and evokes. I try to exalt the meaning inherent in ordinary things.

RR: *What are you currently working on?*

SPdaC: I am returning to work on my new novel after some disruptions with COVID-19 and illness. I'm a bit superstitious about talking about my work while its being written, but I can say that this new work is set between Goa and Australia; it particularly concerns the ecological catastrophe we face, as well as issues of gender violence and the crisis of democratic citizenship. There are a variety of expatriate, migrant and local Goan characters whose lives it explores. I have also been working on an essay about technology and some poems about travel in India, family, fertility and reproduction which I hope to publish as a collection. And just now, this interview ...

Acknowledgments

This conversation was supported by an Australian Government Research Training Program Scholarship at The University of New South Wales, Sydney. Ms Peres da Costa extends her gratitude to Dr Vishvesh Kandolkar for his insights on an earlier draft.

Bibliography

Australian Prime Minister's Literary Awards. 2019. "Judges' Comments on *Saudade*." https://www.arts.gov.au/pm-literary-awards/current-awards/saudade.

de Souza, Eunice. 2009. *A Necklace of Skulls: Collected Poems*. New Delhi: Penguin Books India.

Dwivedi, Divya, Shaj Mohan, and J. Reghu. 2021. "The Hindu Hoax: How Upper Castes Invented a Hindu Majority." *The Caravan*, Jan. 1. https://caravanmagazine.in/religion/how-upper-castes-invented-hindu-majority

Fernandes, Sujatha. 2019. "Orphans of Empire: *Saudade* by Suneeta Peres da Costa." *Sydney Review of Books*, April 29.

Foucault, Michel. 1980. "Two Lectures." In *Power/Knowledge: Selected Interviews and other Writings 1972–1977*, edited by Colin Gordon, 78–109. New York: Pantheon Books.

Ghosh, Amitav. 2016. *The Great Derangement: Climate Change and the Unthinkable*. Chicago: University of Chicago Press.

Neruda, Pablo. 1966. *The Heights of Macchu Picchu*. Translated by Nathaniel Tarn. London: Jonathan Cape.

---. 1970. *Selected Poems: A Bilingual Edition*. Translated by Nathaniel Tarn. London: Jonathan Cape.

Peres da Costa, Suneeta. 1999. *Homework*. New York: Bloomsbury, 1999.

---. 2016a. "A Home in Ananda and the World." *Sydney Review of Books*, Oct. 7.

---. 2016b. "Yoga Diary." *Southern Crossings*, April 28. http://southerncrossings.com.au/arts-and-culture/yoga-diary/.

---. 2018. *Saudade*. Artarmon NSW: Giramondo.

Rilke, Rainer Maria. 1981. *Selected Poems*. Translated by Robert Bly. New York: Harper and Row.

Rogers, Athena. 2019. "Dislocation and Longing: A Review of *Saudade*." *Right Now*, March 8. http://rightnow.org.au/review-3/dislocation-belonging-review-saudade/.

Thapar, Romila. 1978. *Ancient Indian Social History: Some Interpretations*, Hyderabad: Orient Blackswan.

---. [1992] 1999. *Interpreting Early India*. Oxford: Oxford University Press.

Wikramanayake, Marisa. 2018. "*Saudade* Review." *Books and Publishing*, Jan. 25. https://www.booksandpublishing.com.au/articles/2018/01/25/101019/saudade-suneeta-peres-da-costa-giramondo/.

Woodhead, Cameron. 2018. "*Saudade* Review: Suneeta Peres da Costa's Bold Evocation of Childhood." *Sydney Morning Herald*, August 30.

The Delicious Indulgences of Writing: Sulari Gentill in Conversation with Angela Savage

Photograph of Sulari Gentill copyright 2021 by Edmund Blenkins

Sulari Gentill's biographical note, written for her website at the time of her first contract with Pantera Press, begins: "I'm Australian. I was born in Sri Lanka, learned to speak English in Zambia and grew up in Brisbane. I went to university to study Astrophysics, graduated in Law and after years of corporate contracts, realized I just wanted to tell stories". Nine years later, in 2019, she had published 13 novels and was in print in Australia, New Zealand, the USA and Canada. Much of this output was down to the award-winning Rowland Sinclair series of historical crime fiction, the first of which, *A Few Right Thinking Men* (Gentill 2010), was shortlisted for the Commonwealth Writers Prize for Best First Book. Set in Sydney in 1931, it combines crime investigation with well-researched historical context concerning competing factions—violently anti-communist fascists and communist cadres—in pre-World War II Australia. (The stimulus for Gentill's initial interest in the politics of this period is explored in her interview here with Angela Savage.) The figure of Rowland Sinclair, well-heeled, artistic and politically astute, proved immediately appealing to readers and reviewers, with Laurie Steed (2010) remarking in *The Australian Book Review* that "it takes a talented writer to imbue history with colour and vivacity. It is all the more impressive when the author creates a compelling narrative". Gentill continued to document Sinclair's adventures in the decade that followed the publication of *A Few Right Thinking Men*. The ninth book in the series, *All the Tears in China* (Gentill 2019), is set in 1935 Shanghai.

As S.D. Gentill, Sulari has also published The Hero Trilogy, a YA fantasy series based on a retelling of ancient Greek myths. In August 2018, she won the Australian Crime Writers Association's Ned Kelly Award for her standalone novel, *Crossing the Lines* (Gentill 2017a). In it, Gentill takes a witty and metafictional route into murder and detection; popular crime writer Madeleine d'Leon mischievously casts the more sober "literary" author Edward McGinnity in her latest work, just as he is considering a change of direction and a crime-writer protagonist. He is drawn to d'Leon as a model for his central character. *Crossing the Lines* drew warm praise from US novelist Dean Koontz, who found it "a pure delight, a swift yet psychologically complex read, cleverly conceived and brilliantly executed".

Sulari Gentill was interviewed by fellow writer Dr Angela Savage the day after the 2018 Ned Kelly awards night. In this interview, she talks about "the deliciousness of writing", reflecting on her creative choices, the relationship between authors and their characters, the ramifications of the category of WOC (woman of colour) author and the disturbing parallels between Australia in the 1930s and today.

The interviewer, Angela Savage is an award-winning writer, former director of Writers Victoria, and current CEO of Public Libraries Victoria. Her debut novel, *Behind the Night Bazaar* (2013), won the Victorian Premier's Literary Award for Unpublished Manuscript, and all three of her Jayne Keeney PI novels were shortlisted for Ned Kelly Awards. Angela's short stories have been published in Australia and the UK, and she won the 2011 Scarlett Stiletto Award for short crime fiction. Angela holds a PhD in Creative Writing from Monash University. Her most recent novel is *Mother of Pearl*, published in 2019 by Transit Lounge.

Angela Savage (AS): *Sulari, congratulations on winning the 2018 Ned Kelly Award for Best Crime Novel for* Crossing the Line *(Gentill 2017). By my calculations, you are only the third woman, and the first woman of colour, to* win in this category since the awards began in 1995. For some time, you were the only South Asian diasporic writer working in the crime genre in Australia, and you are still one of only two that we know of. How do you account for this?

Sulari Gentill (SG): Well, I don't account for it, to be honest; I'm not sure that I can. I did have a discussion about this some time ago with Malla Nunn, another writer of colour who writes in this genre, and we were talking tongue in cheek about the fact that quite often writers of colour, particularly writers of South Asian origin, are too snobby to write anything but literature.

AS: Well, I did wonder if it reflects a lack of prestige accorded to genre fiction over literary fiction in South Asian diasporic communities.

SG: Perhaps, but I don't know whether people necessarily think in those terms. It did not occur to me when I started writing that I was choosing to write genre fiction. I was just writing. I can't imagine people sitting down and thinking, "I want to write. What am I going to write? I'm going to write something worthy". It seems to me a very artificial construct. I do wonder whether it is a feeling of where you will be welcomed. I know we had this discussion recently about the concept of "the other" and I do think that literature, and high literature in particular, whilst it is viewed as worthy, and award worthy, and grant worthy, and something to be aspired to, is also considered as the "other". It is not something you necessarily read when you're tired or in need of comfort. You don't necessarily read it to feel at home, indeed, quite often it's the opposite—you read it when you want to be extended or challenged or made to learn. When you are tired and you need comfort or a good laugh you turn to genre, and genre is family. So, perhaps it is that writers of colour in the western context are more easily accepted into a writing form that is other, that is expected to be exotic and unfamiliar, rather than a writing form that is "family".

AS: I felt that this was a really interesting point when you made it. I am curious to know whether you think it reflects the whiteness of the industry or the whiteness of the readership for genre fiction. That is the other question. How diverse do you think the readership is, based on your own fan-base?

SG: My fan-base is white, generally. I don't go through and catalogue them but generally the people I've encountered tend to be older, white people, male and female.

AS: *And of course, we should point out that the characters in your Rowland Sinclair series are, for the most part, white.*

SG: Well, someone did ask me about that, and I said, "You know? It's funny because I've never actually said they were white". In my head they are, but I think it is interesting that we default to whiteness unless we're told otherwise, because the alternative is "otherness", and whiteness is home and family. I'm not saying that this is necessarily an issue about white people versus not-white people, but I think it is an issue of white culture and it is so subliminal, so hidden, and passive, that I don't know that anyone even considers it and thinks about it until they are confronted with a writer like me who is writing historical crime fiction and is a writer of colour. I don't escape either—I often default to white, too, despite being brown myself. I do remember the first time someone called me a writer of colour on a blog and I was a little bit surprised. I thought, "What is a WOC? Why are they calling me a WOC?" It wasn't that I didn't know I was brown … I just didn't realize that it put me into a subset.

AS: *I think that was probably Marisa Wikramanayake.*[1] *She wrote on her blog, back in 2012, "The discovery of her work" (meaning you) "in this genre" (meaning crime fiction) "being shortlisted for and winning various awards, published by major publishers, all of this makes me feel far more optimistic and encouraged about the chances and representation and audiences that WOC [women of colour] authors in this country will have in future": a lovely compliment.*

SG: It is lovely, and I am delighted and gratified and proud that my career gives comfort to a generation of writers of colour coming up. When I started writing, it did not even occur to me and I don't know whether that's a particular naivety about me, or a blinkeredness, but it just didn't occur.

---

1   Marisa Wikramanayake is an Australia-based journalist, writer and editor. Her blog is still current in 2021 and can be read at http://www.marisa.com.au

AS: *That's interesting because you are published under what is a pseudonym, not your actual name.*

SG: Yes, my real name is Sulari Goonetilleke, and Gentill is just a pen name. In my real life, I'm Sulari Goonetilleke and happily so. The reason I became Sulari Gentill is so trivial and mundane. It wasn't a great statement to mask my writer of coloured-ness, or an attempt to fit in. It was just that I tend to write books with long titles, like *Gentlemen Formerly Dressed* (2017b), and I have a really long name and a book spine is only so long. So, my publishers at the time said to me, "Look, Sulari, we're going have to shorten your titles because we can't fit your name and your titles on there". And, for me, it was more important that the book had the perfect title than my name be on the spine. So, I took letters out of my name until it sounded OK and it fitted. "Gentill" is just Goonetilleke with several letters taken out.

AS: *You mentioned before that when you started out, being a writer of colour wasn't a burning issue. How did you get started as a writer?*

SG: I just picked up a pen and started—well, I actually picked up a laptop and started writing. I just thought I would write a novel.

AS: *At what point was this in your life?*

SG: Well, I had been a lawyer for many years, and I was working quite successfully, as a lawyer but I was just one of those people who was a serial hobbyist. So, I would pick up a hobby and I'd do it intensely for six months, until I mastered it, and then I'd move on to another one. I've quilted, and I've lead-lighted, and I've gardened …

AS: *And you are a painter as well.*

SG: Yes. I can weld too and do all of those sorts of things. And it was just along the same lines: I'd finished the welding course, I needed something to do, and I thought I would write a novel. But it was one of those moments where you wander down the path thinking you're meandering, and you realize that you've found your way. So, this little frolic into writing turned out, very quickly, to be something that was the essence of me, and I realized, also very quickly, that I wouldn't stop. What also happened, unfortunately, was that I started losing interest in the law, and that is a very dangerous place for a lawyer to be. So I wound back my practice and went completely to writing. I tend to be an all or nothing person. I greatly admire writers who can work and write but I can't. When I write, I am so totally immersed in the writing that I can think of nothing else, which is why my books come out so quickly. But it also means that I am useless for any other pastime.

AS: *Let's talk about your creative choices. Your Rowland Sinclair novels are set in the 1930s and 1940s, largely in Australia but not exclusively. Tell us about why you chose that period of Australian history.*

SG: Well, that was really very pragmatic. My husband, Michael, happens to be a historian and his particular area of expertise is the extreme political movements of the 1930s in New South Wales. So, once I'd started writing, I was in that place where, you know, you experience that first realization of writing, that first falling in love, and I was completely, completely in love. A writer's head is a very seductive place. That is all very well for the writer of course—there are people in there, and worlds, and we can disappear in there for days at a time—but it is difficult for the people we live with. I was going into my head and I didn't want to come out, but I was aware that it was difficult for Michael, because I was suddenly just not there mentally. I knew I was never going stop writing, and as I had no plans for getting rid of Michael, I had to make the two work. So, I actively went looking for a subject that I could write about that would engage him and that would bring him into my head so that I would have to come out of it less. I basically grabbed his history thesis and I found a novel in it.

AS: Right.

SG: And that turned into *A Few Right Thinking Men*. But once I started delving in to the 1930s, I realized what a rich source it was for fiction and I also saw immediately the parallels between the 1930s and what we're going through today and that really, really interested me. I was intrigued to explore that notion of where we could have stopped it. At what point could we have stopped what was happening so that it did not end in World War II—the carnage that we saw—and the Holocaust. That is what has kept me writing the series. It is a constant exploration of what happened then and the more I write, the more parallels are being drawn and the more we seem to be hurtling towards that same place.

AS: The rise of the strong men, the rise of the right, the polarization ...

SG: Even things as simple as the financial crisis, the segregation of society, the scapegoating of certain groups, the tension between women demanding more independence and the need for the right to stomp them back. All of those things. The seeming Teflon-ness of certain figures. And I am really interested in the way people justified things and how they lived with things. On a completely personal level, I always wondered how people could have known—that Germans could have known—what was happening and done nothing. How you could live down the road from a concentration camp and not do anything? And then, you know, Australia started building its own concentration camps ["detention centres"] and I realized how that can happen, and how good people can be mentally battered into complacency. So, that interests me, that alarms me, and that motivates me to keep writing about it in the hope that, in some small way, even through reading my books, people might actually see what they aren't willing to see. Sometimes people are not willing to see something if you tell it to them directly. But if you tell it to them in the way of a story, sometimes they stumble upon that truth themselves.

AS: *Absolutely. On the question of the story, you mentioned that you are a prolific writer. You produce one Rowland Sinclair novel a year. You have published eight in the series so far, and the ninth,* All the Tears in China, *set in Shanghai, came out in January 2019. The first,* A Few Right Thinking Men, *takes place in 1932, I think, and I remember you saying you thought you might set one per year, but I don't think we're out of 1935 yet, are we?*

SG: Not yet.

AS: *So, what is your vision for the series in terms of the story arc, do you actually have an end goal?*

SG: The end will be 1945. My intention was to write Rowly through the 1930s, but having written Rowly through the build-up to war, it would be cowardly not to write him through the war. And I am actually interested to see how he will survive the war and how he will go. So, my notion is that the series will finish in 1945 with the end of the war.

AS: *You hinted at something important about your process there, which is what scholars call the illusion of independent agency ...*

SG: Yes.

AS: ... *which describes a certain kind of relationship between some authors and their characters. Rowland is very real to you, so when you say you want to see what he's going to do—*

SG: Well, look, I know that I have made him up. But for me, the joy of writing is allowing him to be real, is allowing my brain to carry that illusion. I think I could probably write without that illusion, but I wouldn't have as much fun. For me, that is the indulgence and that is the deliciousness of writing: it's going into another world and letting him tell me his story rather than consciously believing I am writing it. Of course, I am writing it, I know that. But there are some delusions that humanity allows itself.

AS: *Which is actually the theme of* Crossing the Lines, *your standalone novel which won the Ned Kelly Award. Just unpack that a little bit. Tell us how that book came about.*

SG: Well, I often get asked at writer's festivals about my relationship with Rowland and people seem quite fascinated with the notion of a writer's relationship with their protagonist. So, I started to think a little bit more about it and how it worked, and to me, Rowland feels quite real. It feels like I can almost see him, like he is just out of my periphery. And I have a comfort that he is there.

AS: *Your sons report that you talk to Rowland in the car.*

SG: Yes, I guess I do. But at all times, I do know that's something that I've allowed myself to believe, which is completely harmless if you don't let it get in the way of life. But I always wondered where that line was: where things became difficult, where things became awkward, and where you started to lose your grip. So, *Crossing the Lines* is a book about two writers, each writing about the other. The narrative does not so much flip, but weaves, so that you go from the perspective of one writer to the other and the two stories start to interweave and intertwine. In the beginning, they're both independent writers who choose the other as a protagonist for particularly sensible reasons—they are literary constructs—and as they write, they get more and more embedded in each other and then all of a sudden, they cross that line, and the imagined walks into reality.

AS: *I love the way you describe it as the weaving of stories, because the narrative is seamless. While I was reading it, I was thinking, "How is she doing* this? I don't even understand how she's getting away with this". Technically, it is an extraordinary achievement.

SG: Thank you. A couple of people have said that to me, but I wrote it exactly the way I write Rowly. I don't plot. I was not conscious of any technical artifice or skill while I was doing it. It just seemed to flow that way and I just moved from one head to another. Quite often, when I am writing Rowly, I know that I'm plotting something in some part of my subconscious, but my subconscious has become good enough at fooling me into thinking I'm just following Rowland around. It was very much like that, but I wanted to explore that whole notion and take it to its extreme end. A lot of writing is about taking something of your own experience to a more extreme point to see what will happen, because what we would not do as humans, we allow our characters to do.

AS: *That is interesting because in a way you're confessing that* Crossing the Lines *is more consciously motivated by your own experience, and it's also the first time you've overtly written a woman of colour, Madeleine, who has a Sri Lankan background.*

SG: Yes.

AS: *And I have just had the privilege of reading a short story of yours that features a woman whose ethnicity is not specified but whom you describe as, "Brown, overweight, and orthodontically uncorrected". Is there a reason why it has taken nearly ten years for South Asian characters to appear in your work and is it something that you see a momentum building around? Or are there other factors governing who appears?*

SG: I think it was just those stories. So, the short piece that you were reading, it was because I was talking about what relatability and sympathy is in terms of the public.

AS: *And the different value placed on different women's lives.*

SG: Yes, exactly. So that was enabled by my using a protagonist who was not-white. I don't actually actively go out to use a particular protagonist—they serve the story. I did not set out to write a white man in Rowland, but the story was served by having a protagonist who was. In *Crossing the Lines*, I did not decide that Madeleine was a woman of colour until you find out in the book that she's a woman of colour, and part of it was about trying to explore that hegemonic default. And I have it, too. Unless someone tells me that a character is black, I tend to assume they're white, and I'm a woman of colour. I don't necessarily judge it as a failing—it is just interesting when thinking about why society and human beings do that. I know that there has always got to be some kind of social structure. There has always got to be some kind of distinguishing and categorization and stereotyping. That's just how human beings work. Our minds probably would not be able to deal with the amount of information they have to process if we couldn't categorize. The point at which it becomes difficult is when we start giving some people more benefits than others.

AS: *When we impose a hierarchy on them—of worth or value.*

SG: Exactly. So in *Crossing the Lines*, when Edward decides that Madeleine is a woman of colour, he's thinking about using it as a twist, and the conversation is, "Maybe it's just not a twist, maybe it's just what it is". What I wanted to play with was the reader having this image of Madeleine as a white woman, and the shock of suddenly realizing, "Hold on, this person we've been following all along is black, or is brown" ... and asking questions of themselves: "Why did I think she was white? Why did I decide she was white when nothing in the narrative defined her as such?" It wasn't necessarily that I identified with her any more as a woman of colour than I would have identified with her as ...

AS: *A writer?*

SG: A writer.

AS: *Well, that's interesting because my next question, which is a bit tongue in cheek, is to ask you whether you consider yourself primarily as a crime writer, a writer of historical fiction, a woman writer, or a writer of colour. Or, perhaps it is easier to ask you, if you were being programmed at a writers' festival, what sort of panels would you most like to appear on?*

SG: I would not like to appear on diversity panels. I don't love diversity panels for a number of reasons, primarily, because when someone is invited to appear on a diversity panel at a writers' festival, they are being asked to talk about being brown, or not being white, as opposed to talking about their books. I am a professional and if I go to a writers' festival I want to talk about my books. I want to talk about art, and I want to talk about literature, and I want to talk about other people's books. I do not want to talk about the colour of my skin. So, I have a really ambiguous relationship with diversity panels. I understand the good intentions behind them. But I don't think it serves those writers being asked to appear, particularly if that's all they are being asked to appear as. If you really want to talk about diversity, it should be diverse panels across the board.

AS: *On topics such as crime fiction, historical fiction ...*

SG: Exactly, exactly. It is a bit like having women's panels. Women crime writers. Here are the men, here are the real crime writers, and here is a subset, the women. I know that is not the intention, I know these panels are put together with the best of intentions and with a notion of really highlighting writers who are there. But I was talking to some of my fellow panellists on a diversity panel recently and some of them had not appeared on a panel that wasn't about diversity, ever. And it was my first diversity panel.

AS: *First and last, by the sounds of it?*

SG: Well, my fellow panellists were envious that I got to go on other panels and talk about my books. It is one of those double-edged swords. You don't want people to pretend that you're white, but you don't want being brown to be the biggest thing about your writing. I love appearing on crime panels. I find crime writers are generous, and they are kind, and they're supportive, and tend to also know each other's work. Combined, these elements make good panels, supporting interesting conversations. I am quite happy to talk about who I am as a person, quite happy to talk about being a brown person, but I don't know that simply being brown is enough for a panel.

AS: *I did want to ask about the Ned Kelly Award, or prizes in general, because the Ned Kelly Award is only your latest accolade. You won the 2012 Sisters in Crime Davitt Award, which is awarded to women's crime writing, for Best Adult Novel for* A Decline in Prophets *(Gentill 2011), the second novel in the Rowland Sinclair series, too. How significant are these awards for you?*

SG: In terms of how I feel about my own writing, *Crossing the Lines* was the same book a couple of days ago before it won the Ned Kelly.

AS: And we should also note, for the record, that you had a lot of trouble finding a publisher for that book.

SG: In as much as I was discouraged from writing it in the first place, I think. People were keen for me to write more Rowly, or write something that was very similar to Rowly, because of its reasonable commercial success and something for which I am already "branded". And, of course, the writing community likes to categorize writers, and so you fall into boxes.

AS: Do you think that is more the publishing industry or the writing community? Or the reading community?

SG: It's really hard to tell. The pressure is to keep doing what you are doing, or what they think you should be doing.

AS: And not to deviate.

SG: Yes. It probably is the publishing industry, and I can understand that. They have spent a lot of money building your brand as a certain kind of writer and then you decide you want to write something else. It must be irritating. It's like the Volkswagen who suddenly wants to be a Jeep. In the end, I wrote *Crossing the Lines* because I felt compelled to write it despite the advice to the contrary. Then I just happened to show it to my American publisher—more because they asked what I was working on than because I was actually submitting it—and they signed it within 24 hours. Once that happened, things changed; there was interest here and eventually I signed the Australia and New Zealand rights to my Australian publisher, Pantera.

AS: So, does this prize make you feel vindicated?

SG: Oh, yes. Very vindicated.

AS: For sticking it out?

SG: Yes. There is a kind of embarrassment, particularly in Australia, associated with saying "I can do this". The potential for humiliation is great. It's terrifying. You are plagued with the notion that perhaps you've overreached, perhaps the world is laughing at your arrogance, until you find someone who believes in that work as much as you do. It is a lot easier to just keep doing what's expected because there is a mechanism of support, both practical and emotional, for that. Having been actively discouraged from writing outside of my established brand, and having overcome the self-doubt to do it anyway, I am glad and relieved and delighted that this worked out. Awards for a novel that deviates from your stock-in-trade do give you chance to go into other fields. Already I'm being talked to about writing more of this kind of book, which is I suppose literary crime.

AS: *It's been called metafiction.*

SG: Yes, metafiction and what is the other one?—postmodern. Honestly, Angela, I write the story I want to tell, as it appears to me—while the categorization is done by the industry. In the Rowly series, every book is quite different, even though they have the same characters. My American audience seems more comfortable with that. They seem to like that each book from the Rowly series is different in format: one is almost cosy, another a political thriller …

AS: *Some have a darker edge.*

SG: Yes, they do. My US publishers highlight the diversity in the structure of the different books in the Rowland Sinclair Mysteries. But not so much here [Australia] where it is easier to market when everything's the same.

AS: *Absolutely. It goes back to that point you were making before about our obsession with categorization.*

SG: Yes, well, the other thing about prizes is that, like a lot of writers, I suffer from imposter syndrome. I suffer from this notion that I'm not really meant to be here, everybody here is better than me and I've slipped in somehow when no one was looking. Things like prizes actually help you feel stronger against the vagaries of the imposter syndrome. And I understand how the imposter syndrome works, so I try to ignore it, but the fact is that it still stalks most of us at various times. It haunts us most when we're trying to do something new.

AS: *Yes. At the same time, you are famous for saying—and I often quote you on this—that awards are not a meritocracy.*

SG: No, they're not. My theory with awards is that a group of people, [judging] panels, choose to shine a light on someone's work. That is a show of support, but it does not necessarily mean that your book is better than every other book on the shortlist. It just means that, at the time, you were lucky enough to be the one they chose to shine the light on. And I am grateful for that, I'm honored by that, but I do not ever rest on that.

AS: *Nicely put. Well, my last question is simply what is on the horizon for you?*

SG: I am writing two books at the moment.

AS: *Of course you are.*

SG: One is a standalone thriller which was inspired by the politics of today. It's a contemporary novel and I was intrigued by—I don't want to throw any spoilers in—but I was intrigued with how certain movements were playing out and I wanted to take them to their natural end.

AS: *Social movements?*

SG: Yes. And the other one concerns mythology.

AS: *Right.*

SG: Not Greek mythology; this one is Old Testament. And it is an indulgence because I don't know that there's a huge market for that kind of book. But it is a story that occurred to me, that wanted to be written and so I'll write it. It is always lovely when someone wants to publish your work, but sometimes you just need to write the story because the story's there, whether or not it actually finds a place in your lifetime. I can always leave it to my sons. They will need something. Here's a manuscript …

AS: *Take it out of the desk drawer.*

SG: Indeed. Here is your inheritance, boys. Good luck!

Bibliography

Gentill. Sulari. 2010. *A Few Right Thinking Men.* Sydney, NSW: Pantera Press.
---. 2011. *A Decline in Prophets.* Sydney, NSW: Pantera Press.
---. 2017a. *Crossing the Lines.* Sydney, NSW: Pantera Press.
---. 2017b. *Gentlemen Formerly Dressed.* Sydney, NSW: Pantera Press.
---. 2019. *All the Tears in China.* Sydney, NSW: Pantera Press.
Steed, Laurie. 2010. "*A Few Right Thinking Men* by Sulari Gentill." *Australian Book Review* 305 (October).

"An Island is a World": Romesh Gunesekera in Conversation with Susheila Nasta

Photograph of Romesh Gunesekera copyright 2021 by Helen Gunesekera

The internationally distinguished writer Romesh Gunesekera was born in 1954 in Sri Lanka, where he lived till the 1960s before moving to the Philippines. He studied at the University of Liverpool, eventually settling in London.

Romesh Gunesekera is one of the great stylists of South Asian fiction, and a writer who makes subtle connections between art, life, memory, loss, death, at the same time negotiating the crucial relationship between the present and the past, the personal and the political. Ever since the publication of his first collection of short stories *Monkfish Moon* in 1992, Gunesekera has sought to extend his fictions in new directions in terms of theme and subject. The relationship between master and servant, a common theme in Gunesekera and first explored in "A House in the Country", is taken up again in his brilliant novel *Reef*, shortlisted for the 1994 Booker Prize, and set in Sri Lanka in the 1960s and 1970s. One of the subjects of *Reef* is the close connection between the "master" Mr. Salgado, a somewhat indolent marine biologist, the environmentally-threatened reef of the title, and Salgado's houseboy, Triton, 11 years old at the start of the book, who becomes his gifted chef. Through them, the political unrest and disintegration of their country is glimpsed until it forces their departure for Britain. As many readers testified, food has seldom been as ravishingly described as it is in *Reef*, where it also serves as a metaphor for the relationship between Triton and Salgado.

The Sandglass (1998) also draws on postcolonial Sri Lanka, but takes place primarily in London, when the Sri Lankan narrator Prins Ducal arrives for his mother's funeral. It is story of a family feud and of Ducal's investigation of the family's past in Sri Lanka, and rivalry with the Vatunas dynasty. The revelation of family secrets leads to an exploration of the nature of exile and mortality, the universals of human experience and the vanishing of time and art, as implied in the title. This is presented through finely-handled conversations.

In *Heaven's Edge* (2002), the protagonist Marc leaves London seeking his family origins in an unnamed island (which appears to be a futuristic version of Sri Lanka). He falls in love but also has to risk everything, within a beautiful landscape that is in the process of being destroyed by armed conflict. Much of the novel's power comes from the combination of desperate situations with Gunesekera's characteristically lyrical and reflective voice.

For *The Match* (2006), Gunesekera had the ingenious idea of starting and ending the story with a cricket match—the first held in Manila and one 30 years later at the Oval in London, where Sri Lanka was playing India during the summer of 2002. As Paul Binding (2006) said in his review in *The Independent on Sunday*,

> This is a most intimately and precisely imagined novel. Those who have followed Gunesekera from the debut stories of *Monkfish Moon* and his subtle first novel, *Reef*, won't be surprised. Yet so complete a match (to use the novel's central image) between empathy and artistry, between lively observation and intellectual grasp of cultural tensions, always surprises.

The Prisoner of Paradise (2012), which Romesh Gunesekera discusses here, represents a further departure in being a novel set on the island of Mauritius in the 1820s, highlighting the complex layers of its mixed cultural history, which includes that of Africans, Indians, Ceylonese, English and Dutch. The novel focuses on the working out of the complex relationship between youthful British Lucy and Don Lambodar, a young translator from Ceylon.

Vasantha is the narrator of the stories in the themed collection *Noontide Toll* (2014). Having bought a van with his savings, he now works as a driver for hire throughout Sri Lanka, carrying NGO workers, businessmen, tourists and others. "Some nights, I just want to drive. We can do that now. No curfew, no roadblocks," he says, but the civil war keeps seeping into his narratives, and threatening to undermine his optimism: "When we first heard the war was over, we believed a line could be drawn", says Vasantha, but the further the reader is drawn into the stories, the more they become aware of the trauma and unspoken histories that underlie the narrative.

Romesh's most recent novel, *Suncatcher* (2019) returns to Sri Lanka in 1964. A wonderful rendition of a relationship between two teenage boys, it traces a heady summer in the life of Kairo and his charismatic and more prosperous friend Jay. It could easily be characterized as a coming-of-age story, but anyone familiar with Gunesekera's work will know that it is about much more: beauty, pleasure, corruption, political unrest and human betrayals of various kinds all have to be dealt with.

Chris Ringrose

The interviewer, Susheila Nasta MBE FRSL, is Founder of *Wasafiri*, the magazine of international contemporary writing she launched in 1984 and led as Editor-in-Chief till 2019. A literary activist, writer and presenter, she is Professor of Contemporary and Modern Literatures at Queen Mary and Professor Emerita at the Open University. She has judged a number of national and international prizes and is currently one of the judges for the 2021 David Cohen prize for a lifetime's work. She has published widely, especially in the field of Caribbean, South Asian and black British writing. Recent books include: *Home Truths: Fictions of the South Asian Diaspora in Britain* (2002), *Writing Across Worlds: Contemporary Writers Talk* (2004), *India in Britain* (2012), *Asian Britain: A Photographic History* (2013), *Brave New Words: The Power of Writing Now* (2019) and with Mark Stein, *The Cambridge History of Black and Asian British Writing* (2020). Current projects include a biography of *The Bloomsbury Indians*. In 2011 she received an MBE for her services to black and Asian literatures and in 2019, the

Benson Medal from the Royal Society of Literature for a lifetime's achievement. In 2020 she was awarded an Honorary Fellowship from the English Association recognizing her contribution to English Studies.

Susheila Nasta writes of her discussion with Romesh, which began live at the 2018 NGC Bocas Festival in Trinidad and continued in London, that

> islands, whether real or imagined, have inspired many of Romesh Gunesekera's works, as has a preoccupation with migration, and the effects of the passage of time and the role of language as symbolic vessel of the imagination in the transformation of human lives.

Susheila Nasta (SN): *We have talked a lot about islands in the last few days: island cultures, island nations, islands as imaginative repositories framed by the sea and islands as porous worlds. Islands have certainly been powerful literary symbols across many histories, especially in Trinidad and the Caribbean where we are today; I am thinking of Homer, John Donne, Derek Walcott, Earl Lovelace, George Lamming and so many others.*

I know the epigraph to Reef, *your first novel—"Of his bones are coral made"—stems from* The Tempest. *Can you talk about islands and why they have been such an inspiration? I know you spent many years of your childhood in Sri Lanka.*

Romesh Gunesekera (RG): The island is first and foremost an artistic construct. For any writer, a book is a kind of island. An island in the mind is the place you go to when you read a book. I find that notion interesting: islands contained within covers. Places you travel to in your imagination. I love that.

Growing up in Sri Lanka, I didn't think about the "islandness" of the place. There were children I knew, living in central parts of the island, who had never seen the sea. I had travelled out of the country by ship and by plane and could see we all lived in our own islands of the mind. In small groups, separated by language, by experience, by reading.

When I started writing in London, I became more conscious of my island heritage. I was writing about island people, from Sri Lanka and the Philippines but also other places like Cyprus, who had come to Britain, either temporarily as I thought I had, or permanently. Maybe they were a little like Sam Selvon and his lonely Londoners. Perhaps we all start out like that. My characters have different backgrounds and different imperatives, but they are all trying to make a life in difficult circumstances. And Britain itself is an island.

SN: *Migrant characters certainly feature widely in your fictions. Such stories of movement and diaspora are even more urgent in our contemporary moment. Yet, it seems some people are only just beginning to recognize their pressing relevance?*

RG: Yes. People have always written such stories, but the subject is now very current. But I want to go back, to something in the 1980s, which changed my writing. I was thinking about issues we all still talk about: moving places, dislocation, migration, racism—all pressing in the 1970s and 1980s and now. But then, in 1983, Sri Lanka erupted into a violent maelstrom while I was writing a story—this changed my priorities. What was happening in Britain was simply not as important or consequential to me as what was taking place in Sri Lanka, 6,000 miles away. You could describe it in all sorts of ways: people talk about pogroms, communal violence, rioting. It was racism expressed in a particularly horrible, violent form. Hundreds, possibly thousands, of people died; thousands of people were burnt out of their homes. And unlike previously, it was witnessed around the world. We did not have the internet and social media, but the televised images of smoke and mobs were just as powerful.

So inventing a story at that time about a Sri Lankan man in London, an immigrant who'd changed his mind and was planning to return home before that Black July to a better life, I knew it had to engage with that world. I had begun the story months before, but I was finishing it weeks after that eruption. The story could no longer be isolated. I began to see that the story, the island and the world were permanently connected.

SN: *Geologically, islands change shape; they are fluid.* Reef, *your first novel, plays on this—highlighting time, erosion, the fragility of the land and the island's potential dissolution by the sea as well as the actions of mankind. The reef frames and changes the world within it. Would you like to talk about that?*

RG: All writers here in the audience will recognize the process. One often starts off writing about one thing but ends up with something quite different. I don't think I started with some grand idea about coral or metaphors about islands. I was really writing a story about a power relationship and someone who was subservient to a dominant figure. As it happens, the book turned out to be about a man in Sri Lanka—a bachelor and his servant boy. The story is told from the servant's point of view and becomes a story of that time and place, of a person finding their place in the world.

The book was set at a moment in history when things were changing socially in Sri Lanka. It was the late 1960s, just before another watershed moment of political upheaval and unprecedented violence in 1971, when a Marxist youth uprising started an attempt at a revolution, crushed by the left-wing government of the day. It was the first time that politics had turned so violent. Several thousand young people died. The numbers were contested, as in subsequent violent encounters. Violence was not new. There had been communal riots in the 1950s. The Prime Minister was assassinated in 1959, but this was different: large numbers were killed for political reasons. For both the young and older generations, it was 1971 that changed their view of the world. The level of violence was a huge shock. My novel explores the period leading right up to that moment.

My starting point was Mr. Salgado, a sort of accidental marine biologist. One of those obsessive people who couldn't quite direct his obsessions; he gets obsessed with coral and then with Miss Nili and so on.

In the 1960s, people knew little about coral and had not thought about climate change. At one point, I realized that I had read everything that had been published on coral reefs during the time the novel is set. I went to university science libraries; I wrote to research institutions. I even managed to get to marine conservation areas where you could see how things could be made better. We did not have the internet databases we have now. You had to physically go and find books, see things. People were just beginning to be aware that coral reefs were vulnerable and might easily die. But no one quite knew what would happen as a result of their degradation. We have since discovered how devastating the consequences can be, especially following the aftermath of the 2004 tsunami. Writing this in the 1990s, I saw the dangers and I could imagine Mr Salgado seeing those dangers 25 years earlier.

SN: *You described your main focus in the book earlier as the power relationship between Salgado and his servant narrator, Triton, caught as they are in* the turbulence of social and political change. Is the book also preoccupied with the process of writing itself and voice?

RG: There is a symbiotic dependency. The powerful and the not-so-powerful. This was the main thing. But in the course of the novel, there's a reversal. Salgado, the dominant figure, turns out to be weak and unsuited to the modern world, whereas Triton, the servant narrator, makes himself into the sort of person who can survive. Triton doesn't even have his own name. He is given his name, which turns out to be appropriate. Triton, of course, is the messenger, an ancient mariner and God who comes out of the sea, with a human voice. The God of poetry with a conch shell. Triton, finding his voice as the narrator, also connects to the book finding its own voice. So, it becomes a book about art and writing as well, charting the control an artist needs to gain over his or her material and instruments. In this case over language. But I try to do this exploration through character. I wanted Triton, my narrator, to be not just a new character but a new type of character as well. A rare creature. He slowly gains control over the narrative of his life, and the language in which he expresses it. So, the English he uses changes as he grows; he makes it his own language. He takes control: his sentences become more complex in the later pages; he introduces new words to the language. It is a process of gaining ownership. And as a writer that is what you have to do. And then the elements fall into place.

But sometimes these things happen by accident. So, even the epigraph from *The Tempest* that you mentioned happened by chance. I was desperately looking for something. It was the last week before publication. I was on the tube in London ... I happened to look up and there it was straight in front of me, "Ariel's Song" with its wonderful line: "Of his bones are coral made". I knew this was it.

SN: Politics is always hovering ... Triton, a seemingly simple character is very much a natural philosopher, who says many wise things. His cooking links to the process of writing too—what to leave in, what to take out etc. And towards the end, he makes an observation which resonates across your work: "Human history is always a story of somebody's diaspora. A struggle between those who expel, repel or curtail, possess, divide and rule, and those who keep the flame alive from night to night, mouth to mouth". Given the simplicity of the tale on the one hand, I wonder how you keep the balance, maintain the integrity of Salgado and Triton yet manage to set these political issues within broad human contexts?

RG: This is how I learnt to write. As I mentioned before, just when my writing started to find itself, the politics of the day, of what turned out to be a long war in Sri Lanka, invaded the page. I felt my fiction had to work within this. Fiction had to be meaningful even in the direst circumstances, at least for myself—never mind any other reader.

SN: *Let's move to the different island world in* The Prisoner of Paradise *(2012), set on Mauritius in 1825. The subject once again seems to chime with large themes: migration and diaspora, but also the wider history of indenture and global slavery. You focus on a romantic tale about Lucy, an almost Orientalist young woman, who travels there from early 19th-century England. Can you tell us about this and the book's intriguing title?*

RG: Lucy features prominently on the front cover and that's Don Lambodar, the translator she meets, on the back. They are looking in opposite directions. Perhaps that is indicative of the direction of the novel. Each of my books seems to emerge as a sort of reaction to the previous one. For example, the book before this, *Heaven's Edge*, is a dystopian futuristic novel. That in turn came about because of the previous one, *The Sandglass*, a contemporary London novel with a big hinterland: Sri Lanka throughout the 20th century.

SN: *Why Mauritius? I remember we were both at a British Council conference there in the late 1990s. A special Mauritian issue of* Wasafiri *also came out of that trip.*

RG: On that trip I read that in the early 1800s, when the British took over Mauritius from the French, there was actually Indian slavery, not just indentured labour. There were equivalent numbers of African enslaved people and Indians. The system was the same: the way people were brought there, the conditions they lived in on the sugar plantations and so on. This was news to me.

It is a period of history that isn't much written about, because it was soon overshadowed. In the 1830s, indentured labour was brought from India—a bigger story involving far larger numbers of people. So, the slave period which preceded it has been almost completely forgotten. I also discovered that the British used Mauritius as a place for prisoners, including political prisoners, from what was then Ceylon, now Sri Lanka.

I became fascinated by learning that a key figure from Sri Lankan history had been brought to Mauritius for the last days of his life. He was a collaborator and helped the British take over in Ceylon; afterwards, they regarded him as a danger. He had been the King's first minister. So, he was exiled to Mauritius, but he was the kind of prisoner we all want to be. He had the freedom of the island, a house, staff and an interpreter. He was invited to tea in the grand houses, including the governor's and lived a most comfortable life. He didn't speak English. He would make visits and his entourage would put on little concerts for entertainment. They sang very badly; everybody would try not to listen.

All of this is reported in about two paragraphs (as an aside) in a tiny book that the governor's wife wrote. A journal. There's nothing else. I wanted to write a book about those paragraphs. In the end, I became less interested in the original story—and became engaged with the character I had introduced from England. A young girl of 19, Lucy, who arrives in Mauritius, like one of Dickens's orphan children. Her parents have died, and she goes to live with her aunt. And, yes, she comes with a lot of orientalist stuff in her head because she is 19; it's 1820 in England and that's what a lot of young girls talked about. They read racy stories about oriental princes and were thrilled by books like *Lalla Rookh*, written by Thomas Moore (1859); a mixture of poems and stories about a young princess who is captured by a prince pretending to be a poet in Kashmir. All young women of a certain class were reading it. It was the bestseller of its time, which of course then disappeared. No one knows much about it anymore, but it was the equivalent of the *Fifty Shades of Grey* of their time!

I brought Lucy to Mauritius and she meets Don—a flamboyant translator and interpreter for an ageing Ceylonese prince, exiled in Mauritius by the British who had taken control of both islands. I won't tell you much more but there's tragedy, there's comedy and love. The backdrop is the tragic French story of *Paul et Virginie*.[1]

---

[1] Jacques-Henri Bernardin de Saint-Pierre's novel *Paul et Virginie* (1788) is set on Mauritius, then under French rule and named Île de France. Paul and Virginie are friends since birth who become lovers.

SN: *So is it primarily a love story but set amidst brewing racial and political unrest?*

RG: What was so interesting is that Mauritius is one of the few places on the planet which doesn't have an indigenous population. It was an island with no people; nobody has a prior claim of ownership by birthright. Everybody there has been an invader. Or migrant, I should say. In 1825, you had people there who were enslaved from Africa and from India, but you also had free people from both places. The moment is fascinating. There were black scientists and agriculturalists. Prisoners who were murderers and political exiles. Society was multi-layered. I wanted to navigate this mixed world through Lucy's young eyes.

SN: *Her aunt comes from the West Indies, doesn't she? It is interesting, given empire, that she doesn't want to go to England, but prefers to go Mauritius.*

RG: Well, that was the system—it is the same in the UK's Foreign Office even now. People get posted within different tiers of countries categorized by importance. So, you will find that at this time, the West Indies, Mauritius, Sri Lanka, were an island network. They were places that attracted a certain level of administrative class, who often moved between them until they were promoted to the next tier: Canada, Australia or India—larger countries.

SN: *I want to discuss* The Match, *set in Britain. It came out in 2006, not that long after the tsunami had wreaked further havoc on a Sri Lanka already traumatized by war. Were you inspired by C.L.R. James's (1963)* Beyond a Boundary *and the relationship between cricket, empire and the politics of independence?* The Match *is certainly a good example of the political always being present, even if not explicitly so?*

RG: I have often had to deal with this. Events do politicize fiction. I should add, though, that I don't see myself primarily as a political writer. Sri Lanka came up in early books because of the communal violence and the beginnings of a civil war—lasting nearly 30 years. The violence confused me. Growing up in the 1960s, with peace movements, I thought we were moving away from violence. I was naïve. We now know that violence is present all over the world. But, that first recognition of the precipice and consequences of politics came, as I mentioned before, in my 1980s story, "Storm

Petrel".[2] Since then, a lot of my writing has dealt with this issue of how people can turn into such violent creatures in the personal and domestic sphere as well as the political. I explore why we end up doing the things we do, why the world is the way it is.

Anyhow ... a nicer story from that time is the cricket story. In 1996, Sri Lanka suddenly became the world champions. Cricket became the thing Sri Lanka was good at; it offered a different kind of notoriety, a more positive story than tourism, mob violence and bombs. Cricket was important enough to even stop the war for a big international match. I'm not a cricketer but I'm greatly indebted to cricket—not least because after Sri Lankan cricket became famous, people in England no longer had a problem with Sri Lankan names like Gunesekera (*Laughter*). You suddenly had commentators all over the BBC who could put out Sri Lankan cricketers' names just like that—perfectly. So, we became normalized, if you like. I wanted to write a story where cricket wasn't just an episode but metaphorically important. I did not think anyone had done that. I thought it would happen soon. I wanted to do it before anyone else. Now of course there are lots of cricket novels.

SN: *That is true, but few have such a wide canvas and weave in about art and aesthetics?*

RG: When *The Match* appeared there weren't any novels like it. Only the sort of P.G. Wodehouse-type novel. These concerned the early 20th century: English village cricket, rather than the passionate international game celebrated here and in South Asia. I knew the work of C.L.R. James and his wonderful essays on cricket as an art. Fabulous pieces, where he likens cricket to Greek tragedy. It's a spectacle. You know the tragedy at the end—for your team, usually! Yet as you watch it, everyone in the game acts as though they are performing in a theatre. I discovered that cricket works as a game, but it also works on a different level. It's an art form that photographers love. If you look into the photography of sports, you'll find all

---

2   "Storm Petrel" is a story from Gunesekera's first collection *Monkfish Moon* (1992). In London, the narrator encounters a friend, CK, also from Sri Lanka, who enthuses about his recent trip home, ironically unaware of any darker side to life there. But the dream of Sri Lanka cannot endure: "in just two months the whole island would be engulfed in flames".

sorts of pictures of footballers, right? Snaps. But if you look at a photographer who photographs cricketers, you'll see a completely different art form, one concerned with composition. Pictures of bowlers are depicted with perfect balance. The art comes through the eye of the camera. I just loved that.

My character Sunny is a person who doesn't play cricket and is not a good photographer but gets obsessed with both. He tries to discover why he likes cricket, what makes this allegiance and why you might support a team, particularly teams that lose. He also tries to become a photographer and these strands come together in his life.

SN: *The epigraph is important again. Here, you frame the novel with words by Cartier-Bresson, who once said: "shooting a picture is like holding your breath". Is Sunny trying to hold his life and control it in some way through photography like the artist?*

RG: I'm writing about two things I hadn't addressed before: one is sport, cricket; the other is the Philippines. The book begins in the Philippines, probably one of the few countries where cricket isn't played. I wanted to write about the Philippines, where I spent my adolescence. So, I put both challenges together. I'm not an autobiographical writer. I don't use personal experience often. But in *The Match* I do use regions I know. The times and places I have inhabited: the Philippines, Britain, Sri Lanka.

There's a real match too. Sri Lanka and India were touring England for the NatWest series. I went to the matches and got involved, just like Sunny was. I was trying to capture that moment in words, as Sunny was trying to capture it in film. I wasn't sure why, other than the feeling I have of life flowing past and the need to capture it without stopping it. Doing the impossible ... that is why I write novels. To stay alive by keeping my imagination alive. This takes me back to *Reef*. A reef, like a human being, is strong, but only strong because it is alive, and it is only alive while the most delicate part of it, the coral polyps, are alive; in our case, we are alive only when our most sensitive tissue, our brain cells, are alive. And the brain is alive—for me at least—when the imagination is alive.

SN: *There is also the idea of capturing memory in* The Match. *Indeed, the idea of holding time, preventing that final full-stop as you put it in* The Sandglass, *seems a key preoccupation. We can see that in relation to* Noontide

Toll, *your recent cycle of stories also. Vasantha, your van driver narrator, enables a multiplicity of perspectives. He also implicitly engages the reader with the difficulties of narrating modern-day Sri Lanka, a country reeling from the war. Was it challenging telling these stories and finding a form to narrate experiences that are so raw and relate to such atrocities?*

RG: When the war came to an end ten years ago, it ended in a very difficult way. It was very contentious. No one has established to everyone's satisfaction what exactly happened. Basically, the Tamil Tigers, the Liberation Tigers of Tamil Eelam, were defeated by the Sri Lankan army. But in the last stages, several people were pushed into a coastal area in the east. There were no-fire zones, which turned out to be possibly fire zones. No one knows how many people died, how many innocent people and how many civilians. Claims and counter claims: "fake news". There had been talk about war crimes. There had been talk about that being too extreme a charge. It remains an extremely murky area.

The period immediately after was tense. People did not want to talk about what had happened. There was triumphalism among some groups, but also trepidation. I know writers in Sri Lanka were finding it difficult to talk about things that troubled them ... there was a sense of required silence. One response to trauma is silence. But there is also a political tactic to do with erasure of the past. We know that from the Cold War era, when historical figures were "airbrushed" out. Now with Photoshop and Facebook, people alter not only history but their own self-image. Selective amnesia does seem part of the political programme in many parts of the world. In Sri Lanka, it was happening in relation to the war that had just ended. So, I wanted to use fiction to shine a light on what was happening, and what that might feel like for someone like my narrator Vasantha.

SN: *The episodic form you use is intriguing in terms of its shifts between the light, humorous and the dark. So many of the characters are holding grief and pain. Yet, at one point, Vasantha tellingly comments: "The driver's job is to stay in control behind the wheel and that is all. The past is what you leave as you go. There is nothing more to it".*

RG: Form interests me. I was working with two dimensions of it. The first was to push the boundaries of the novel and the short story. In *Noontide Toll* you have 14 stand-alone stories, but when they are read sequentially, they form a narrative arc that could be a novel. I wanted to see if I could satisfy our different needs for short stories and novels in the same book. I wanted readers who prefer short stories to read these and then discover they have consumed a novel, and for those readers who prefer novels to read this as a novel and then discover they do appreciate short stories too.

The other dimension concerned time and fiction. A novel exists in its own time; it creates its own time. It is a complex thing, because the novel exists only through language and language itself changes with time. In this book, I wanted to deal with a reality that is changing fast because of the political and social changes happening after the end of something as traumatic as war, and because the language used to describe it is also changing. I wanted a novel that worked immediately with the world as it was at the end of the war but which would still have resonance after some time had passed and language took on different meanings. The best example is the word "Toll" in the title. In Sri Lanka, immediately after the war and while the tsunami was still in our minds, the connotations of this word were all to do with death and casualty. It was the toll we recognized. But soon after the war, we had an increase in the traffic of people travelling around the country and new roads being built. On these new highways appeared a new phenomenon: toll plazas. These were not part of common experience in Sri Lanka during the war years, but now they are. So, for Vasantha, the van driver, constantly on the road and on the highway, the word "toll" itself begins to change its meaning. I wanted to capture that, and the form for doing it was not Cartier-Bresson's camera as we discussed earlier, but this collection of words that morph from short stories into a sort of novel.

SN: *I think one of the most wonderful things about Vasantha and his telling of the stories is that he is the vehicle of the narration throughout. This both enables a lightness of touch, whilst opening up the broken landscape of lives lost and destroyed.*

RG: There is always an amnesia about history. In Britain too: just look at Brexit and the fantasies people conjure on both sides of what they think are the "good old days". It is the way people and societies cope, or not. I wanted to deal with this moment at the end of an extremely traumatic period. Trying to work out how to deal with it, and how to put that into fiction. So, I ended up with a van driver who goes around the country to places he had never been before because of the war. He goes to the North and the East, where most of the fighting took place, though violence was everywhere. He sees these places and talks about them in his own way, trying to work out how to deal with memory, especially painful memory. But also political pressure. For him, humour is important. I realized this was an effective way of dealing with dark and threatening things. A lesson I remembered from writers I've known who have had to deal with difficult times in Eastern Europe during the Soviet era.

SN: *Does his lightness of voice act as a thin cover for a wilful amnesia? This is tricky territory to travel.*

RG: On memory, I think Vasantha takes the view that it is better to remember. As a driver, he knows he has to remember where he started from to get where he is going, otherwise he'll just go round in circles. Towards the end, he says he carries all these stories in his head and mustn't lose them—they "make us who we are". If he forgets them, he will drift into oblivion. It takes us right back to islands and mistrustful memories, as in *The Odyssey*, where Odysseus and his sailors become in effect lotus-eaters and forget who they are.

Sri Lanka's mythology has a very similar story with the legendary queen Kuveni casting spells on shipwrecked sailors. I have written a couple of poems on Kuveni and *The Odyssey*'s sorceress Circe, published in anthologies, so it is an enduring concern. In *Heaven's Edge* I try to bring some of those parallel myths and legends (religious and cultural) together to weave something new. Islands are magical places, but they are also dangerous.

SN: *So, what are you writing now? The title of your new novel,* Suncatcher *(Gunesekera 2019), sounds intriguing?*

RG: My new book is set in Sri Lanka, or Ceylon as it was called then. It is set in 1964 before some of the watershed moments of Sri Lankan history we have discussed but reflects a moment in time when the political landscape was in upheaval. The story is about two boys: the charismatic Jay, who comes from a wealthy, privileged family and Kairo, who comes from a more ordinary middle-class family, but whose father is very left-wing, and their unexpected friendship. The situation in the country is remarkably familiar today: the government is in disarray, politicians change sides week-by-week, there is a sense of crisis, schools are closed, the religious right are on the rise. Socialism is having a resurgence. The world's first elected Trotskyites have joined the government of the world's first woman prime minister. These two boys find that they have to grow up fast and their childhood games suddenly have serious consequences. Much of what we've talked about comes to a head in this novel. It has been a long time coming; there are hints of its concerns in my earliest writing in the 1980s, but it now suddenly seems to be hurtling out. It is a coming-of-age novel, but also about political and ecological awakening in a beautiful but fragile world. A world where a young boy learns the price of growing up and the difficulty with which we evolve into what we eventually become.

SN: *Political and ideological awakening seems like an important subject given our present-day lives in "Brexit Britain". Do you have any comments on this, and more importantly on the Easter Sunday bombings in Sri Lanka on April 21, 2019?*

RG: Regarding Brexit, there too we can see underlying fault lines in society, linked to the failing and faulty memories of what happened, who we are and where we have come from. And the recent Easter bombings were a vicious reminder of the dangerous world we live in. Many say it was completely unexpected. Sadly, it was not unexpected because there was intelligence that an Easter attack on churches was planned. The alert was ignored, as similar warnings have been disregarded so many times elsewhere in the world. Over the years, as bad things happen, you learn to live with a sense of dread. Sri Lanka has been heading for a catastrophe like this. We have talked about amnesia, how quickly problems get forgotten rather than solved. Regrettably, despite the end of the war, and the high hopes of the 2015 election which was an extraordinary expression of democracy, many serious problems have not been addressed. This atrocity will have huge consequences. The bombings will raise the stakes even higher during the 2019 Presidential elections soon to be underway: how to ensure safety without sacrificing hard-won precious civil liberties? Politicians will be tempted to offer tougher authoritarian options. And brutal violence might again become an imaginable course of action for fundamentalists of all kinds—they are all waiting in the wings, political and religious. But as with the aftermath of the tsunami, we have also seen heartening examples of kindness and generosity: queues of blood donors, solidarity between communities. People wanting to reach across and find empathy. I hope this will prevail and people will recognize just how malleable memory is, how we unconsciously mould it to suit present inclinations. Novels and imaginative writing may help us here, holding up a mirror for us to see ourselves, or even how we want to see ourselves.

In writing *Suncatcher*, I thought I was immersed in the strange past of a secret, special place. But when I open the novel, I find it begins with two boys meeting in a church car-park halfway between a mosque and a temple; the rest of the country is in turmoil. Things are on the brink. Alarm bells ring. We could be stepping into the island of Ceylon in 1964—or the world of today.

Bibliography

Binding, Paul. 2006. "*The Match*, by Romesh Gunesekera." *The Independent on Sunday*, March 19.
Gunesekera, Romesh. 1992. *Monkfish Moon*. London: Granta Books.
---. 1994. *Reef*. London: Granta Books.
---. 1998. *The Sandglass*. London: Granta Books.
---. 2002. *Heaven's Edge*. London and New York: Bloomsbury.
---. 2006. *The Match*. London and New York: Bloomsbury.
---. 2012. *The Prisoner of Paradise*. London and New York: Bloomsbury.
---. 2014. *Noontide Toll*. London: Granta Books.
---. 2019. *Suncatcher*. London and New York: Bloomsbury.
James, C.L.R. 1963. *Beyond a Boundary*. London: Hutchinson.
Moore, Thomas. 1859. *Lalla Rookh: An Oriental Romance*. London: Longman, Brown and Green.

A Highbrow "Hijra":
Kaiser Haq in Conversation with Mohammad A. Quayum

Photograph of Kaiser Haq copyright 2021 by Kaiser Haq

Kaiser Haq (b. 1950)—described by Khushwant Singh as "a jovial litterateur [with a] macabre sense of humour" and by Alamgir Hashmi as a master of "derisive imagery"—is arguably the most internationally renowned Bangladeshi poet in the English language. He began writing while in school, but his first two collections of poetry, *Starting Lines: Poems 1968–1975* and *A Little Ado: Poems*, came out in 1978. Haq has since published several volumes of poetry, including two Collected editions: *Published in the Streets of Dhaka: Collected Poems 1966–2006* (Haq [2007] 2017) and *Pariah and Other Poems* (Haq 2013). He also has a significant body of more recent and previously uncollected poems to his credit. His poems have appeared in several distinguished journals and anthologies, including *London Magazine*, *The Arnold Anthology of Postcolonial Literatures*, *The Journal of Commonwealth Literature*, *The Cambridge Review*, *Wasafiri* and *World Literature Written in English (WLWE)*.

Haq is also a veteran translator and currently the director of the Dhaka Translation Centre. He excels in translating Bengali works from multiple genres into English: poetry, prose and fiction. His translated works include *Selected Poems of Shamsur Rahman* (Rahman [1985] 2016), *Quartet* (Tagore 1993; a translation of Rabindranath Tagore's novella *Chaturanga*), *The Wonders of Vilayet* (Mirza Sheikh I'tesamuddin 2002; a translation of the first Indian travel book on Europe), Nasreen Jahan's (2012) novel *The Woman Who Flew*, *The Triumph of the Snake Goddess* (Haq 2015; a comprehensive prose rendition of the Bengali folk tradition of Manasa, the snake goddess) and Shaheed Quaderi's (2018) *Selected Poems*.

Haq completed his Bachelor's and Master's degrees in English literature at the University of Dhaka and went to Warwick University, in the UK, on a Commonwealth Scholarship to study for his PhD. He received the degree in 1981 for his critical biography of the Australian-born writer Frederic Manning (1882–1935). On returning to Bangladesh, Haq began teaching at the University of Dhaka and went on to become a professor there. In 2015 he moved to the University of Liberal Arts Bangladesh (ULAB), where he is currently Dean of the School of Arts and Humanities. He was a Senior Fulbright Scholar at the Centre for Twentieth-Century Studies, the University of Wisconsin-Milwaukee, in 1986–87; Regional Chairperson (Eurasia) for the Commonwealth Writers Prize in 1996–97; and a resident at the Hawthornden Castle Writers' Retreat and the Ledig House Writers Colony in upstate New York in 2001. He has also held a Royal Literary Fund fellowship at the School of Oriental and African Studies, London.

Haq fought in the Bangladesh Liberation War in 1970–71 "as a freshly commissioned subaltern in command of a company". He is recipient of the Bangla Academy Award for translation (2013) and the South Asian Literary Association's Distinguished Achievement Award for Creative Writing (2019).

The interviewer, Mohammad A. Quayum is of Bangladeshi origin and now resides in Adelaide, Australia and works as Adjunct Professor at Flinders University and the University of South Australia. He taught over four decades at tertiary institutions in Bangladesh, Malaysia, Singapore and the US before hastily retiring from International Islamic University Malaysia because of the 2020 pandemic. Author, editor and translator of 34 books,

Quayum has also published more than 120 journal articles, book chapters, and encyclopaedia entries in the areas of American literature, South Asian literature and Southeast Asian Literature. In 2019, he edited a festschrift for the distinguished Asian-American writer Shirley Geok-lin Lim, published in the *Journal of Transnational American Studies* (UC Santa Barbara and Stanford University). He has forthcoming books with Routledge, Springer and the Asiatic Society of Bangladesh, respectively on Rabindranath Tagore's educational ideas and experiments, Malaysian Literature in English and Bangladeshi Literature in English.

A note on the interview title:

Dictionary.com defines "Hijra" as "1. a person whose gender identity is neither male nor female, typically a person who was assigned male at birth but whose gender expression is female. 2. a person who is transgender". In Urdu, the word refers to a eunuch. Kaiser Haq adopts the problematic identity of this group of people, who belong neither to one category nor another, to describe the status of Bangladeshi writers in English. This is because, although English is widely used by the country's middle-class and adopted by a group of writers as their creative medium, it has no official standing in the culture or the Constitution of Bangladesh. The word is used in the title only to highlight, playfully, Haq's ambiguity about himself as a writer.

Mohammad A. Quayum (MAQ): *Let me begin with a couple of questions arising from an earlier interview I conducted with you (in 1997 in* World Literature Written in English, *later renamed the* Journal of Postcolonial Writing*), if I may. In that interview, I asked you about the state of Anglophone writing in Bangladesh and followed up by asking whether you were optimistic about the future of this tradition. Your answer then was an unequivocal "no". It seems that your opinion has changed in the interim period, as in an article in* Wasafiri *(2015) you suggest that both English and English writing have made strides in the country and that a whole body of new writers has emerged in recent years. This is undoubtedly welcome news. Please tell us a bit more about these positive changes and the contribution such new writers have made to the development of the tradition.*

Kaiser Haq (KH): First, I wish to thank you for keeping in mind the previous interview, published in *World Literature Written in English* (*WLWE*).

With that as a point of reference, we can see if and how my attitudes have changed. When I gave that interview, the prospects of Bangladeshi literature in English did look dim. In the *Wasafiri* article, published just a few years back, I note certain dramatic developments. A large number of books, mainly fiction, have been published in this century. While working on my chapter on "The Novel of Bangladesh" (Haq 2019) in Volume 10 of the *Oxford History of the Novel in English* I was pleasantly surprised to discover that about 60 books of fiction in English by Bangladeshi writers have appeared since independence in 1971. Interestingly, all but half a dozen or so have appeared in this century. This is mainly because a number of the young people going through the IGCSE (International General Certificate of Secondary Education) and then going abroad to study are interested in writing. A dozen or more have gone through university Creative Writing programmes or taken writing courses. Having said that, I think the basic problem that I had in mind all those years back is still there: and that is, there is no officially recognized place for English in the country. It is the de facto second language of the educated classes, but the constitution regards it as a foreign language and the official view, as well as the view of the cultural establishment, is that it is desirable that English should be replaced by Bengali at all levels of national life. Such sheer blindness to the need for English in order to function in the world is being ignored. Meanwhile, those who say these things send their children to English-medium schools.

MAQ: *In the same interview, I also asked you whether Bengali literature and writers have inspired you in any way. Your reply was again in the negative. You are the foremost translator of Bengali works and writers in the country, and I wonder if all the time and energy you invest into it does not, somehow, feed into your thought processes, even if in an intuitive way.*

KH: I think I have done my share of translating. The modern and contemporary authors I have translated have been friends or acquaintances. We would have "addas" where literary chatter predominated, so you could say we belonged to the same coterie, and have shared concerns. But I doubt if you can find much direct influence. Rather, a shared sensibility found expression in Bengali in my friends' works, and in English in mine. One factor which distinguished my work from theirs is that I have related to the tradition of South Asian Anglophone writing as my primary tradition. This is a literary tradition Bengali poets are willfully ignorant of. To them, it is a perverse outgrowth of colonialism. I'm afraid I have to disagree with that entirely. My view, shared by everyone in the subcontinent interested in writing in English, is that the language has gone native. Otherwise, the most prominent bestseller in the subcontinent would not have been an Anglophone writer—that is, the popular writer of pulp fiction Chetan Bhagat.

MAQ: *Since English and English writing are now making some headway, should we reconsider the use of tropes like "hijrah" and "pariah" to describe these writers?*

KH: As I have explained already, the cultural establishment continues to look askance at English writing; hence my use of these terms. The situation will not change until we as a nation are pragmatic enough to make English the national second language. If we did that, the millions of workers sending home precious remittances would be earning more. I have it on good authority that Bangladeshi nurses working in the Middle East do well as station nurses, but cannot qualify in the examination for promotion to Head Nurse because of their lack of command of English. If they did qualify, their income would leap from, say $20,000 to $50,000 per annum. What I am arguing for is that the state schools should teach English as a second language in an efficient manner, and not perfunctorily as they do now.

MAQ: *But do we have the resources for that? Apart from the lack of political will, there is also a lack of trained and qualified English teachers in the country. English has taken a heavy beating from the nationalist upsurge that began with the Language Movement in the 1950s, and the political leaders from both sides of the aisle have used that to their advantage in the aftermath of the country's independence in 1971. Would you agree?*

KH: I do agree. A lot of damage has been done, but the sad thing is that wholehearted efforts to rectify the situation are not being made. The English-medium schools preparing students for the IGCSE are at one extreme; at the other, you have badly funded state schools that cannot provide adequate language teaching—not only in English but in Bengali too. We have an expanding economy, so we should be able to spend more on school education. As you know, schooling is the bedrock of an educational system, and no amount of remedial courses at higher levels can remedy defects in schooling.

MAQ: *While researching for this interview, I realized that, unfortunately, not much is available on Bangladeshi literature in Australian libraries. This is perhaps because, as you have said yourself elsewhere, Bangladeshi books are not often marketed outside the country, even to India. Given this situation, have you considered the possibility of setting up a website or an electronic platform for Bangladeshi poetry in English? Wouldn't this make the writers and their works more visible and accessible to international readers and thus create a win-win situation for both readers and writers?*

KH: You have identified a crucial problem faced by our Anglophone writers. Nowadays, an increasing number of fiction writers are finding takers among the international publishing houses that have set up branches in India, and a few have been published in the UK and the US; but except for, say, Zia Haider Rahman or Monica Ali, they don't have a sizeable readership. Books published in Bangladesh have hardly any distribution abroad. I agree with you entirely regarding the use of the online platform and e-books. As you know, we at ULAB have a Translation Centre and a publishing house. We are seriously exploring the possibility of marketing publications abroad, and also of producing e-books and audiobooks. If we can do this, we will be able to extend our reach enormously. It's not the number of titles sold alone that matters, but also whether our publications are easily accessible to anyone interested, no matter where they are located. In a globalized world, it is imperative that we make our literature available globally; and electronic methods are the most convenient way to achieve this goal.

MAQ: *Echoing Buddhadev Bose, you once said that authentic poetry could only be written in one's mother tongue. Does such poetry also have to come from one's motherland?*

KH: No, no, I suspect there was a degree of misunderstanding. Buddhadev Bose was very dogmatic in his assertion. All that I said or meant, and this was in my essay "An Apology for Bangladeshi Poetry in English", a postscript to my *Collected Poems* (Haq [2007] 2017), and that too in a rather tongue-in-cheek manner, is that for a poet it is an advantage to write in a language one has been familiar with since one's early years; and this is true of English for those of us who have been educated in English from kindergarten onwards. There is also increasing transnationality, i.e. greater mobility of people in a globalized world, more migration, more changes of address for professional reasons. Such movement is bound to lead to the creation of literature in acquired languages. The important thing is to judge the poetry, not the poet on the basis of their mother tongue or nationality. There are many instances where fine poets have written in a language they were not born to. They include all the successful Anglophone poets in the subcontinent and poets like Charles Simic and Andrei Codrescu in America.

As for the writer's relationship with their motherland, in a globalized world with increasing transnationality, it makes no sense to privilege writing from the motherland over diasporic writing. Whether it is a diaspora text or something produced in the motherland, it should be judged on its merits.

MAQ: *How has Anglophone poetry developed in the country? Who are the new poets, and what are they writing about?*

KH: The history of English language poetry in Bangladesh can be easily sketched. Our teacher Razia Khan Amin is the first we should mention. My friend Feroze Ahmed-ud-din published a promising debut collection, *This Handful of Dust*, in 1974. I had started writing in the late 1960s but did not publish my first collections till 1978, and have carried on ever since, though sometimes in fits and starts. Among younger compatriots, several of my colleagues published debut collections (Azfar Husain, Nuzhat Mannan, Rumana Siddique, Shamsad Mortuza, Shafiqul Islam); young friends like Sadaf Saz and Ahsan Akbar have brought out their first collections; a young poet called Sofiul Azam has published several volumes. But the most outstanding new voice is that of Nausheen Eusuf (2017), whose collection, *Not Elegy but Eros* includes a Pushcart prize-winning poem. Then there are several diaspora poets of Bangladeshi origin.

MAQ: *You once said, "writing was a process of playing around with words till one struck what seemed the right note". I fully agree with this. It sounds a bit like Coleridge's "Prose: words in their best order; poetry: the best words in the best order". But is poetry entirely a language game, aesthetic playfulness, or is there more to it? Are writers in any way "doctors" of culture as Begum Rokeya claimed?*

KH: "Doctors" of culture, or those who try to "purify the dialect of the tribe", as Mallarmé put it. I think there is always a mysterious element in poetry; the poet scribbles, revises, puts away, plays around, then suddenly feels that a piece sounds right. Of course, we should be open to differences of opinion; what sounds right to me may not to the reader.

MAQ: *I sometimes think that the metaphor in the title of your first poem, "Nature on a Leash", has remained central to your poetry; it implies that we live in a circumscribed and diminished world, and not in one of freedom, subjectivity, grandiose nobility that the Romantics envisaged or the grand narratives and ideologies associated with the Modernists. Would that be an acceptable way of approaching your work?*

KH: I wouldn't quarrel with your insight. I should like to add that the "diminished world" that you mention has specific roots in our society. I was born in 1950 in Dhaka city when it had a population of only 335,000. Our locality was partly urban and partly village-like, and yet it was just a mile from the city centre. As the city grew, with half a million people in 1960, and 1.3 million in 1970, a walk in Ramna Park produced the line you quote. Now Dhaka is a huge conurbation with an estimated 21 million people, and yet it does not really have the feel of a modern city. The sense of being constricted has increased.

MAQ: *Your poems highlight the moral decadence of the place as well, as in "Poor Man Eating" and "As Usual"—the blights of abuse, corruption, poverty, bigotry and so forth in the country.*

KH: Isn't that unavoidable? In fact, I consider satire and social criticism to be the most significant aspects of literature in the world today. I couldn't be mystical or philosophical even if I tried. When I focus on the self, it is a self beleaguered by everything that is rotten in the state of the world.

MAQ: *"Ode on the Lungi" and "How Many Buddhas Can They Destroy" are easily two of my favourite poems. I am not surprised that they have received a lot of attention in the US and elsewhere because they are both fairly serious pieces. There is no doubt that you have achieved considerable comic depth and intertextuality in the first one, while the second one reads more like an occasional poem. Would you mind telling us about the creative process involved in these two poems?*

KH: Looking back, I would acknowledge Lawrence Ferlinghetti's "Underwear" as an inspiration behind "Lungi". The poem took a while to germinate, but once I hit upon the idea of bringing in Walt Whitman, everything fell into place. It actually went through several versions before reaching its present form. Let me quote here a few lines from Ferlinghetti's "Underwear", followed by some lines from "Lungi", so that you can see how these two poems are connected and how I generally share Whitman's democratic spirit in my poem:

Underwear

I didn't get much sleep last night
thinking about underwear
Have you ever stopped to consider
underwear in the abstract
When you really dig into it
some shocking problems are raised
Underwear is something
we all have to deal with
Everyone wears
some kind of underwear
The Pope wears underwear I hope
The Governor of Louisiana
wears underwear
I saw him on TV
He must have had tight underwear
He squirmed a lot
Underwear can really get you in a bind
You have seen the underwear ads
for men and women
so alike but so different
Women's underwear holds things up
Men's underwear holds things down
Underwear is one thing
men and women have in common
Underwear is all we have between us ...

Ode on the Lungi

Grandpa Walt, allow me to share my thoughts
with you, if only because every time
I read "Passage to India" and come across
the phrase "passage to more than India"

I fancy, anachronistically, that you wanted
to overshoot the target
by a shadow line
and land in Bangladesh

Lately, I've been thinking a lot
about sartorial equality
How far we are from
this democratic ideal!
And how hypocritical!
"All clothes have equal rights" –
this nobody will deny
and yet, some obviously
are more equal than others
No, I'm not complaining about
the jacket and tie
required in certain places –
that, like fancy dress parties,
is in the spirit of a game

I'm talking of something more fundamental
Hundreds of millions
from East Africa to Indonesia
wear the lungi, also known variously
as the sarong, munda, htamain, saaram,
ma'awaiis, kitenge. kanga. kaiki
They wear it day in day out,
indoors and out
Just think –
at any one moment
there are more people in lungis
than the population of the USA
Now try wearing one
to a White House appointment –
not even you. Grandpa Walt,
laureate of democracy,
will make it in
You would if you
affected a kilt –
but a lungi? No way.
But why? – this is the question
I ask all to ponder

"Buddha" was a response to the senseless vandalizing of Buddhist temples in Cox's Bazar some years back.[1] You will recall that someone tampered with the Facebook page of a Buddhist youth and uploaded an image calculated to anger Muslims. This was circulated, and a mob went on a rampage without bothering to investigate the matter. Mercifully, no one was killed. Unfortunately, similar things happened across the border in Myanmar, where Muslims were the victims; a monk notorious for his Islamophobia has even been dubbed "the Buddhist Bin Laden". The poem is a desperate act of affirmation of the better angels of our nature. Here are the concluding stanzas of the poem:

> Who can tell
> How many Buddhas there must be
> In our overpopulated world
> For us to hear the voice so often every day
>
> Social scientists might find it interesting
> To conduct a worldwide survey
> They needn't bother
> I can give you the answer straightaway
> It's over six billion
>
> There are over six billion of us
> Each with a living Buddha
> In a tiny yet immeasurable space
> Within the heart
>
> Now tell me
> What can they do to so many
> Those merchants of calculated hatred
> Those engineers of irrationality
> Tell me What can they do against six billion Buddhas
> Tell me
> How many Buddhas can they destroy

---

[1] Mobs attacked Buddhist monasteries, shrines, as well as the houses of Buddhist inhabitants in Ramu Upazila in Cox's Bazar District, Bangladesh on the night of September 29, 2012. They destroyed 12 Buddhist temples and monasteries and 50 houses, in response to the tagging of an image depicting the desecration of a Quran on the Facebook site of a Buddhist youth. As Kaiser Haq says here, investigations by local media later revealed the youth had nothing to do with the Facebook posting.

MAQ*: I was reading your poem "East And West: A Plan for World Peace" the other night and I must say that I was taken aback by its dark humour and deadpan style. It immediately brought to mind Jonathan Swift's depiction of the Yahoos in* Gulliver's Travels *and also his essay "A Modest Proposal" (especially the ironic title). We have come to expect a degree of wit, ambiguity and sarcasm in your poetry, but it all reaches a new level in this poem. If the idea was to deflate human pride and bring us back to the sordid world of reality, it has succeeded dramatically. May I please ask what prompted you to write this poem?*

KH: Thank you for drawing attention to this poem, which has been overshadowed by "Lungi", even though the two are in a sense companion poems. My immersion in the work of V.S. Naipaul, my favourite prose writer, may have had something to do with the poem. (You will remember how he highlights the toilet habits of Indians in "An Area of Darkness".) Then, a friend did actually have an argument with a westerner over toilet practices. That led me to Rudyard Kipling's "East-West" dichotomy, and Allen Ginsberg's affirmation of the holiness of shit, which of course is a big Yea for man the natural animal.

MAQ*: Would you please briefly introduce your two Collected volumes—*Published in the Streets of Dhaka *([2007] 2017) and* Pariah and Other Poems *(2013)—for the benefit of our international readers, and explain how your poetry has evolved over the years.*

KH: The first book has a title poem, which I consider rather significant, as a declaration of literary independence, so to speak. It includes all but a few of the poems in my first five collections, plus some additional ones. The present edition is the third, and with each new edition there has been some augmentation. The second collection contains nearly all the poems I wrote after the appearance of the first Collected volume. It has a few autobiographical poems that resuscitate the locality I was born in. Since this book, I have published just a few poems. One can be found in in *The Gollancz Book of South Asian Science Fiction* (2019) edited by Tarun K. Saint, and another is forthcoming in a follow-up volume; both volumes are from Hachette. The first of these takes off from the Partition and looks forward another 70 years; the second was prompted by the corona pandemic.

Judging from my unpublished drafts, I think I will be moving in a new direction before long; but I can't say exactly which way.

MAQ: *Since you mention the current pandemic, I am curious to know if it has affected your writing in any way, especially since Bangladesh has been hit quite hard by the virus.*

KH: The poem I have just mentioned, though prompted by the pandemic, moves on to critique the pitiless world in which we find ourselves. The pandemic per se hasn't yet produced anything from my pen. I suppose the enormity of it will take time to sink in and then emerge in lines of verse. I think non-fiction will register it better. Already, the Chinese novelist Fang Fang (2020) has published *Wuhan Diary: Dispatches from a Quarantined City*. Such works offer a more interesting treatment of the subject than fiction or poetry.

MAQ: *You told me previously that you wanted to be a novelist like Hemingway, but took up poetry because you lacked "the temperament to become a fiction writer". Now that you have published to international critical acclaim* The Triumph of the Snake Goddess *(2015), a transcreation of the story of the snake goddess Manasa in a "punchy prose narrative" (Korom), described by Tabish Khair in* The Hindu *as "essential reading for all of us who grew up with stories of snakes as objects not just of fear and fascination, but also of veneration, respect, even worship", would you reconsider trying the novel form?*

KH: Thank you for the appreciative comments on *Snake Goddess*. But I still don't think I have the temperament of a novelist. Another couple of retellings may emerge; and I hope there will be a lot more non-fiction, which in fact interests me more than fiction. I actually enjoy reading non-fiction more than most fiction. The fiction I really love I enjoy rereading.

MAQ: *What is the state of your translation of Tagore's* Yogayog *and the memoir you mentioned in the first interview? By the way, I have read your prose piece "English-medium Boy: A Post-commonwealth Memoir" in* Griffith Review *59 (Haq 2018). Is this meant as one of the earlier chapters of the memoir? The opening paragraph is memorable:*

> I loved the smell of the cotton cloth measured out from bolts that made a soft, slapping sound as they were unrolled: white for half-sleeved shirts, navy blue gabardine for shorts. I enjoyed being measured out for two sets of the uniform at the

tailor's. It was fun trying on the black Naughty Boy shoes at Bata, with white cotton socks; picking up a navy blue silk tie fastened with a rubber band; filling a brown canvas satchel with books and copies, and pencil, eraser, ruler. How sweet the bouquet of the new books, how exotic the coloured illustrations, how musical the crisp rustle of paper at the stationer's. None of the other boys in our locality were experiencing such exquisite delights; I was the only one who had been admitted into an English-medium school. Looking back, I identify it as the defining moment in my life. (283)

KH: A bit of the *Yogayog* translation appeared in *The Essential Tagore* (Tagore 2014); the complete draft is in my drawer. I don't know if anyone would be interested in publishing it.

I have published another memoir titled "Testament of a Pseudo-Translator" in a journal in Odisha; and an autobiographical essay on my experience of our food culture has come out from Pan Macmillan Picador India and Beacon Books (UK) in an anthology titled *Desi Delicacies,* edited by Claire Chambers (2020). There was an essay in *London Magazine* in 1986 that is a sort of intellectual autobiography; and an essay titled "Karl Marx vs. Nux Vomica 200" in *Bengal Lights* (Haq 2012) that would fit into a memoir. I published a memoir of Berlin on the eve of reunification in the Edinburgh journal *Chapman* and travel pieces in *Six Seasons Review* and *Bengal Lights.* I have a longish memoir of my father's experiences in World War II. All of these could be collected; a full-length autobiography could be attempted too. Let's see how the chips fall.

MAQ*: Since the relationship between literature and criticism is symbiotic, could you reflect briefly about the state of criticism of Anglophone writing in Bangladesh. Is it contributing to the positive growth of creative activity in the medium?*

KH: Generally speaking, criticism in Bangladesh is rather weak. This applies to Anglophone writing as well as Bengali writing. I hear the same complaint about Indian writing.

MAQ*: But hasn't India produced a number of outstanding critics in postcolonial literature, many of whom currently teach at western universities? I notice that many talented Bangladeshi scholars are more interested in journal-*

istic writing than serious criticism. Is this something that has affected our critical tradition adversely?

KH: There are more theorists than critics; and when they are ensconced in western academia, their work becomes part of the academic discourse there. Literary journalism, as in the *Times Literary Supplement* (*TLS*), the *London Review of Books* (*LRB*) or the *New York Review Books* (*NYRB*), is of more value to the writer and the common reader than jargon-ridden academic writing. India has *Biblio*, which is very good, but it's a quarterly when it ought to be a weekly. The literary culture couldn't sustain it as a weekly, which tells you a lot. In criticism as in creative writing, ultimately the quality of the writing and the insights matter. The best critics, whether outside or inside academia, have been good writers: Lionel Trilling, Matthew Arnold, Harold Bloom, John Carey, just to take a few names at random.

MAQ: *What are you working on now? What can we expect from your several spheres of creativity in the near future?*

KH: I have suddenly taken up a big academic project: as you know, for you are one of its contributors, I am co-editing *The Routledge Handbook of Bangladeshi Literary Culture*. But I hope I can make time to do what I enjoy most. I want to retell the 17th-century Bengali Sufi classic, *Nabi Bangsha*, and the tales in *Mymensingh Geetika*. And write more poems.

Two New Poems by Kaiser Haq

Words
A sense of exaltation
      heralds a new poem

Words fall in
      like soldiers in a conscript army

The orders are clear –
    storm the ramparts
      of a rotten state

letting in sweet light –
    then
      wearied
        rest
          in a drawer

Next time I pull the drawer open
        termites have had them all –

I'm left with the exaltation

Belated Mirror Stage

Born in a bamboo hut
one winter evening
in the amber light of hurricane lanterns,
I grew up playing in dirt,
the dry dust of autumn, winter, spring
or monsoon puddles
when grey skies hung low
and the field sagged underfoot
as we struggled
with a football of cheap leather
that had soaked up a deluge
and lay heavy as lead
and stung at every kick,
moving and not moving,
and we'd have thought of Zeno's paradox
if we'd heard of it,
but goalless draw notwithstanding,
I sloshed buckets of well water
over my skinny body,
happy as the rain was cool,
and raked wet hair with bazaar comb,
marking the parting
without help of looking-glass:
there were a couple of them around,
one A5 sized for mother
to oil and plait her hair,
the other roundish, five inches across,
for father to shave and scissor-trim whiskers;
my sense of being was complete
without one: Indian, Bengali, Muslim,
I looked inward towards
atman or *rooh*, a centre
insubstantial yet firm.
At fifteen a passion

for self-refashioning
drove me to study hard and work out harder.
Since Charles Atlas was too pricey
I followed a routine of my own devising:
starting with ten Indian-style push-ups
and adding one more each day
I counted two hundred before the year was out.
I didn't take a break
except for festivals or flu.
Once I saw an American body-building magazine:
page after coloured page of incredible hulks
posing with fancy barbells before mirrors. No,
my modest physical culture routine wouldn't pass muster
in the land of the bigger and better; enough
that it worked for me, though I never
checked out results before a mirror.
I liked it for it made me feel good
just as it felt good when I wrote a poem;
I had time for both every day.
But nothing runs steady all through life:
workouts slacken, trousers grow tight,
the muse plays hard to get,
you're happier nursing a drink,
but just when you think
this is the drab prosody of life,
doomsday shadows creep across the page;
press-ganged into a masked carnival of death
old lessons kick in: fitness and strength
are at a premium when the reaper plays with loaded dice.
Desperately swinging Indian clubs
I stand sweating before my wife's dressing table,
examine the pecs, biceps, faintly visible four-pack,
and not out of vanity: having rounded off
the biblical three score years and ten,
and no longer sure of *atman* or *rooh*,
I look hard at the mirror just to see –
I'm still here.
Next time friends ask
if I've got a Covid-inspired poem, I'll say
yes: I'm still here.

Bibliography

Chambers, Claire, ed. 2020. *Desi Delicacies*. New Delhi: Pan Macmillan.
Eusuf, Nausheen. 2017. *Not Elegy but Eros*. New York: NYQ Books.
Fang, Fang. 2020. *Wuhan Diary: Dispatches from a Quarantined City*. New York: HarperVia.
Haq, Kaiser. [2007] 2017. *Published in the Streets of Dhaka: Collected Poems*. Dhaka: The University Press Limited (UPL).
---. 2012. "Karl Marx vs. Nux Vomica 200." In *Bengal Lights*, edited by Khademul Islam. Dhaka: University of Liberal Arts.
---. 2013. *Pariah and Other Poems*. Dhaka: Bengal Lights Books.
---. 2015. *The Triumph of the Snake Goddess*. Cambridge, MA: Harvard University Press.
---. 2018. "English-medium Boy: A Post-commonwealth Memoir." *Griffith Review* 59: 283–90.
---. 2019. "The Novel of Bangladesh." In *The Oxford History of the Novel in English, Volume 10: The Novel in South and South-East Asia Since 1945*, edited by Alex Tickell, 74–87. Oxford: Oxford University Press.
Jahan, Nasreen. 2012. *The Woman Who Flew*. Translated by Kaiser Haq. London: Penguin.
Mirza Sheikh I'tesamuddin. 2002. *The Wonders of Vilayet*. Translated by Kaiser Haq. Leeds: Peepal Tree Press.
Quaderi, Shaheed. 2012. *Selected Poems*. Translated by Kaiser Haq. Dhaka: Bengal Lights Books.
Rahman, Shamsur. [1985] 2016. *Selected Poems*. Translated with an Introduction by Kaiser Haq. Dhaka: Pathak Shamabesh Books.
Tagore, Rabindranath. 1993. *Quartet [Chaturanga]*. Translated by Kaiser Haq. Oxford: Heinemann Asian Writers Series.
---. 2014. *The Essential Tagore*. Edited by Fakrul Alam and Radha Chakravarty. Cambridge, MA: Harvard University Press.

Nomadic Thinking:
Tabish Khair in Conversation with Pavan Kumar Malreddy

Photograph of Tabish Khair by Christopher Thomsen

> Literature remains the best antidote to fundamentalism
> —religious, political or economic. I would just define myself as
> someone who reads this kind of literature, and tries to write it
> —Tabish Khair (2019, 280)

Tabish Khair is a novelist, poet, and an academic based in Denmark. He was born in a small provincial town (Gaya, in Bihar) in India, and has spoken of its tolerant environment:

> I grew up in an open and religious Muslim family, going to a Roman Catholic school and surrounded by Hindu friends and neighbours. The idea that one has to show respect for other religions is not new to me; one just did so, it was a lifestyle. (2019, 274)

He studied for his masters at the local university and worked there for a number of years before relocating to Denmark for personal reasons. There, he gained his PhD from Copenhagen University and a DPhil from Aarhus University, where he is currently an associate professor. He maintains his connection with India in a number of ways, including his role as a columnist for *The Hindu* and as a regular speaker at Indian universities.

Khair is the author of seven novels, five poetry collections, over half a dozen monographs and edited collections, and numerous essays on subjects as wide-ranging as racism, postcolonial Gothic, travel writing and new xenophobia. He has been awarded the All India Poetry Prize and his novels have been shortlisted for more than a dozen major awards, such as the Man Asian Literary Prize, the Hindu Fiction Prize, the Encore Prize and the DSC Prize—twice, for *The Thing About Thugs* (Khair 2012) and *Night of Happiness* (Khair 2018). While declining to be drawn into pronouncements on the vicissitudes of the diasporic and migratory experiences ("I do not consider my alienation or loneliness, to the extent that they exist, as due to my experience of a foreign land. I felt lonely and often alienated when growing up in Gaya too" [2019, 222]), he has written insightfully about both. His fiction is remarkable for its willingness to embark on new and distinctive projects, and deal with them in direct and unexpected ways. *Just Another Jihadi Jane* is convincingly narrated in the voice of Jamilla, a teenager who leaves England for Islamist Syria. The story of Amir Ali in *The Thing About Thugs* engages with *thuggee* to address the fallacy of the common colonial claim to know everything about the colonized; as Khair says, "what the colonizer sees and what the colonized experiences are two different things" (2019, 277).

Tabish Khair is a household name in the field of postcolonial studies, both within and outside of South Asia, and his work has been the subject of various edited volumes, readers, and essays. As Khair's writings make evident, both his academic and fictional imagination is shaped by a seamless blending of his childhood formations in Bihar, and his later years in Europe and beyond. In this interview, which took place in the city of Surat (India) in January 2019, Khair reflects on many themes familiar to his readers: exile, migration, racism, and capitalism.

For biographical notes on the interviewer, Pavan Kumar Malreddy, see his interview with Amit Chaudhuri in this volume.

Pavan Kumar Malreddy (PKM): I will start by registering your aversion to the term "diaspora", but when I think about your work, it is hard for me to avoid the figure of the "migrant". In his piece on intellectual exile, Edward

Said says something to the effect that migrants learn to be happy with the idea of unhappiness "so that dissatisfaction bordering on dyspepsia, a kind of curmudgeonly disagreeableness, can become not only a style of thought, but also a new, if temporary habitation" (1993, 117). To what extent would this be true in your case—that is, the idea of never being complacent with the fraternal and filial association, and always occupying a position of "temporary habitation"?

Tabish Khair (TK): It's a complex idea. I would like to start by viewing it from a slightly different perspective than this notion of intellectual exile. I would think that in some ways we are all exiled from ourselves: even at your best, you might feel that you ought to be better than what you are or you want to be something else at times. On the other hand, I wouldn't say that this is necessarily something that makes you unhappy, because the desire to be actually something more than what you are, something different than what you are, is also an impetus. So, in that sense, I wouldn't necessarily see intellectual exile in terms of happiness or unhappiness. Maybe I would have 15 or 20 years ago before I became a father. But I would see intellectual exile now as this paradoxical state of being *in* the world and *not in* the world at the same time. I think intellectual exile enables this necessary (dis)junction of being more or less visible, and one uses it creatively in a form that can be seen as being rooted in a degree of dissatisfaction about what exists in the world and …

PKM: … and being more politically aware?

TK: Politically aware, yes. But unhappiness is not a word I would use again; at the same time, happiness is not a word I would use either.

PKM: I agree, there is no rule that one has *to be happy or unhappy about exile. I think it is interesting that Said himself employed these terms, including the aspects of "inner exile" you talk about.*

TK: Yes, exactly.

PKM: The idea of "inner exile" is pertinent to our discussion. Here, I am thinking of your fictional characters who are always on the move, all the way from The Bus Stopped *(Khair 2004) to* Just Another Jihadi Jane *(Khair 2016); even in* The Thing about Thugs *(Khair 2012), there is a movement within the nation, across the nations, and across strange unimaginable shores, and* the seamless, at times unassuming collision of these worlds. So throughout your work, there are people moving from village to city, and city to foreign lands—just as in your own life trajectory—and I wonder if this urge for movement between different "selves" is something you are very conscious of, or does it come to you naturally?

TK: Some of it I can consider as coming naturally because I myself grew up in a small town (Gaya) in Bihar. I left the town for the first time when I was 24, and by then I had started writing and I had started publishing. I hadn't yet published a novel but I had been publishing poems and working as a journalist and in the course of doing this, I also read a lot. And one thing that struck me was the fact I had grown up in a place which, in some ways, was extremely mobile: people from villages coming to the town, people from the town moving around, and also being mobile in an intellectual sense. When I started writing, I wanted to focus on that kind of mobility; *The Bus Stopped* is an example of that because I realized that a lot of discussions of mobility or diaspora tend to be across national borders, which tend to focus on a metropolitan space and confuse it with cosmopolitanism (of the European kind).

PKM: It camouflages the inequalities as well as the diversity of small towns?

TK: Diversity, yes, and I realized that in some ways small towns have their own characters and limitations just as big cities have, but what if small towns also contain cosmopolitan traditions and spaces? I wanted to focus on that. By cosmopolitan, I simply mean the ability of people to live with things, traditions and other people who are different from them. What more could we attribute to cosmopolitanism, apart from that? A metropolitan space might not *grant* you that ability, as one might be living with upper class people in a neighbourhood, or might be working with them, or you might never have had anything to do with a villager. In a small town, you would invariably have something to do with a villager because there is always a village around the corner, in a ten-kilometre periphery or so.

PKM: This is interesting to hear from you directly. In some ways you might disagree with me on this because in The Bus Stopped, *you blend the village imagination with the city imagination, and as I argued elsewhere (Malreddy 2011), cosmopolitanism is something you cannot always discuss in relation to the west. If you look at R.K. Narayan's fictional town Malgudi, in spite of* its Hinducentric characters and southern focus, it converges various pan-Indian characters and experiences. This is something I have called "localpolitanism".

TK: And that tends to be neglected sometimes by critics who read Narayan's Malgudi as a town stuck in the past. It's actually far from static.

PKM: *Yes, it's dynamic and that brings me to a very important aspect of your work. You have always been a champion for the recognition of minority voices, traditions and needs—be it in physical or artistic spaces—including Muslims and Dalits and other endangered communities. At the same time, you have never dismissed the heritage of whatever might be called "the Indian tradition" in the literary context. How do you go about achieving that balance between the representation of minorities and set traditions in India? Is it something that goes back to your origins in these intra-communal spaces?*

TK: I am not seriously conscious of that. I think that is the way I experienced India. That is the way I continue to experience India, and there is certainly a kind of collection of dominant ethos and discourses, and then of course minority discourses against that. These two are inseparable. Sometimes they clash, but sometimes they interpenetrate and even shape each other. So, in that sense, to think of these differences only in terms of black and white wouldn't really do justice to the reality I've experienced.

PKM: *The perspective you offer on diasporic difference as something locally bred, not necessarily beyond the national borders or beyond nations, is quite refreshing. Very few people have explored this angle of internal diaspora. Sometimes, we tend to forget that India is a country that was put together.*

TK: Like most countries.

PKM: *Yes, of course, but don't you think that the scale of diversity here in India is something else?*

TK: Definitely.

PKM: *Greater here?*

TK: Definitely, it is greater here for various reasons, first of all, for its expanse. But also bear in mind that when we talk of the USA, it's also a country that is very big but a country whose past was largely erased by a certain kind of colonization. But, in India, no past has been totally erased.

Hegemonies, yes, but much less erasure. It is a palette of pasts and cultures. I'm not saying that there have not been differences but that doesn't matter because most of them have survived at different levels. Whether you think of it in terms of aboriginality, caste, religion, or region, most of the layers are still out there, which makes it a much more vast, and much more complex social fabric than the USA can ever be. There, native Americans have been pushed into marginal spaces and restrictive spheres of political and cultural significance.

PKM: Your response leads me to think about the literary techniques used / required for representing such diverse, palimpsestic and, at times, extremely polarized cultures. There is Salman Rushdie's so-called "cinematic novel", and then we have Bollywood melodrama, which works with extreme polarities, of say, a billionaire's granddaughter falling in love with the Dalit driver. So, in the process of representing such extreme polarities, a realistic mode of writing spills over into other genres and modes of writing—be it melodramatic, irrealist or even magic realist. Do you think that this palimpsestic diversity is one of the reasons why South Asia has produced so much fiction, and so many creative writers?

TK: It is one of the factors but there are other factors as well, like how literary traditions are shaped by the levels and styles of writing both at micro and macro levels. People talk of "writing India", as if "writing Gaya" is a simpler matter: the layers are as complex at the local level and language is as frayed and contentious. Moreover, there is much interpenetration at all levels, and at an almost subconscious level at times. That's a rare situation. Also, historically, despite the fact that South Asia was exploited under colonization, there were still spaces of political and poetical freedom. These spaces have survived—sometimes blossoming, sometimes shrinking—after Independence. Here, I would stress particularly in India because in some ways our neighbors have greater restrictions in terms of cultural ideologies, especially in Pakistan where Wahabi Islam is on the rise. It could well be that India will go that way in the future, but it hasn't happened yet. Like India, Bangladesh and Pakistan, too, have great literary traditions except that Pakistan has a lot of unresolved problems which do relate to the way one reads what is written.

PKM: *But still it is not able to contain the mushrooming of a new generation of writers both in Pakistan and Bangladesh.*

TK: Bangladesh, in particular, is a vibrant culture. Pakistan, I must say, I don't follow it closely now. With some exceptions, the currently visible generation of Pakistani writers are all writing in English and in the literary circles *in* Pakistan, especially from what I see of Urdu writing, my impression is that the trajectory has actually gone the wrong way. I mean there was more contentious writing in the past: would someone like Manto[1] come up today? Not that he was not dragged to court, but still ... On the other hand, maybe I am just ignorant. I do not follow the scene in Pakistan.

PKM: *Manto, Faiz Ahmed Faiz,[2] all were rather popular in India.*

TK: Faiz Ahmed Faiz was a committed socialist. Would it be possible for many Urdu writers to be openly socialist today? Though, I must add, there are exceptions in India, such as the outspoken Javed Akhtar.

PKM: *Also a cosmopolitan and humanist of the highest order, he became the editor of* Lotus *magazine, and championed the Palestinian cause.*

TK: The sort of cosmopolitanism that was distinctive of Urdu writing is gradually disappearing as well. Another example of such a rich tradition would be Iran. Iran has gone the wrong way but it still has a vital intellectual culture. I just hope that it is not bombed to smithereens, like Iraq or Libya, because of the power politics of Saudi, Israel and Trumpist USA.

PKM: *Since you bring in the cosmopolitan aspect of Urdu and Iranian / Farsi literature, I want to bring in my own upbringing in the Urdu milieu in post-Nizam Hyderabad. In the Hindu villages under Nizam, Muslims became another caste, known as "Turkas" (after Turks), and the Irani cafes were brewing Indian chai, and Telugu bagara fused with Mughul pulav gave birth to the famous Hyderabadi Biryani. My Pakistani friends find my Urdu funny and*

---

1   Saadat Hasan Manto (1912–55) was an Indian and Pakistani writer whose short stories in Urdu are often cited as some of the greatest produced in South Asia. He also authored a novel, radio plays, essays and personal sketches
2   Faiz Ahmad Faiz (1911–84), born in Sialkot, India, which is now part of Pakistan. was a celebrated Pakistani poet and author in Urdu, who was widely read in both India and Pakistan. He was noted for his ability to use traditional forms such as the ghazal to explore political and social issues.

entertaining, and my North Indian friends find my Hindi to be Pakistani Urdu.

TK: Especially keeping in mind that in South India Hindi is a completely unfamiliar language.

PKM: *Even that. Now, when I try to tell my Telugu friends that biryani is more Turkish than Indian, or chai is more Irani than Hyderabadi, they would frown at me. You have hinted at this cosmopolitan curiosity that shapes your work and I do think that's what cosmopolitanism should be, not always absorbing things into "our tradition" or "our culture", but orienting ourselves to the possibility that what is ours might relationally be somebody else's—just as in Edward Said's idea of "contrapuntality". But there is this deeply entrenched ethnocentrism in the South Asian culture of things that are ours, that we make traditions. How do you think that our literary traditions reinforce this notion to some extent?*

TK: You see these tendencies always exist side by side in any field of history: for certain political reasons, one of the two tendencies gets *strengthened*. At the moment, it's true that there is a tendency in India, and in a lot of other countries too, to insist on their own specific identity. Whether it's done in terms of "America is great" or the "glorious British Empire", or "Danish values" or some kind of "Indianness" or some kind of "Islamic culture in Pakistan", that tendency exists and has become more prominent and exacerbated in recent years for various reasons. The reasons are political, economic, and also perhaps to a certain degree a disappointment with metro-cosmopolitan forms of intellectual engagements—a failure of certain kinds of progressive movements, especially on the left. And the more I think of it, the failure is largely due to the fact that economic issues are often left out of the debates. People around the world are worried; they are living in a world where capital penetrates every aspect of their lives and disrupts their traditional means of income and bargaining power. And they want to hang onto something that no one can take away from them: some narrow parochial definition of culture, nation, and so on.

PKM: *Nation?*

TK: Yes, these things function as safety nets, as long as we have politicians and ideologies assuring people that capital won't be able to penetrate their lives and rip them apart. These are politicians hand in glove with elite, finance capital (which is essential to stay in power these days), and hence they have to point at other, partly or entirely, imaginary monsters. Nation, religion, even "democracy" or "free speech", all can be used to distract attention from the real monster.

PKM: *I think that is very interesting, but what if capitalism is doing that very same thing, i.e. granting people a false sense of safety?*

TK: It is doing that because of larger political failure. That's why when people talk to me about the rise of "bad things" such as new nationalism—as they call it in Europe—I often feel that the distinction between good and bad politicians today is very much a deception. Should we call politicians good because they say "oh we need immigrants, we need to let some refugees in, and immigrants are good for the economy", and bad if they say "keep them out, build a wall"? But the fact of the matter is that politicians today—whether inherently good or bad—don't really talk about the main issue. The main issue here is the capital that does not really need to be put into production, especially when labour is becoming increasingly vestigial. In that situation, politicians feel that the only thing they can do is to keep the bankrupt corporations happy, the banks running. So every time a corporation fails, money is pumped into it, but where does the money come from? Obviously, from the taxpayers' wallets. This is how the money is being created for the corporations: by cutting down on social welfare and other services. So obviously citizens feel the crunch. Then they look for someone to blame.

PKM: *And use the Other as a threat, an excuse?*

TK: The real reason is too abstract. No politician is interested in focusing on that, so they simply blame the immigrants and refugees.

PKM: *I think this is the gist of your book* The New Xenophobia *(2016), where you bring the element of capital to the centre, where you try to blend new modes of capital and capitalism with the old ones. It's not that one replaces the other?*

TK: Old kinds of capitalism are still there but new forms are dominant, especially in the centres of finance. I'm not an economist, so I'm not even sure if this new form should be called capitalism because capitalism meant a certain relationship between capital, labour and production. Now that relationship has ceased to exist. So maybe we need another word for it. Maybe capitalism is dead or comatose, and that explains why its sharpest critics, Marxism-influenced parties, can make no headway politically in the world today.

PKM: But I am sure you will agree with the view that there is no capitalism without the processes of production?

TK: At some level. What people do on Wall Street is that they look at the numbers flashing on screens; they're not concerned with how these numbers are connected to the real world of production out there. It's just a play of speculation and numbers and you can earn billions by just moving the numbers around. So, in that sense, even though there is of course at one level the connection between capital and production, today capital does not need labour as much as it did under classical capitalism. It replicates on its own. But this doesn't mean old forms of exchange, or even commodity exchange, have died out; they still co-exist. They are just not sufficient; power is slipping from their grasp.

PKM: This is like disposable capitalism, or "use and throw" capitalism, to put it in lay terms. When you talk about the new xenophobia, one also observes similar tendencies. Hamid Dabashi (2009) terms these tendencies "post-Orientalism", which he defines against the 19th-century classical Orientalism that Said was concerned with. For Dabashi, classical Orientalism has exhausted itself, having served its colonial mission. Now you have a different kind of Orientalism which is subject to epistemic instability depending on the region, skin colour, or the religion that it deems a "threat".

TK: Yes, it changes its shape quickly.

PKM: Yes, the Chinese, for example, are not in the fold of such post-Orientalism.

TK: Neither are the Japanese.

PKM: Empire politics. I recall a page from one of Ananta Pramoedya Toer's novels that the Meiji emperor, at the height of Japanese imperialism, demanded that the Japanese in East Asian colonies be recognized as "whites", on a par with the European status. There is this formulaic understanding of racism in India, it seems, where one is conditioned to think racism is a colonial invention of import, not something we did to our own people.

TK: We are pretty good at that.

PKM: *If we take the question of untouchability, you take the Otherization of minorities, or even racialisation of Muslims, one could make a strong case for internal racism. I find it very difficult to articulate, and even in the postcolonial pedagogies I don't think this is an aspect that is adequately addressed. There are people like Kancha Ilaiah,[3] who argue that caste is race, but these are marginalized views.*

TK: No. But you see that's because postcolonialism works across national borders, which I call the colonial bridge. If you write a novel that tracks forward the colonial bridge, it gets much more visibility. So, in some ways, many postcolonialists just do that: institutionally they privilege the colonial bridge, even in their critique of it. For instance, postcolonialism notices the modern world only when "modernity" crosses that bridge. The connection is with an Indian who writes in English, that's the bridge, but not with a Malayali who writes in Hindi, or a Bihari who writes in Tamil.

PKM: *It's an event.*

TK: Yes. There is very little institutional space for that in postcolonial discourse.

PKM: *All the publishing spaces, all the marketing spaces are not conducive to any sort of internal criticism as well.*

TK: Yes, the problem is there. But to go back to your earlier point, I was recently told in Kolkata that "one of your novels contains elements of Islamophobia". I gave my reading anyway, but because I have been critical of internal problems in Muslim or Indian societies, I am suddenly faced with these questions. I think it's important to factually register and acknowledge what we do to other Indians, which is seriously problematic.

---

3   Kancha Ilaiah's ([1996] 2019) *Why I Am Not a Hindu* is advertised by its publisher as "a manifesto for the downtrodden [that] examines the socio-economic and cultural differences between the Dalitbahujans (the majority, the so-called low castes) and other Hindus in the contexts of childhood, family life, market relations, power relations, [and the] ideology of the Hindu Right".

Say, the easy explaining away of restrictions imposed on women by religious Muslims. There are other examples too, not confined to Muslims. The way we treat our aboriginal communities is in some ways as bad, if not much worse than how the British treated them. And we tend to totally forget about it because we see this space as an "Indian" space and them as throwbacks from a past that should be erased. Everyone should be middle class and urban and invest in shares seems to be the mantra of this kind of India.

PKM: *What of religious prejudices?*

TK: Well, I'm not even talking of Hindu, Muslim, or Christian divisions. I'm talking of intra-communal aspects, an area that we typically ignore: within the same community. I mean you might be a Muslim. But you might be treating certain other Muslims in a questionable way. You might be assuming that certain things are an abuse of Islam, so you don't allow any discussion of that. Even when two things can be proved scripturally not to be part of Islam. One good example is the ongoing triple talaq[4] controversy, since it is not practised in most Muslim countries.

PKM: *But in India.*

TK: And there is no scriptural sanction, not that I care about scriptural sanction or its lack in such matters of human rights. And there are people up there fighting against it. Some of them argue this is because the Bharatiya Janata Party (BJP) is pushing us but whatever the reason, the fact is that there is no reason to justify triple talaq, you know. But within the community, in many Muslim circles, I would not say this openly because I don't want to get into an argument.

PKM: *Absolutely. I have been sceptical of the popular left argument on this as well. I am reminded here of Dipesh Chakrabarty's caveat in* Provincializing Europe *(2008) that not everything that came out of colonialism has to be painted in a Eurocentric light. He says that even "the most trenchant critic[s]*

---

4   Triple talaq is a legally protected practice of instant divorce, used predominantly by Indian Muslims, in which the married man can divorce his wife by uttering the world talaq three times, which can be done in the presence or in the absence (via electronic media) of his conjugal partner. In 2018, and again in 2019, the BJP-led Indian government has made concerted but unsuccessful attempts to pass laws against this practice.

of the institution of 'Untouchability' in British India refer us back to some originally European ideas about liberty and human equality" (5). And so, this poses a daunting challenge to the writing tradition of the colonial bridge that you just spoke of.

TK: I totally agree with that. I would just like to add to that before I forget it. Yes, not everything that came through colonialism needs to be dismissed. There are a lot of these things that came through colonialism, and I'm not talking of the train or the plane, I'm talking about cultural aspects. The resistance to untouchability is one thing. But these progressive traditions also existed in India before the arrival of the colonizers. It is also important to make the connection that it wasn't as if we were an obtuse people who had no awareness of our own oppression, no. There had been resistance; there was an entire movement of social reformism in Bengal and elsewhere. But this has been either absorbed or erased in discourses of an anti-colonial movement. So it is also important to maintain a critical perspective on what the colonizers claimed: that they were the people who made us civilized or modern. That is not true. It is important not to dismiss what they enabled, whether collaboratively or contentiously, but also not to hand over all the credit to them!

PKM: *I think it is important to maintain a critical edge rather than bending the stick too far in the other direction? I don't think Dipesh was doing that.*

TK: No, I've read his book and I'm very sure he doesn't. It is an admirable study.

PKM: *But it's very interesting how the fetish of the east or the west is played out in postcolonialism, often in extreme ways that claim everything that came from colonialism is horrible, and everything that is native is noble.*

TK: Which is basically a double-bind and that's the failure. I mean before the current notion that the Muslim world is all military Islamist, we drummed up the notion that the west was even more violent. Sweeping generalisations that construct clashes of "civilizations" in a world that interpenetrates in actuality.

PKM: *And the militant Islamists use the same rocket launchers developed and supplied by the western powers.*

TK: They do use the same rocket launchers, the same tanks, the same vehicles, and the same mobile phones. They even use the same anti-semitism at times.

PKM: *I have seen and heard this long enough in Indian villages, where there is a toxic blend of ethnocentrism and an insatiable appetite for all things western and capitalist: technology, roads, infrastructure. So, I found this paradox quite striking, which brings me to your earlier point that capitalism, or the infiltration of capitalism into everyday lives, makes people cling to their religious or nationalist credos. But let us concede the fact that untouchability and feudalism went hand-in-hand. So one could argue that all these cultural infirmities were there even before the advent of capitalism?*

TK: All countries have had their structures of power; some people have ruled over some others. That's the way it still is, and it was more so in the imperialist past. I mean just because the British were not here didn't mean that we were not exploiting each other, and killing each other. It also doesn't mean that we weren't helping each other and trying to make things better. It's just that the British, when they came here, obviously wanted to make profit. They made a profit. But some of them also came here for other reasons. And they tried to do some good, in their own distinct ways. I think one problem that we have not faced up to, and in certain circles it's very difficult to articulate—I keep on planning on writing about it and then I don't know how to put it in the context of an interview—are the consequences of the positive intentions of the best people for the rest. I'll give you an example. Recently, I wrote a piece about corruption. And my point was that corruption is connected to socioeconomic disparities. I said that everywhere in the world, the more the socioeconomic disparities, the greater the chance of corruption. Of course, there are cultural factors that might mitigate it, but if socioeconomic disparities increase, corruption increases. I also said that there are certain societies, usually democratic European welfare states, that are seen as the least corrupt. Of course, there are certain kinds of connection between parliament and corporations in such countries of the first world that have been so long established that they are no longer seen as corrupt.

PKM: *Yes, they are being normalized.*

TK: But I didn't go into that when I was talking about corruption in general. So I got a response from a couple of well-meaning people in the west saying "oh but the west is corrupt too and look at corporations". I got emails from more well-meaning people who were concerned about corporate corruption. I did write back to them saying that yes, I know all these things exist but it makes no difference to India, or to Pakistan, or to Turkey. The fact is that we have to face our forms of corruption, and we cannot tell ourselves that "we have corruption but look—these people also have corruption".

PKM: *As if it is a zero-sum game.*

TK: That's an endless situation to be in. And we always end up doing that. We have to face the problems we have and we cannot just bracket the problems or pass the burden onto someone else and think "look it's so bad there, too" or "we're not really corrupt, that's just the way it works". Then we are never going to get any better. That's the consequence of good intention at the worst on the left today. They do that all the time instead of facing the problems that exist. They mean well, but they often end up providing excuses rather than solutions.

PKM: *Let me now move from India to Europe because, in many ways, Europe has shaped your literary imagination and you produced a lot of fiction and poetry from there, especially after the September 11 attacks—an event that seems to be central to your work.*

TK: Yeah, it was an "in-your-face" event for me, definitely.

PKM: *And what was your experience? I ask this because you have written about new xenophobia, the inverted terror in colonialism, the Gothic, all of which bear the traces of post-9 / 11 cultural politics.*

TK: Look, when the buildings went down, there were two ways in which people reacted to it. People who had actually experienced New York, physically or culturally—those who had seen those buildings—saw it as an actual event, a horrific tragedy. And then there were the people who had hardly seen a photo of them except for TV footage. For me, it was like watching a movie. And it took me about two minutes before I realized that these are not just buildings crashing, but that there are people dying. And then the horrific hit me. I think there was a difference in the way people from immigrant backgrounds might have experienced the aftermath. People from India and the Middle East might not have had the same experiences.

PKM: *As a last question, let me return to where we started: the notion of exile. The Somali writer Nuruddin Farah (1988) says that being in exile has given him a clearer vision with which to look at his place and his country. Does this hold true in your case?*

TK: You see, if you move to another space, you do experience a different set of things. Which means that it changes what you are to some extent. There, you do look back from that space to your previous space and you see it slightly differently. This is of course entirely necessary, and I think it is necessary for all writers; whether you move physically or not, you have to do it intellectually. To move away—and this moving away can also make you appreciate certain things in the world which you would not have appreciated. So, I think it's not just a question of distance. It is also a question of closeness at the same time. By moving away, you also come close to other things. I think it's a very creative position to occupy. Of course, if you are lucky enough to move away and be able to come back any time, as in my case, it's better. But if you're forced to move away and cannot go back, it will probably affect the way you connect to other places. I can only talk of my own experience here.

PKM: *Thank you so much for this conversation, Tabish.*

Acknowledgements

This publication is supported by a grant from the German Research Foundation (DFG): MA 7119 / 1-1.

Bibliography

Chakrabarty, Dipesh. 2008. *Provincializing Europe: Postcolonial Thought and Historical Difference*. Princeton, NJ: Princeton University Press.
Dabashi, Hamid. 2009. *Post-Orientalism: Knowledge and Power in Time of Terror*. New Brunswick, NJ and London: Transaction Publishers.
Farah, Nuruddin. 1988. "An Interview with Nuruddin Farah [with Maggie Jonas]." *Journal of Refugee Studies* 1 (1): 74–77.
Ilaiah, Kancha. [1996] 2019. *Why I Am Not a Hindu*. 2nd ed. New York: Sage.
Khair, Tabish. 2004. *The Bus Stopped*. London: Picador.

---. 2012. *The Thing About Thugs*. Boston: Houghton Mifflin Harcourt.
---. 2016. *Just Another Jihadi Jane*. Reading: Periscope.
---. 2016. *The New Xenophobia*. Oxford: Oxford University Press.
---. 2018. *Night of Happiness*. New Delhi: Pan Macmillan India.
---. 2019. "'Literature is the Best Antidote to Fundamentalism': Tabish Khair in Conversation [with Goutam Karmakar]." *Journal of Postcolonial Writing* 55 (2): 269–81.
Malreddy, Pavan Kumar. 2011. "'Cosmopolitanism Within': The Case of RK Narayan's Fictional Malgudi." *Journal of Postcolonial Writing* 47 (5): 558–70.
Said, Edward W. 1993. "Intellectual Exile: Expatriates and Marginals." *Grand Street* 47: 112–24.

Reading, Writing and the Contours of Power: Mridula Koshy in Conversation with Maryam Mirza

Photograph of Mridula Koshy copyright 2021 by Tejinder Singh

Described by the poet and novelist Jeet Thayil as "an extraordinary Indian moralist with an unmistakable gift", Mridula Koshy is the author of several short stories and two novels. She was awarded the 2009 Shakti Bhatt First Book Prize for her collection of short stories *If It Is Sweet* (Koshy [2009] 2011), which was also shortlisted for the Vodafone Crossword Book Award. Her varied stories show how Koshy embraces resilience rather than despair in her depiction of her characters' misfortunes and triumphs. They emerge from different class backgrounds to interact and connect with one another (a feature of Delhi life that she explores in this interview). The stories can end surprisingly (as in the fate of the sons' ashes in "The Good Mother" or the outcome of the resentments of Suraj, the domestic help in "Today Is the Day"). They can conclude movingly ("Passage") or poignantly, as in the final sentences of "The Large Girl": "A thousand and one chances will come and go in this small city, in this small world. I will never see you again".

Her debut novel, *Not Only the Things That Have Happened* (Koshy 2012), was shortlisted for the Crossword Book Award in 2013, and Janice Pariat's (2013) review in *The Sunday Guardian* compared its structure to that of "a diptych, a painting hinged in the middle, linking two images, telling a story that works its way across the canvas". One half of the diptych concerns Annakutty Verghese, from Kerala, who gives up her four-year-old son Madhu for adoption by a German tourist couple, and the way she is affected life-long by this action, which had been largely out of her control. The other half engages with Mahdu himself (now Asa Gardner) and the vicissitudes of his life in the Midwest of the USA. Many readers have commented on the rewarding complexity of the book's handling of past, present and future. A distinctive essay on its powerful treatment of adoption can be found in the blog of Marijane Nguyen (2013) a self-identifying "Taiwanese-American Adoptee". Nguyen responds feelingly to the histories of both Annakutty and Madhu / Asa, saying of the latter that: "At the root of Asa's turmoil is the lack of any tangible history, in essence, a lack of true identity. With only fragmented memories of his past, Asa wanders like a lost soul, searching for missing pieces and reinventing stories to fill in the gaps".

Koshy's latest novel is *Bicycle Dreaming* (Koshy 2016). Thirteen-year-old Noor, who lives with her family in a one-room home in the Chirag Dilli district of Delhi, yearns to possess a green bicycle so she can become India's first kabaadiwali. Her father, Mohammad Saidullah, a kabadiwala, who pedals his bicycle door-to-door to collect discarded household objects, loses his job and is left with no option but to scavenge in the city's landfills. Noor falls for Ajith, a Dalit boy, and takes steps to find her own place in the world. The point, says Mridula Koshy in a comment to Tishani Doshi (2016), is precisely not to document the story of an exceptional individual; instead, she aimed to write "an unexceptional poor person into a novel; [not] a poor person deserving their place in literature by some trick of cleverness or sensitivity" (para. 7).

Mridula Koshy's short stories have appeared in journals such as *Wasafiri*, *The Dalhousie Review* and *Existere*. Born in India in 1969, she moved to the USA as a teenager and lived there for 20 years before returning to her country of birth. She now resides in New Delhi and is the co-founder of The Community Library Project. In this interview with Maryam Mirza, conducted between August 2018 and February 2019, Mridula

Koshy discusses the pressing impulses, themes and causes that have animated her life as a writer and community worker.

For biographical notes on the interviewer, Maryam Mirza, see her interview with Rukhsana Ahmad in this volume.

Maryam Mirza (MM): Ms. Koshy, did you always want to be a writer? I believe you have had numerous, fairly disparate, jobs in the past.

Mridula Koshy (MK): No, I have not always wanted to be a writer. Although yes, I have been told from an early age that I would-could-should become a writer. And this was because my grand aunt was a poet. I fear this idea of writing as something you inherit because it implies a lack of agency. A gift visited on you is a gift that can be withdrawn as easily. I feared and avoided writing because I was certain that anything I wrote would be evidence that I wasn't a writer. When I began writing it was somewhat reluctantly in response to a move to Delhi, a city I had left 20 years in the past. I had no other means to figure out how to be a part of the collective thinking of this city other than by writing. Subsequently I have always thought of writing as something you do, like any other work, and of course as something you struggle to do well. I don't subscribe to the idea of talent.

MM: While your debut novel was published in 2012, you have been writing short fiction for much longer. This is perhaps an unfair question, but which one among your many short stories is your favourite and why?

MK: I don't have a favourite short story, but some of them mean more to me than others. "The Good Mother" (Koshy 2008) was written at a time when I was going from being the mother of two to the mother of three—a death of sorts of the two, which I then treated literally and literarily. Most of the time my stories are about images and ideas that I see out there in the world. The stories that mean more to me are the ones that deal with things I am working out within myself. Similarly, I feel close to the emotions of the story, "Passage" (in Koshy 2011). I woke up one morning and there was an email from my brother-in-law. My sister had been hospitalized. She is alive and well today, but I wrote the story to figure out how I would have dealt with the grief if I had lost her. To my surprise the story ended with the narrator's husband comforting her. I suppose that's what I think would happen to me. Would I be comforted? I still don't know. A story can tell you a lot but it is also ultimately apart from you.

MM: *Do you usually know how a story will end before you put pen to paper, or fingertips to keyboard?*

MK: Yes, I almost always know. Whatever idea I am working with is the end of the story I then set out to write. Most of the time I write because I have felt something confounding or seen something amazing, often an image, sometimes a feeling, and this image or emotion is something I want to hold and turn in my hand, to examine and understand it. I want above all to experience it again. Writing allows me to do that. I write to get back to that moment and so, of course, that moment is the end of a story I am writing.

MM: *How has your return to India from the USA shaped the direction that your writing has taken over the last few years?*

MK: I no longer write. I wrote to join the conversation about who we are in India and in the world. I have been frustrated to see that in India literature is the purview of the few. The many are excluded from it. How or why would I write under these circumstances? All the bemoaning about "people" no longer reading refers only to the select who are viewed as "people". Those who have for centuries been forbidden literacy on pain of punishment—Dalits and lower caste citizens—and those who are taught poorly in schools so that they are literate but not fluent—the working class—are the majority of Indians. In a country of over a billion people an English language best seller is a book that sells 5,000 copies. Most recently my contribution to literature in India has taken the form of working with others in the library movement. Libraries that are free and open to all are sorely missing in India. My work with The Community Library Project addresses this gap by running two free libraries and networking with dozens more spread around the country.

MM: *Are there any contemporary South Asian writers (diasporic or otherwise) with whose style or thematic preoccupations you feel a particular affinity?*

MK: It is difficult not only for me but for many others who write in South Asia to feel that connection to another writer, to feel that we are writing with or against another. This is because we are few and our interests are necessarily divergent as we try to cover the vast swathes of what needs to be covered thematically. Contemporary Indian literature in English is a series of small points of light in the dark—dim and distant from one another. Literature in a few of the other Indian languages fares only a little better. The many points of light that could have been were never realized because those who could-would-should have been writing have been excluded from it. That said there are some writers whose voices resonate for me and whose thematic preoccupations I share. To name a few: Rajathi Salma, P. Sivakami, Benyamin. And I admire too many writers to name here.

MM: *Your work often examines the multi-layered contours of grief and trauma but does not disallow the possibility of humour. I'm thinking, for instance, of the second half of the novel* Not Only the Things That Have Happened *which grapples with a seven-year-old boy's harrowing journey first from Kerala to New Delhi, and then to the US. In Chapter 5, you have poignantly portrayed Madhu / Asa's first day in Los Angeles with his adoptive family, where we see him wailing almost unremittingly, feverish and unable to sleep. Shell-shocked as he is, as Madhu furtively watches his new sisters (and he has four) he observes: "[S]he is supposed to be one of his sisters [...]. What a disappointment to produce girl after girl [...]. The other two sisters come into the room [...]. This one will get married soon. She should. She looks old and tired". Do you find it challenging to weave humour and irony into representations of deeply distressing human situations such as Madhu's?*

MK: Humour is a great way to show multiple perspectives. What is funny to Madhu would never be seen as funny by the Gardners. We readers can see both perspectives. Fiction depends on such devices to achieve its greatest accomplishment—fluid movement of readers' sympathy from one character to the next and ultimately the ability to hold opposite truths without fracturing the universe. Humour is also about resilience. And resilience is a powerful idea, which I want to convey in my writing.

MM: *Please tell us about your interest in the theme of (transnational) adoption which, in addition to* Not Only the Things That Have Happened, *you have explored in the short story "Jane Eyre" (in Koshy 2011).*

MK: I am interested in literature as one space in which power difference and corruption can be addressed. Good literature has always been literature committed to examining how we structure our lives and the ideas to which we subscribe. In any relationship, a power difference creates the possibility of exploitation. In an adoption, the child by virtue of being a child, the biological mother by virtue of being poor and disenfranchised, are at the mercy of the adoptive family. Add to this the power difference between the state and the individual, between the countries that adopt and the countries from which children are adopted, and you have a potent mix designed to oppress. Children of the poor, children of the poor nations, children of nations at war are transported across the world and removed from their parents, families, language, religion, culture, all in the name of saving them. There is the fiction that they are orphans and an additional fiction that this is the way to save them. For the individual adoptee these multiple fictions add up to psychic harm. Adoption as an institution is known to be rife with corruption of the kind practised by middlemen who coerce biological parents to relinquish their children. Various legal structures are put in place to address this corruption. But in the end such corruption cannot be addressed completely and satisfactorily. I contend that the institution is itself corrupt in its embrace of the inequality built into the triad—adoptive parent, biological parent and child / adoptee.

MM: *Your work is peopled by a vast array of "subaltern" characters, such as refuse collectors, working-class single mothers and domestic workers, but you also often also endow them with the determination to put up a spirited fight. One such character is Aruna, the protagonist of your short story "Almost Valentine's Day". As a lower-class Indian immigrant in the US, Aruna does not hesitate from resorting to manipulation and blackmail to secure her future. How do you conceive of subaltern agency and resistance?*

MK: People resist injustice. Resistance is defining for people. This resistance can be collective or individual. Fiction as an art form can be quite restrictive of the attempt to tell a collective story, a people's story, while excelling at the story of the individual. I haven't the skill, craft or art to tell the story I would really like to tell, that is, the story of the collective. However, I was pleased with "Almost Valentine's Day". My protagonist is sneaky, maybe even a little unlikable and often baffling to me as a writer and reader. But resistance is like that: simultaneously necessary and baffling in that it even takes place. Why don't people take their beating lying down? Why are the beaten so hell bent on finding the interstices that allow them to fight back, to breathe? It seems to me that in my writing I am expressing the possibility that people aren't necessarily noble or courageous in their resistance to injustice, but yes, they are resistant. "By any means necessary" is one way to look at subaltern struggle.

MM: *Would you agree that a major "character" in some of your works of fiction, including the short story "Romancing the Koodawalla" (in Koshy 2011), is the bustling Indian metropolis, a place which is at once terrifying and full of possibilities, especially with respect to how intimate relationships are imagined and lived?*

MK: I have lived in a couple of very different cultures in my life: the American culture and the Indian. The latter is more pluralistic in its outlook, more embracing of contradictions than the former. However, the same fascistic tendencies in politics are present in both countries and their governments: both are characterized by powerful states that embrace surveillance, enforce homogeneity and nationalism through the instrument of the police and the military. Having seen differences and similarities within two cultures, I do not make the assumption that the status quo is given. People exercise choice at every turn, individually and collectively. My narratives are about such choices. The metropolis of Delhi figures strongly in my first book and again in my third. It is a place where people from different classes and different levels of power and powerlessness live in close proximity to one another. Delhi is especially fascinating for the way in which the powerful and the powerless share household space. The contradictions of their lives are laid bare in such intimacy. As is the understanding that power is mediated in these characters' lives through class, or gender or caste.

I think about a writer like Ian McEwan, who must either hope for an accident or go to great lengths to contrive to bring an upper middle-class character in contact with a working-class character. So, in his novel *Saturday* (2005) the first contact between neurosurgeon Perowne and the working-class Baxter is through a collision in traffic. Later, Baxter rather unbelievably invades Perowne's home, holds the family hostage, attempts to kidnap Perowne's daughter etc. In Delhi, characters meet across class and caste lines without recourse to accidents and kidnappings. In the first world much of what would previously have been described as domestic work is rendered invisible. Food is cooked, packaged etc. elsewhere and the middle and upper class consume it without seeing those who have prepared it. This is not so in Delhi. This proximity is what I focused on in my writing. Much of what I write about is the intimacy of small moments within the context of this proximity. In my story "Today is the Day" (in Koshy 2011), the narrator, a little boy, is a servant in a household. He sleeps on the floor beside an elderly member of the household and asks her what he should do in the event of a fire. She tells him to save himself. I find such moments between people explosive. This intimacy in which a character is laid bare to another is more powerful and more sustainable than grander narratives, for example the narrative of love across class and caste lines. Other writers who have concerned themselves with this narrative have dealt with the impossibility of such love by killing off their characters, which is rather problematic for the argument of resilience with which my writing is concerned. So Velutha in Arundhati Roy's (1997) *The God of Small Things* is killed off and so Robbie and Cecilia are dead in Ian McEwan's (2001) *Atonement*.

MM: *You are actively involved in The Community Library Project in New Delhi. Can you please tell us more about this initiative?*

MK: All over India, organizations and people are engaged in debating the purpose and need for minimal literacy versus the need for fluency in reading and the attendant access to books as a powerful tool for thinking. We hear from the government and from non-governmental organizations that we are a poor country and it is best to confine our limited resources to education that produces a skilled workforce. We hear from multinational corporations and other international authorities that literacy must include digital literacy. They are interested in India for the cheap labour pool it provides. In the future this labour pool will have to possess some digital fluency. India as an unthinking market is another attraction. Some of us are interested in building a citizenry that is more than an obedient workforce and market. A publicly owned and operated library system that allows people access to free books and builds their fluency as readers and thinkers is key to developing citizenship that is empowered by its ability to think critically.

      Having said all that, which sounds lofty to me and must sound lofty to the reader, I will add that the group of us who created The Community Library Project are realistic folk who run two small libraries in the National Capital Region (New Delhi). The libraries are free and open to all, and owned and operated by their members. It is a small revolution that allies with similar libraries throughout the country to create a larger revolution. An open door, a warm welcome and a rich collection of books and a rich ecosystem of programming ensures thousands of our poorest citizens are reading and thinking in New Delhi. They are children who will soon enough be adults. Member ownership and leadership in the library means that this will be a generational project that not only equips its members with books and reading but also with politics that allows them to continue as adults to raise the issue of access to books. We are building a library movement, thankfully not alone, but rather in partnership with dozens of other library leaders.

MM: In what ways has your activism informed your fiction, and vice versa?

MK: I talked a little bit about resilience in my answer to an earlier question. My activism has put me in close touch with this resilience. It is from my activism that I derived the need to portray the resilience of my characters. In my home, we have a wonderful Woody Guthrie quote on a poster. He talks about not wanting to write the "kind [of songs] that knock you down". I too don't want to write that kind of "no good song". Instead, my stories are like Guthrie's songs, interested in saying to you that "this is your world".

MM: Ms. Koshy, thank you very much.

Bibliography

Doshi, Tishani. 2016. "Allure of the Unexceptional." *The Hindu*, Feb. 27. https://www.thehindu.com/books/literary-review/tishani-doshi-talks-to-mridula-koshy-about-bicycle-dreaming/article8285187.ece.

Koshy, Mridula. 2008. "The Good Mother." *India Currents*, July 4. https://indiacurrents.com/the-good-mother/.

---. [2009] 2011. *If It Is Sweet*. Melbourne: Brass Monkey Books.

---. 2012. *Not Only the Things That Have Happened*. Noida, Uttar Pradesh: HarperCollins India.

---. 2016. *Bicycle Dreaming*. Delhi: Speaking Tiger Publishing.

McEwan, Ian. 2001. *Atonement*. London: Jonathan Cape.

---. 2005. *Saturday*. London: Jonathan Cape.

Nguyen, Marijane. 2013. "Book Review: *Not the Only Things That Have Happened*." *Beyond Two Worlds: Musings of a Taiwanese-American Adoptee*, Oct. 7. https://beyondtwoworlds.com/2013/10/07/book-review-not-only-the-things-that-have-happened/#comments.

Pariat, Janice. 2013. "Memory and its Makeshift, Fragmented Mechanisms." *The Sunday Guardian*, Feb. 2. http://www.sunday-guardian.com/bookbeat/memory-and-its-makeshift-fragmented-mechanisms.

Roy, Arundhati. 1997. *The God of Small Things*. London: Flamingo.

"To want to know the world, to look outward": Neel Mukherjee in Conversation with Anjali Joseph

Photograph of Neel Mukherjee copyright 2021 by Nick Tucker Photography

Neel Mukherjee is an award-winning novelist and reviewer who currently lives in London. He was born in Kolkata (formerly Calcutta) in 1970, and his education took him from Jadavpur University to Oxford (as a Rhodes Scholar) and then to Cambridge for his doctoral studies. His work is striking, formally varied and challenging, and its concern for "underdogs" has often been noted. His first novel, *A Life Apart* (2010) was first published in India as *Past Continuous*. It follows the fortunes and struggles of Ritwik, a student from Calcutta living in Oxford and London, but challenges the *Bildungsroman* form through a series of formal shifts that include segments of Ritwik's own fiction about the British governess Maud Gilby—a walk-on character in Tagore's novel, *Gharey Bairey* (*At Home and in The World*)—and her experiences in Bengal at the turn of the century, together with time shifts that plunge us into the protagonist's memories of his abusive upbringing at the hands of his mother. The connection with India is also pursued through Ritwik's tender and surprising relationship as he cares for Anne Cameron, his elderly landlady. "I poured my heart into Anne Cameron", said Neel Mukherjee in an earlier interview (Mukherjee 2009) "she has suffered so much and the character Ritwik has a lot of me in him".

His second novel, the 500-page *The Lives of Others*, is the closest Mukherjee has come to a classic realist novel, in its portrayal of the lives of three generations of the Ghosh family in Bengal. It was short-listed for the Man Booker Prize in 2014. In the interview that follows, he expresses some dissatisfaction with conventional notions of plot, character and narrative, much as Amit Chaudhuri does in his interview in this volume. The two novelists' responses to this challenge are quite different, however, and the brutal, poignant savagery of the deaths in the opening chapter of *The Lives of Others* takes us into confronting territory.

The current interview was conducted by Anjali Joseph at the time of the publication of Mukherjee's third book *A State of Freedom* (2017). Its five stories set in contemporary India are as challenging, searching and compassionate as one has come to expect from this talented and original writer.

Chris Ringrose

Anjali Joseph writes:
I have known Neel Mukherjee for about eight years. A mutual friend introduced us in Bombay a couple of years after his first novel, *Past Continuous*, was published in India and had gone on to win the Crossword Book Award for Fiction. When Neel and I met, I was working for *ELLE* in Bombay. *Past Continuous*, renamed *A Life Apart*, appeared in Britain in 2010, which was also the year my first novel *Saraswati Park* came out.

When I was asked if I would interview Neel on the occasion of the publication of his third and latest novel, *A State of Freedom*, I was delighted. As I read the novel, I was both surprised and not at all surprised at its spareness, its wilful undoing of its own narrative, and at the authority and wholeness of its characters—among them, a bear tamer, a domestic worker and an expatriate Indian man who spends a month in India each winter and begins to compile a recipe book.

A State of Freedom is the very inverse of one of those "interlinked narratives" which perhaps reached their apogee in a film like *Babel*. A ghost story of sorts runs through the novel, beginning from the opening episode—but who is the ghost? Once I started thinking about it, it seemed to me that every character in the novel is a ghost of sorts, existing but unperceived, marginal but obstinately real. Perhaps the Indian state, free from a colonial ruler but trammelled by its own institutional cruelties, is the ghost. Or perhaps it is the reader, able to watch each of these characters for a time, but never allowed to come to a conclusion or make a simple judgement, any more than an intelligent man or woman of conscience might, these days, be able to give a single satisfactory account of him or herself if asked the question: "Are you a good person?"

About the Interviewer: Anjali Joseph's first novel *Saraswati Park* (2010) won the Desmond Elliott Prize, the Betty Trask Prize, and jointly won the Vodafone Crossword Book Award for Fiction in India. It was shortlisted for the Commonwealth Prize for Best First Book, the Ondaatje Prize, and the Hindu Literary Prize. *Another Country*, published in 2012, was longlisted for the Man Asian Literary Prize. *The Living* (2016) was shortlisted for the DSC Prize. Her fourth novel, *Keeping in Touch*, is a story of dysfunctional love and a lightbulb with unusual properties. The first chapter, under the title "Everlasting Lucifer", was longlisted for the *Sunday Times* Short Story Award in 2017. She lives in Oxfordshire, UK.

Anjali Joseph (AJ): Your second novel, The Lives of Others, *was in some ways a classic novel, almost a 19th-century novel—characters were introduced, a world was beautifully evoked, the terms of the novel were set and then we followed the characters through what unfolded, with all its surprises and shocks.*

A State of Freedom *introduces different characters, different threads, follows the characters through involving and appalling events which they undergo with the stoicism brought on by having no alternative. There are links and parallels between characters, but instead of cohering towards the end, these elements further unravel, fray and fragment. I thought it was such a striking departure both from the previous novel and in general from the current expectations of the novel.*

Of course, the state of disarray of the narrative by the end of the book made me think of the Indian state, so tattered, so indefensible in many of its actions, but somehow still enduring after six decades. It also made me think of the spate a few years ago of people saying "The novel is dead" as though the novel were a monolithic kind of God instead of the loosest possible mode of—telling a story? Not telling a story? Inviting a reader into the experiences of others? Infiltrating the consciousness, the dreams and heart of the reader and reconfiguring his or her capacity for compassion? Whatever it is we do. Can you talk about the kind of novel you wanted to write in A State of Freedom, and why, and your feelings about the novel in general—if you have any, that is?

Neel Mukherjee (NM): You're absolutely right, Anjali. *The Lives of Others* was a self-conscious homage to the 19th-century novel, with some thinking about the ideological foundations of the realist novel smuggled in. I wanted this theoretical thinking to be subsumed entirely within the story, and seamless with it, so I shouldn't have the right to feel surprised, as I did, when no reviewer or critic picked up on it; the Trojan horse was a victim of its own success. I mention all this because you have seen a collocation between *The Lives of Others* and *A State of Freedom* exactly on the site where there is one—on the question of form—and put your finger unerringly on the *formal* difference between the two novels that has led you to ask about the novel form.

Like a lot of novelists, I'm beginning to get slightly impatient with the constraints and artifices of the realist novel at the same time as I find myself endlessly fascinated by the form. The realist novel is anything but realist: mimesis is a process of stylization, of modelling reality, if you will. The selection process involved in picking what should go from life, and in what form, onto the page is an act of stylization, of extreme artifice. Edmund White was once told by a friend that he would never make a great novelist because he was incapable of writing a line such as "The Marquis got dressed to go out every afternoon at five o'clock". How do you move people around, go from one place to another, from one set of characters to another in a realist novel without falling into banality and obtrusive scenery? You have shown a similar impatience in your latest novel, *The Living*, reaching out for a new form in which, instead of events and external matters of lives and plot, you dig under the surface for the real inner life, the small moments of consciousness that, strung out, make what we call a human life. You also bring together two separate and distinct stories, one of a white, working-class single mum in Norwich, the other of a middle-aged *chappal*-maker in Pune, within the covers of one book, and ask very important questions about what gives both cohesion and coherence to what we call a "novel".

I, too, wanted to pursue a similar line of enquiry. What if one were to take away all the things that one conventionally associates with contributing to the cohesiveness and unity of the realist novel, elements such as plot and characters and psychological development? Could we still end up with something that can answer to the term "novel"? In other words, I wanted to write a novel with all the connective tissue taken out, and also to see how much I could push realism towards anti-realist modes (such as the ghost story) while working within the realist framework and with its accepted generic *topoi*. What would a love-child between realism and anti-realism look like?

But, of course, if you're an Indian writer, you are seen as capable of writing only "good yarns", which are family sagas, or about inequality / crushing poverty / the "New India". The term "experimentation with form" is reserved for white guys only (or when black people are allowed a look in, they have to be, first, the toast of the New York Scene). It's a battle we have lost; there's no point engaging with it any longer; one writes what one can or what wants to, the rest is chance.

AJ: *I also wanted to talk about the idea of Indianness. You grew up in India, but your entire adult life has been outside, mostly in Britain, and you're a British national. And yet of course your imaginative engagement with India remains. How does that work? More interestingly, you've been drawn to the fissures, the broken bits of the Indian experience, whether looking at the experience of an English governess in Bengal during the freedom struggle in* A Life Apart *(whose initial title* Past Continuous *I continue to like, by the way), or following Naxalites in 1960s Bengal in* The Lives of Others, *or in this novel you include for example figures like a poor man who almost accidentally becomes the keeper of a dancing bear—a bear whose terrible mutilation you show us, one of the scenes in fiction that I think I will remember until I die— or a desperately poor woman who goes through a chain of miserable jobs as a domestic servant.*

I didn't know much about how a bear is tortured to the point of becoming a performing animal, but I do know the stories of figures like Milly, the domestic worker. At one point she is trapped with an elderly couple in their house in Bombay, not allowed to go outside, mistreated and physically abused. Stories like this are in the newspapers in Indian cities all the time. Then, the scene of the bear's mutilation—in one extraordinary moment the pain the animal goes through as men hold him down and drive an incandescent stake through his nose is so intense that his eyes swim out of focus—it's as though what the human species is inflicting on him is just too cruel for the animal to comprehend. Reading this, or reading about Milly, I felt what the novelist Evie Wyld calls "the familiar shame of being human" but also the familiar shame of being an Indian. Maybe the cruelty inflicted on the bear is less shameful than the way the middle class couple treats Milly, or maybe the two things are related because in both cases the perpetrator sees the victim as fundamentally other, undeserving of basic kindness. I know you aren't trying to present a snapshot or write a sociological essay on contemporary India, but what feelings does "Indianness" evoke in you? As a supplementary question, what are your feelings about Bengaliness?

NM: I feel I could be here forever with this one. But, to begin: yes, I've lived more than half my life away from India now but I left India at the age of 22, so as a fully formed—one hopes—adult. For better or for worse, that place made me. That is something immutable and irreversible. We can, of course, parse "made" in many ways: not just the obvious things such as the socioeconomic bracket you inhabited, the school you went to, what your parents did for a living, the language(s) you spoke, but also more "micro" things—childhood reading, friendships and enmities, the food you ate, the domestic helps who worked in your house, the radio stations you listened to, the climate you dealt with, the fact of *Nyctanthes arbor-tristis* flowers—or night blooming jasmine—in the autumn ... in other words, everything that makes up the texture, the thickness and density and the "thisness" of life. By the time you are 22, all those hard-wirings are in place; what happens afterwards is top dressing.

I got myself a British passport out of expediency: it's so much easier to travel the world if you are a UK passport holder. For a start, you don't get treated like a dog at the Italian High Commission in London when you go to get a visa. But I've never considered myself British; I never could be. Britain entirely lacks an assimilationist narrative or impulse. Besides, of all the things in the world one could be, why would one want to "be" British, especially if one comes from India? I consider myself an Indian writer who lives and works in London and spends part of the year in the USA.

Having said that, we return once more to the notion of "Indianness". The notion of experiencing a nationality-ness is something I find opaque. It begs the question, "What is Indianness?" The moment you begin to answer it, or any such question about what constitutes the essence of the people of a nation, everything dissolves. I am suspicious of such totalisations. Yes, sure, an American walking down a supermarket aisle might find the availability of only a dozen kinds of muesli disappointing, whereas I, in the same situation, would find the same fact, at different times, overwhelming, gratifying, wasteful, unnecessary. But does that constitute some kind of essential "Americanness" or "Indianness"? Besides, what does it mean to feel or experience that?

The only thing I can say about my continuing interest in India is that I find the country intellectually fascinating in a way I do not find stable, liberal, first-world, capitalist democracies fascinating. India is so plural, so shifting, so one thing and its opposite simultaneously ... how on earth has that country cohered? I cannot even speak of an "India" as a monolithic entity but only of shreds and patches of it. To be an Indian is to be in material all your life. Look at the turn the novel has taken in the west, particularly in the US. The lauded books of our times are books about fucking divorce and relationship dramas! Or about the endless fascination with looking at oneself in the mirror. Oh, fuck off!

As for concentrating on the fractures and fissures of the Indian experience, well, how could one not? It's a *moral* duty, I feel. What is the experience of India for the vast majority of its people, even the middle classes, if not of what you call "the broken bits"? Rose Tremain used to tell her students, "Don't write about what you know, write about what you *want* to know". I think that's not just an invaluable piece of advice, but a moral one too. To want to know the world, to look outward—why write if you can't or don't want to do that? But, of course, to write about "the broken bits" is inevitably to have a reckoning with "the familiar shame of being human". To that phrase by Evie Wyld I would add Coetzee's "the disgrace of living in these times". Nowhere do you come so up close against those sentiments as in India. Is there *anything*, any one thing, that you see in India that makes you feel proud, at least at this particular juncture in history, when the country has been hijacked by foaming-at-the-mouth rabid, monkey- and cow-worshipping murderers?

AJ: Well, I've been living in the north east of India for the last three years, in Assam, and travelling a little bit, mostly in Assam but also in Meghalaya, Mizoram and Arunachal. And that position of being literally on the side of things—away from what, in the north east, we call the "mainland" of the country—has given me pride in that region, and in a larger sense, in some essential bloody-mindedness and scepticism in Indian ways of thinking. There is a cleaving towards irony, paradox and humour that I really love. You see it in the sarcasm of Hindi humour or the silken irony of upper Assam. Among other things, for me it is an antidote to the present political narrative of nationalism, which flattens out perspectives and, ridiculously, demands loyalty. For me, the very fact of belonging, of being at home, means that I shouldn't have to prove that I have a right to be there. That is what it is to be abroad—to be polite, to be in some senses a guest. And yet it is what the Indian government is increasingly trying to demand from us. It seems so self-defeating to me as a strategy. I mean, when at home one shouldn't have to ask oneself if one belongs. And when one has to ask the question, surely the sense of belonging is already ruptured?

But if this thought is new to me, it's not a new experience for a large number of Indian citizens. In the north east, for example, people have a tendency to look at you sidelong and say, very politely, "Oh, we like Indians. We like Indians very much". Then you obviously think, And what are you? But the fact is, people in that area, although sometimes they benefit from special privileges (tribals from the region don't, for example, pay income tax) have also undergone the most peculiar and estranging treatment from the Indian government. In Mizoram for example, during the independence movement of the 1980s, the Mizos were hiding in the forests to avoid air strikes by the Indian air force. When Assam was invaded in the 1960s by China, Jawaharlal Nehru made an announcement on the radio saying, "Our heart goes out to the people of Assam. The fall of Assam is not the fall of India". Not very reassuring for the Assamese, who fled their homes, rightly thinking they'd been abandoned. So the Indian government—not just the present one, but various governments since 1947—has often behaved like an abusive parent, a fact that has somewhat dislodged my attachment to an idea of Indianness at the level of national identity.

Moving on, though, I wanted to ask a technical question, about craft. In A State of Freedom, as well as The Lives of Others and A Life Apart, you don't flinch from the close description of actions. I think of Ritwik bathing his elderly landlady in A Life Apart, or the blowjob he gives a man in the first few pages of the novel; of the exact description of a young Naxalite from Kolkata learning to do a poor job of harvesting paddy in country fields in Medinipur; of the bear's mutilation in A State of Freedom. What is your feeling about detail, about research, when to zoom in?

NM: Ah, details. I know the term "world-building" is used exclusively of speculative and science fiction and fantasy, but why should only worlds different from the one we inhabit have to be created on the page? Isn't world-building also something central to the realist novel? Here is a passage from Naipaul's (1971) great masterpiece, *In a Free State*:

> The filling station Bobby turned into belonged to an old company that had come to the country after independence. A tall yellow-and-black board announced the amenities in bold international symbols. But one of the symbols, the telephone, had been partly covered over with a square of brown paper; and another symbol, the crossed knife and fork, had been crossed out, apparently by a finger dipped in engine oil. Along the lower edge of the yellow board, as on the white walls of the office, were the marks of oily fingers and sometimes whole hands that had tried to wipe or roll themselves clean. The covered part of the asphalted yard was black with oil; the exposed part, still wet after the rain, was iridescent.

A whole world in there, utterly precise, fleet-footed yet with all the weight of history, in cinematic sharp focus.

The idea is not to tip and shake out your entire research notebook onto the pages of your novel, but to give enough so that the solidity of the world the novel depicts is conveyed. Think of the temple of Narsoba in the forests of the Western *ghats* towards the end of *The Living*: so unexpected, but so necessary, almost inevitable, when you discover it on the page, rendering the world you've built at once familiar and different, original. I think that's what details should do: they should allow readers to feel they're inhabiting a real world, a world solid, dense and, above all, convincing and truthful. If it's an unfamiliar, foreign world they are entering, as was the case with most readers of *The Lives of Others*, the accumulation of details creates simultaneously the sense of difference, otherness (used in a benign way!) and the feeling of gradual familiarity with this new world. Penelope Fitzgerald, more than any author I know, has mastered the trick of the correct detail in the correct place, making even the notion of detail become unobtrusive, even invisible, to the reader; all that remained was the truthfulness of the world she was writing about, be it early 20th-century Cambridge or Thuringia in the closing years of the 18th century.

I think the work often dictates where to zoom in on details, where to put in things that will confer three-dimensionality. I feel my guide in this is that startling sentence from *Middlemarch*: "to conceive with that distinctness which is no longer reflection but feeling—an idea wrought back to the directness of sense, like the solidity of objects".

AJ: This is a shorter novel—how did that feel? Did you write an enormous quantity of words that you then as it were filleted, or did it emerge in this form?

NM: I've recently been advised not to make the kind of pronouncements that I'm about to make, so I feel almost obliged to do it: I may be done with the long novel. I hope my future books will be shorter than *A State of Freedom*. And it emerged in this form, as five narratives, to reflect the novella, the "two supporting narratives" and the bookends of the prologue and the epilogue of V.S. Naipaul's *In a Free State*, with which, I'd like to fancy, my book is a conversation.

AJ: Finally, the idea of England. At the time of writing these questions I was sitting in a friend's house reading your novel, contemplating moving back to England, a place I've spent over half my life. By the time your answers arrived, I already had returned. It's a funny time to do it, perhaps, in the light of the present mood in England—but then we're in a certain historical moment all over the world. Being in England after a few months after living largely in Assam for the last three years has also given me a chance to think about the things I love and appreciate about England: inclusiveness, magnanimity, a quiet generosity and a willingness to accept people, even people from outside, as they are. (I keep using the term England not to exclude Wales or Scotland or Northern Ireland but because my idea of Englishness is different from the idea of Britishness, which seems at times to connote the coercion inevitable in holding together an empire.) Now those qualities seem to be in question as one of the dominant ideas is that there isn't enough to go round—enough money but also enough time or enough patience to put up with people who are different. How do you feel about England at this moment?

NM: I have felt bleak and pessimistic about Britain for a long time and Brexit has driven the final nail into the coffin. A great unravelling of the country is on its way. Two of its greatest 20th-century achievements, the NHS and the BBC, especially the former, are being filleted to nothing and there appears to be no significant political mobilisation against it. If you look at the absolutely shamingly appalling healthcare system of the USA, you realize what we have and what we need to save, not to go down the route of the USA. That single subject of the destruction of the NHS, I feel, could be made a loud, relentless issue on which an election could stand or fall.

I don't know why you've chosen this moment to come back to the UK. I suppose if it's a choice between a small or a large sewer you choose the smaller one because the amount of effluents you are exposed to is smaller. At least the stripe of nationalism in the UK has not degenerated to vigilante mobs hunting down people and groups they do not like. I am reminded of what the great pianist, Alfred Brendel, once said about Britain—that the English mind is not given to any form of extremism, which rules out the possibility of ultra-nationalism or any kind of fascism in government and power. But the stunted, morally impoverished, stupid, lying, half-formed humans in government in both countries are essentially similar and remind me of that wonderful Bengali phrase, "the recto and verso of shit are identical".

Brexit could potentially make Britain realize its absolute insignificance in the world but I don't think the collective consciousness and the ruling classes (government, press) are going to update. Besides, I feel the cost of Brexit will be borne, as it always is, by people who can least afford it, not the Eton-Oxbridge-educated Conservatives who, hand in hand with a lying press, landed us in this shit; and that is too high a cost for the extremely slim possibility of a nation coming to its senses about its position and power and uniqueness. Then there is the collective, willed, obstinate ignorance and amnesia about colonialism. Unlike Germany, which has had, and continues to have, such an extraordinary reckoning with its history, Britain has never had one and will never have one. Highly intelligent and educated people still trot out that line, "But we gave them the railways". That's where the level of the "thinking" is still stuck.

Still, there are some hopeful beginnings: the stranglehold of the feral and profoundly mendacious right-wing press in the UK seems to be slackening, especially on the younger generation; a new kind of grassroots politics is beginning to emerge (I worry about the might of the forces—by which I mean the British press—ranged against it and its ultimate burgeoning). London, I know, is a bubble, or even an island, but its true cosmopolitanism and spirit of openness and inclusiveness (long live the metropolitan elite!) remain undented, and this is heartening.

Bibliography

Joseph, Anjali. 2010. *Saraswati Park*. London: HarperCollins.
Mukherjee, Neel. 2009. "I Wanted a Gay Protagonist in My Novel: Neel Mukherjee [Interview]." *News 18*, Noida, Uttar Pradesh, India, July 27.
---. 2010. *A Life Apart*. London: Constable, 2010.
---. 2014. *The Lives of Others*. London: Chatto and Windus.
---. 2017. *A State of Freedom*. London: Random House UK.
Naipaul, V.S. 1971. *In a Free State*. London: Andre Deutsch.

This interview was first published in *Wasafiri* online: www.wasafiri.org

Before the Battle:
Karthika Naïr in Conversation with Laetitia Zecchini

Photograph of Karthika Naïr copyright 2021 by Koen Broos

Before god
Before the dead
Before children
Before a world
Dance.
[...]
Before god dies, smile trampled, a thousand arms crushed underfoot
Before the dead return like moonlight, trailing white ash and regrets
Before children swap marbles for slugs and swallow darkness at meals
Before a world of straight lines and ironclad right owns your eyes
Dance, dance on vanishing shores between night and half-light
    Return, return to nest like stacked spoons, lock chest with spine
        Twine hip and thigh, knit ten fingers, purl the lips—once more

    Before the battle. (Naïr 2015a)

Karthika Naïr was born in Kerala and moved to France in 2000, subsequently working for several prestigious cultural institutions (Cité de la musique, Centre national de la danse, Musée national de l'histoire de l'immigration, etc.) as a dance producer / curator, dance-writer or "dance enabler", as she sometimes likes to define herself. Her closest associations have been with choreographers Sidi Larbi Cherkaoui, and Damien Jalet. She was also the principal scriptwriter for Akram Khan's award-winning dance-drama production *DESH* in 2011 (and its adaption for younger audiences, *Chotto Desh*, in 2015). Her organic and creative relationship with dance, with the visual and concrete choreography of words, is at the heart of her poetry, from her first collection *Bearings* (Naïr 2009) to *Until the Lions: Echoes from the Mahabharata* (Naïr 2015a) which won the Tata Literature Live! Book of the Year 2015 (for fiction), and was partially adapted by the choreographer Akram Khan;[1] to *Over and Underground in Mumbai & Paris* (Naïr, Chattarji, Jolivet and Vyam 2018), which is a tale of two cities and four artists (the poets Karthika Naïr and Sampurna Chattarji, the artists Joëlle Jolivet and Roshni Vyam). With Joëlle Jolivet, she also brought out a children's book, *The Honey Hunter / Le Tigre de Miel* (Naïr and Jolivet 2013), which has been translated into French, German and Bangla.

Karthika Naïr's poetry and biography constantly weave together a multitude of contexts, voices, artistic, linguistic and cultural backgrounds. She also situates herself and her work inseparably in a world of texts, and in the turmoil of the political and social world. For instance, as David Shulman (2020) suggests, her poignant retelling of the *Mahabharata* in *Until the Lions: Echoes from the Mahabharata*, is "among other things, a passionate antiwar manifesto". The epic is recast from the perspective of those who have been subjected to erasure and are often the first casualties of war: the faceless, the nameless and unremembered by / of history, many of whom are women. But the "echoes" of the *Mahabharata* are not only the echoes of all the other *Mahabharatas* in whose lineage Karthika Naïr places herself; the ocean of stories and (re)tellings to which

---

1 Akram Khan's acclaimed eponymous piece, *Until the Lions*, premiered in London in 2016. An opera based on the book, scored by Thierry Pécou and directed by Shobana Jeyasingh, was due to open in March 2020 in Strasbourg at the Opéra National du Rhin. It was postponed to September 2022 as a result of the COVID-19 pandemic. An American edition of *Until the Lions* was published in 2019 by Archipelago Books.

the epic continues to give birth. Her poems' unflinching confrontation with the violence of the world, and of India in particular, are about today. In the damaged and enraged voices of *Until the Lions*, we hear echoes of the struggles of Dalits, *adivasis*, women, Muslims, migrants, but also of all the other threatened minorities whose dissenting views or narratives infuriate the sentinels of cultural and religious majoritarianism: activists, journalists, students, artists, writers.

Another collection of intricate echoes is *Over and Underground in Mumbai & Paris*, which not only weaves together the voices and gazes of four women artists, joining poetry lines to visual lines and metro lines, but also connects Paris to Mumbai, joining north to south, east to west, and corners of the world to each other. It's a collection that celebrates the life-throbbing, pulsating vigour of the city, the fragments of stories and memories, songs and "ripples of tongues", wonder and mourning that attach themselves to the train tracks and metro lines over and underground.

In the following interview conducted over Skype, and revised over email in January 2021, which also continues previous conversations (including one conducted for a special issue of the *South Asia Multidisciplinary Academic Journal* [Naïr and Zecchini 2020] from which some passages are excerpted), interviewer and interviewee talk about the different worlds and arts straddled by Karthika Naïr; about the experience of diaspora and nomadism; about the city of Paris, and her relationship to her two countries, France and India; about how "home" can attach itself to certain specific spaces and places; about the "bastardized, eclectic *imaginaire*" she claims as her own; the partnerships and collaborations that sustain her writing and her sense of belonging; about the importance of dance and fable; how the experience of vulnerability and living with a "dysfunctional body" has impacted her writing; about literary activism and how literary texts can "respond" to violence, to terror and damage, and can "give voice" to pain and also chronicle the wonder of living.

The interviewer, Laetitia Zecchini, is a tenured research fellow at the CNRS (Paris). Her research focuses on contemporary Indian poetry, postcolonial modernisms and the politics of literature. She is the author of a monograph on Arun Kolatkar, *Arun Kolatkar and Literary Modernism in India: Moving Lines* (Bloomsbury, 2014), whose works she has also translated into French, and co-edited eight volumes, including "The Worlds of Bombay Poetry" (*Journal of Postcolonial Writing*, 2017) and "The

Locations of (World) Literature: Perspectives from Africa and South Asia" (*Journal of World Literature*, 2019). She is co-investigator of the AHRC-funded project "writers and free expression", and is at work on a monograph around issues of literary activism and struggles for cultural / literary freedoms in postcolonial India.

Laetitia Zecchini (LZ): *Perhaps we can start with your first collection, Karthika, Bearings, which has a section called "Terra Infirma"—and maybe you could explain the title for us?—which largely revolves around exile, but here, as often, you debunk the clichés associated with migration or diaspora, and with ideas of "home" and identity. You write, for instance, that home can be a dubious notion for anyone, not just for diasporic or migrant writers. But you also write that your poetry springs from a "changeable, patched ground", and that uprootedness has been a way of life since childhood. I was wondering if you could talk to us about that foundational uprootedness, and perhaps explain how it influenced your writing ...*

Karthika Naïr (KN): "Terra Infirma" was a deliberate twist on the expression *terra firma*. I wanted to emphasize—at the outset of the section—that the ground beneath the feet (of the narrative self) was not stable, that it was prone to heaving, buckling, to giving way. And, that by extension, the associated themes of belonging, home, identity were just as labile.

Now, I think this sense of nomadism has been integral to my being, primarily because my parents were nomads themselves; they did not have a settled existence. When the Indo-China war happened, my father joined the army, and they spent their first major chunk of their lives, before middle age, as professional nomads. They never lived more than two or three years in a city, and when they had me, that didn't change. So, during the first 14 years of my life, we were constantly moving, every 2 or 3 years. And as you know, in India moving between states also means moving between languages, worlds. So that sense of movement has been perpetual. Being diasporic is just one more step. Of course, there is a difference between being in India and being in Europe or in the US. But when you move to another state—in the microcosm of the world that I consider India to be—you are already experiencing a lot of what would be central to diasporic existence in terms of the change of language, the change of cuisine, the change of customs, religious practices, societal expectations—and the loss of belonging. For instance, to the teen that I was, the move from Shillong to Trivandrum in the late 1980s was a more severe culture-shock than the one to France in 2000.

LZ: *And that mobility, or the forced dialogism in a sense, between worlds, explains the multiplicity of forms in your poetry, but also the freedom it gave you, or that you gave yourself, to use, just like Kolatkar's crow (with which I think you identify), to take or recycle from anywhere, and anything.*

KN: Yes, completely. I always say that I prefer the analogy of Kolatkar's crow—one of my favourite "fictional" animals (probably second only to his Pi-dog, who remains an enduring inspiration!)—to the analogy of the magpie. The crow builds its nest from everything it can find—anything and everything its gaze falls on, and it can get its claws on. I am not really a nest builder, though. Writing may be the closest that there is to a nest, and, yes, everything goes into that, whether dance or cinema, or a pantoum, or a ghazal, or what I grew up with, like the worst of the Hindi cinema's potboilers and Malayalam arthouse cinema, for example! *Everything is fodder.* And I think the forms that I use are not so much a nest as a collage or an assemblage. Ownership is not interesting; what is interesting is chronicling; that may be what I try to do every time I write. The act of writing itself is that of chronicling.

LZ: *That might be why you are so fond of Salman Rushdie! Of Rushdie the story-teller, the chronicler ...*

KN: Oh yes, because inventing is also a way of chronicling, and that's why I love the realm of the fable. The character of Dakkhin-Rai in *The Honey Hunter* is as much a chronicle as a poem on the Line 3 of the Paris Métro, or an essay I write on Dance and Otherness. And that's something I first learnt from him, from *Haroun and the Sea of Stories* (Rushdie 1990), long before I knew I would ever write.

LZ: *That reminds me of something Edward Said was saying, that in Latin, "inventio" is to find again: "It's not creating from nothing, it's reordering". That means that you are always assembling or starting from the voices, the words or the fables of other people?*

KN: Yes, and that again brings me back to Larbi (Sidi Larbi Cherkaoui), like so much of my work does. Because when I first started writing poetry, when I hadn't yet been published (which was just around the time he and I began collaborating), I remember that was one of my existential crises: everything has been already done and said so beautifully, what's the point of my writing? It's something John Steinbeck develops beautifully in *Sweet Thursday* and I blurted that out to Larbi once. He replied that this was true for everything, for every art and discipline. He pointed out that what you can bring in—the only thing, really—is your gaze. That makes the difference, nothing else, at the end of the day. Our individual gaze. That's one of the many things we have in common, the thing we strive towards, Larbi and I; we are both really curious of what has been done, in different points in time, in various parts of the world, in different disciplines, whether pop culture or "high art". There is a constant fermenting that is triggered by other things, other people, by the past and the present.

LZ: *Returning to that question of belonging, there is a city you belong to, today, and that is Paris. In one of your poems in* Over and Underground in Mumbai & Paris, *you write of "the Paris I'd grown to wear like second skin", which can also be taken almost literally, right, Karthika, because Paris has given you a second skin ...*[2]

KN: Yes, and my use of the analogy of skin is not anodyne.

LZ: *Just a side question here, Karthika, did the knowledge of Paris also being a place of medical expertise and excellence, play an important part in your decision to come here?*

KN: It's actually the reverse process. I did not come to Paris knowing that I would get the most extraordinary medical care and the most stable life that I had ever known, despite all the administrative difficulties and the loops I've had to jump through for work permits and for "legitimacy", so to

---

2 Epidermolysis Bullosa, specifically, in Karthika Naïr's case, RDEB, Recessive Dystrophic Epidermolysis Bullosa, is an incurable, often fatal condition that affects the skin and mucous membranes. It is caused by a lack of collagen protein in the skin, which makes the skin extremely fragile, and leads to blisters and lesions at the slightest friction or knock. So anything as banal as a sneeze or inhaling household cleaning products can prompt blisters in the mouth, the throat, the oesophagus, as can actions like twisting keys to open a door or tying shoelaces.

speak. But I've actually never had a life as buttressed as I have in Paris. So I didn't know that I would find the kind of medical home I did in Saint-Louis.[3] And once that happened it was very clear that I would do everything to stay. That I could is thanks to the Parc de la Villette and the Cité de la musique. As I often say, I am extraordinarily and *doubly* privileged, because I had extraordinary employers who did everything they could to help me stay on in Paris, but an equally devoted medical team that intervened actively, that defended the medical reasons for my need to stay on.

LZ: *In the same collection,* Over and Underground, *you have a poem called "Homistan" where your two "homes" (France and India) collide. So "you" are returning from India and fall asleep in the metro, and you are besieged by the threatening image of fluorescent cows. And at the end of this poem, we are given another image: "you" panicking about being late for a performance at Porte de la Villette, and when you arrive, these are the words, transcribed in the poem, of your friends and colleagues: "No sweat, we'll sneak you in through the stage door, stretch the first song or something". And you add: "Yes, here is where and why I belong". I love that line …*

KN: Thank you. Actually, I had just returned from a performance in the Canary Islands, not India. But yes, at the airport—which is where the poem begins—I was on the phone with my mother, who always frets about my getting home safely! Well, the Villette is really home. I think the Villette is how (and why) I fell in love with Paris. It wasn't the Louvre, it wasn't l'Île Saint-Louis. No, I fell in love with the Villette. Even before I first came to Paris, I had heard of the Villette as a cultural mecca through my boss in India, Ashok Adicéam, who is French but of Indian origin, and who was the director of the Alliance Française in Trivandrum at the time, where I had also studied. He pulled me into the whole cultural management stream. He often said that the Villette was the place where he would love to work, and, funnily, it was I who began my career in France there! He also used to call the Villette, Mars. So, you know, I had that image of an incredible place which would be the ideal destination for anyone in my field. And although

---

3   Hôpital Saint-Louis in Paris, a national referral hospital for EB treatment and research.

I've never planned anything in my life because of EB, I did have that clear goal that this would be the place where I'd want to do my internship.[4]

I mean, just imagine, you have the abattoirs (i.e. "slaughterhouses") of Paris in the 19th century, which become an industrial wasteland across 20 or 30 years in the second half of the 20th century, a completely dilapidated, decrepit place, infamous for mugging and prostitution and drug peddling. And then François Mitterrand decides that he is going to turn it around, and he transforms these 55 hectares into the most amazing, the richest cultural / artistic hub you could imagine. Look at the number of theatres and art organizations! There is a conservatory, now a Philharmonie, which was already a cité de la musique with a museum of music, Trabendo for electro music and jazz; and there was the Zenith for rock, and the Cabaret Sauvage for "world music", a big top for visiting circuses, and then this amazing modular shell called the Grande Halle de la Villette which can be an exhibition space, a two-story theatre, a concert hall for rock—anything, really. I was in fairy land! Or Alice in another Wonderland, but without a Red Queen!

LZ: *When I listen to you talking of Paris, I'm (re)discovering my city through your eyes. A bit like in* Over and Underground, *where Paris (and the Metro) are pictured as places for outsiders, for tourists, for foreigners ... And both Paris and Mumbai come alive, and are reinvented through the gaze of outsiders—Bombay in the eyes of Joelle Jolivet, and Paris in the eyes of Roshni Vyam.*

KN: It was really important for me when Larbi and I started working together, to take him there. And when he discovered the Villette, he was equally keen on being there, because this is a place where a child of the suburbs, or of immigrant origin, can come and see a performance, while they would not necessarily feel able (or sometimes welcome) to go to one in a theatre in the heart of Paris. And they can see the same artist and they can say, I can become that man or that woman. And I always tell Larbi, there is no greater dream to share, to hand on ... So, now, we've been

---

4   Karthika Naïr came to France to pursue higher studies in arts management and cultural policy, at the Université Lyon II and ARSEC. The course, then called a DESS, included a 3-month internship in a cultural organization during the second semester.

taking Larbi's work there regularly since 2010. It's a partnership I am truly proud of.

LZ: Returning to the question of belonging, and your belonging to Paris—or rather to certain spaces in Paris, like La Villette, or the metro, there's also this constant feeling in that specific collection that if you can belong to Paris (or to the Metro), it's because it's precisely a place where people "from all shades and stripes" (those are Sampurna Chattarji's words) come together. In what ways does being an outsider allow you to write? Sorry it's a bit of a trite or very general question, but in what ways does this "outsiderness" allow you to write on Paris, in what ways does it define your relationship to India, and perhaps transform the way you write about India?

KN: I think the reason why I like Paris, is that it's almost antipodal to India. My non-Parisian (mostly French, but also Belgian) friends hate—that might be too violent a term; let's say they are wary of—Paris for the same reason I love it. It's a very rough city. It's not polite like London, it's not courteous like Brussels or warm like Antwerp is (I'm talking about cities I know best). But the wonderful thing for me is that it's the city where I discovered freedom. It's a freedom I never had in India, as a woman, as a disabled person, as a person belonging to a certain family, because in India you are always identified by your genealogy, for better and for worse. I am not denying that it brings lots of privileges as well, especially for me. But it comes with its shackles. Wherever you are, you do not exist as yourself.

LZ: But you could have gained that freedom anywhere outside India, couldn't you?

KN: No, not really, no. I could be in the UK, or even in the US, and there would be fewer people who know me than in India, but those countries still contain a lot of family, diasporic communities that often have fixed expectations. So that was specific to France. The people who knew me, knew me because I was a professional. They didn't know me because of my parents, or my relatives, or a caste name or ... or ...

LZ: Yet sometimes this "foreignness" is hurled back at you ...

KN: Oh, all the time. Or rather, all the time outside my milieu—performing arts, which is the most important part of my life. So this feeling of outsiderness was very frequent at the beginning when I was living in France, because I had to get my papers renewed sometimes after six months, sometimes after three months. In the everyday, outside, administrative world I was reminded that I was a foreigner. But in my professional, my personal life (and both are totally interconnected), I never suffered because I was "the outsider".

LZ: *Yes, and in* Over and Underground, *there is this line where in the metro you overhear two passengers talking about the composer Carlos Ott, another immigrant who built Paris, "though one with the rare sense to leave when his job was done" ... Does this often happen, this overhearing of blatant anti-migrant remarks, this experience of everyday racism?*

KN: Well, the metro is also a great place for that! And, you know, I may be a crow or a magpie, but I am also a shameless eavesdropper!

LZ: *In a previous discussion together, you've said that the one force that the COVID pandemic has helped is the force of authoritarianism, that it's the rights of the most fragile sections of society which have suffered during the lockdown. And you talk specifically about refugees, with whom you seem to identify—or at least, since your positions are also very different today—empathize. Is that something that you still live with today?*

KN: Oh absolutely. I was a day away from being an illegal immigrant. With all that support, with the privilege I had of knowing the language, and with some amount of capacity to navigate administration! This was 20 years back, and I had the full support of two state theatres, both of which were doing everything they could to keep me in the country. But still. It takes so little to lose that belonging and that legitimacy. For a great number of people that you are faced with when you are an immigrant, and very often for those who are sitting on the opposite end of a desk, whether it is to renew your work permit, whether it is to decide whether you are worthy of citizenship, there is no such thing as an immigrant who is worthy enough. And this whole question of who belongs "where" and who has the right to be there is something that troubles me constantly. So even when I am very, very privileged, I am equally aware that all it takes is an accident, a natural disaster, a war, things beyond one's control, to go from privileged, established, to being completely devoid of rights ...

I remember being in Monoprix in Pyramides (as you know, a department store in a very rich neighbourhood in the centre of Paris) one day, where there was a food bank drive for homeless people and refugees, and in front of me in the queue stood a mother and a son. The child asked his mother if they were going to buy anything for the drive. And the mother said very clearly: "non, on ne veut pas de réfugiés, nous" (we don't want refugees). These words really stuck in my head. That sense of invulnerability is something I dread, completely. Perhaps part of me envies it too?

LZ: Going back to etymology again, vulnerability is the capacity to be wounded, right? And this vulnerability, along with the fragility of the body, of the skin's surface, which is linked to your everyday personal, autobiographical experience, is omnipresent in your work. For instance, in the poem that you wrote to commemorate the 70th birth anniversary of India, "Pro Salute Patriae" (Naïr 2017), you talk about India's skin, which you describe as hardened, "impervious to tenderness and touch, / fresh breeze and clement rain, or warm earth". And that brings me more specifically to the way you relate to India.

KN: You know I relate to both of my countries, France and India, in the same way. I am fiercely critical of them, and of the directions they are taking, but also really grateful for the person they've made me, because both have, and also very defensive of the founding principles of both countries, principles that are laudable and vital, and were, for a long time, successful against all odds.

LZ: In the same poem you write, "We're strangers / now: you can't recall me, and a dog in the manger / I'd be named if you did" ...

KN: Well, I don't recognize the nation India is becoming, one where there is volitional mass radicalisation. I mean, I know, and recognize what is happening on a cerebral level, but emotionally, it is wrenching to believe this is what the country that I grew up in, is transforming into. I had no illusions about the scale and depth of injustice, casteism, misogyny, structural communalism ... but I did believe in *some* of the secular instruments the Constitution provided, the press and the courts, to some extent. My earliest memories are of the Emergency, so I also remember the resistance there was to it. The dog in the manger bit is a commentary on the criticism I get from some readers in India: their argument being that since I don't live there anymore, I do not have the right to protest or comment.

LZ: *You've just said that ownership was not interesting to you, and in an earlier interview, that the good thing about scripting for dance is that it teaches you that your words are no more and no less than raw material for others to use. I'd love to follow up on that idea with you, because of course that goes against the Hindutva attempts at "governing those who undertake the telling of stories", to cite the poet Jeet Thayil (2015); and goes against all those who want to decide on which story is true, or legitimate; who has the right to tell it, or claim custody over it. I know you've spoken about this before, but since* Until the Lions *is also about challenging majoritarian narratives, would you like to tell us again how it is connected to that specific context?*

KN: Let's put it this way. So many people have said it so much better than I ever can, but the *Mahabharata* is part of a tradition that has thrived in its multiplicity. There are *Mahabharatas* all across Asia. Characters change, equations change, morality changes. What's wonderful about the *Mahabharata* for me, is that it's much more revelatory of the time and place in which it is told; it really mirrors the preoccupations, or the defences, or the reclamations of that particular localized humanity. And for me all these *Mahabharatas* are valid. And the attempt that every majoritarian power, every totalitarian regime makes, which is to homogenize narrative, has to be resisted at all cost.

Until the Lions was primarily driven by the desire to show that the landscape changes depending on where you stand. Like I've said, when you are at the rim of the battle, it looks very different from when you are in the thick of it, surrounded by bodies. It's a very different vision of "glory" or "heroism" than it is for someone who is sitting on a throne and just listening to a narrative of how much has been gained or lost, or someone who listens to this victorious poem 2000 years later and decides to reclaim it because there is some golden past that they want to connect to. So, the poems are about that as well.

LZ: *But when you were writing* Until the Lions, *were all the controversies surrounding those who like the painter M.F. Husain, or the writer and translator A.K. Ramanujan, have retold these epics or celebrated their multiplicity, and have been hounded or censored for those very reasons, at the back of your mind?*

KN: All that was there. But when I wrote *Until the Lions*, I needed to be true to each voice, to inhabit all these different voices. And you know the India I grew up into was so much more plural than it is now ... But I guess it helps to live in France, with a government whose default position is not "you should be behaving yourself as a writer". It's great not to have strictures about what you can or cannot write. Yet, once again, while I was writing it, it was a process of immersion and the only thing that inhabits each poem is hopefully the voice of the person it should be. Now, is that person in an a-historic and insulated world? *No.* For me that person could be here and now. And Sauvali[5] is a Dalit woman today as much as a mythological character in a non-existent kingdom. And when I wrote Sauvali was I thinking about all the *Adivasi* women whose rights to their own bodies have been violated? Yes. Actually, Sauvali could also be an upper-caste woman who is told that she has to bear sons.

LZ: *You said many times that you also belong to a stream of imagination, and that you consider yourself an heiress, who is "only" continuing that stream of imagination. Would you say that this kind of belonging also defines your relationship to India—as the foundry of so many narratives?*

KN: That is indeed what I say in the introduction to the American edition of *Until the Lions: Echoes from the Mahabharata*. I called this book the "mutant, happily illicit child of so many ancestors, with varied provenance".[6] And I am too! You know, for instance, as I said, I grew up learning three languages simultaneously, and my *imaginaire* (that's one of the most

---

[5] Sauvali, one of the 19 characters and voices of *Until the Lions*, who is chosen as a concubine and raped by Dhritarashtra, speaks in the poem "Bedtime Story for a Dasi's Son".

[6] "Until the Lions: Of Myths and Men". The whole passage reads as follows: "Vyaasa himself, whose Mahabharata contains something as radical as an entire book—the Stree Parva—chronicling the laments and tirades of the grieving mothers and widows of both warring clans in the wake of the final carnage. Ovid, with his millennia-old Heroides ... Amir Khusrau, who could sing to his spiritual master in Persian and Braj, alternating languages within the same couplet. Andal of the fierily sensual poetry for her beloved deity, Perumal. Bhâsa, who—almost two thousand years ago—adapted plays from the epics, ones where the motives of the gods are openly challenged, ones imagining alternative scenarios [...]. The 9th-century Tamil poet Perunthevanar ..."

beautiful words in French which has no real translation in English; perhaps "creative ethos" would be the closest), was initially formed as much by Russian fairy tales, because those are the things you read as a child when you lived in Delhi in the late 1970s, as by Kunchan Nambiar, an amazing Malayalam poet and humourist who created this satiric art form called Ottamthullal where you could criticize the king or priests or other authority figures, or by Faiz Ahmed Faiz, and Hindi cinema, and so many others. So, mine really is a bastardized *imaginaire*!

LZ: So, you claim this bastardized, eclectic collective imaginaire *and you place your own voice in that stream of voices, past and present. That also leads me to the collaborative or dialogic dimension which is so omnipresent in your work. Writing is almost never a solitary business, even in* Bearings *or* Until the Lions, *so when you are the only one authoring the book, you include a multitude of footnotes, acknowledgements, even bibliographical references. You always summon all these other people, voices, and texts. And the renga (a Japanese form of collective poetry) in* Over *and* Underground *but also in your present work with the poet Marilyn Hacker, is a form you privilege.[7] The poem becomes a kind of letter addressed to a fellow poet, where you write for someone, just like you do for dance. I wonder if you could reflect on this dialogic dimension. What do you find in these collaborative ventures? Is it also the pleasure of being able to speak to someone in particular, the pleasure of being read by one privileged interlocutor?*

KN: I hadn't thought of that, but that's a really interesting question, because a lot of my poems are written to a "you", even if that "you" keeps changing. So I'd say that the dialogical is intrinsic to pretty much everything I write. Yes, even when it's not a collaboration, there's definitely always a "you" involved, either a you that is evoked through the poem itself, or there is one specific reader that I am usually thinking of. In a sense, there is always a conversation involved. And as far as the collaborations are concerned, that may be because even though I am not a dancer or choreog-

---

7 Karthika Naïr is currently wrapping up a book of *renga* with the American poet Marilyn Hacker, a chronicle of their daily lives through the months of lockdown in Paris.

rapher myself, the artistic discipline in which I have grown, and in which I have spent my adult life, is dance, and that is inherently collaborative.[8]

LZ: Yes, and you start Over and Underground *with a "Duet", right, between Bernard Maris and Dominique Seux, that was "tragically interrupted" by the Charlie Hebdo attacks.[9] And so that leads me to the question of literary texts as responses to specific events. You've written many poems that seem to articulate a kind of response, like your ghazal around Shaheen Bagh, or your texts on the Charlie Hebdo and November 2015 attacks in Paris in* Over and Underground, *or the recent poem triggered by a self-portrait of the photographer Khadija Saye (Naïr 2020), who was killed in the Grenfell Tower fire ... That made me think of a short newspaper column written by Adil Jussawalla ([1993] 2014) called "Poems after Ayodhya", where he takes issue with the fact that you should expect poets to voice their immediate protest or shock at the riots. And he has this fabulous sentence where he writes that "the state of the country is not a workshop that makes poems happen" ...*

KN: Bless him! But whether we like it or not, poetry is political. Take the Romantic movement, for instance, which all seems very innocuous, but for me was intensely political as well, because you were taking the divine out of the established places and the realm of religion, and placing it in nature for instance, or within the discovery of a wider world. But I agree completely with Adil and do get uncomfortable with poems that are for example titled "Kargil" or "Palestine". And very conflicted about what one could call a form of disaster porn. But it's sensitive, isn't it? And I always think of something Larbi (Sidi Larbi Cherkaoui) told me: *should me no shoulds*, in other words, let there be no rules on what can or cannot be tackled by art. So, I also think that everyone responds as he or she can, and the poem will

---

8   "The good thing about coming to scripting / writing for dance after years of working in the field [...] is that you are very clear that your poems and stories, your words, are no more and no less than raw material for each of the collaborators to transform into his or her medium. You are aware of the danger of retaining words just for your own" (Naïr 2013).
9   Bernard Maris was a well-known French journalist, writer and economist who was murdered on January 7, 2015 when the Kouachi brothers stormed into the Charlie Hebdo headquarters, and killed 12 people, including many senior members of the editorial staff. He had a weekly radio program on France Inter with Dominique Seux.

speak for itself. Nothing should come between that compulsion to speak and the page, if you see what I mean. My own take is that I try to situate it in the intersection between the personal and the political and that's the way it's been for Charlie Hebdo for instance ... Even today, I mourn Bernard Maris like somebody I knew. And so I write also from a very personal space, of what I lost in that bloody massacre.

But it took me months, even I'd say an entire year, before I could articulate how I felt to begin with, about Bernard Maris. And it took me about two years before I could talk about what happened on rue de Charonne, and again it's about the guilt of not being there, because I was supposed to be on that street with Damien,[10] and the poem is about him. So, it is about a person in my life who is fortunately still with us, but could so easily not have been. And it's actually a chronicle of the precise events that led us to not be together at that particular moment and place.

LZ: *You've said that Manichaeism is the poison of epics, because they give form to many shades of human nature, and dissolve the predicable binaries of "black" and "white", heroes and villains.[11] And I was thinking that the vocation of the writer is also to nurture complexity, to produce works of art that are open to an inexhaustible plurality of interpretations, or gazes as you say, and perhaps also to struggle (I am here paraphrasing the writer Amit Chaudhuri) against visible, definite or content-driven markers ... So how do you reconcile the writer and the activist within you, and is that a question that you find relevant, if at all?*

KN: I never feel the need to reconcile the two because I don't make a distinction, for myself. But once again, those are personal choices. When Arundhathi Roy talks about the hyphenated writer, i.e. writer-activist, and says that it is a tautology for her, I totally get that, and, in a sense, abide by that. Because, you see, to all intents and purposes, *The Honey Hunter*,[12] which is in principle a children's book, is no less political than *Until the*

---

10   Choreographer and dancer Damien Jalet, whose earlier work Karthika Naïr produced.
11   See, amongst other interviews, the very interesting two-part conversation between Jai Arjun Singh and Karthika Naïr (Naïr and Singh 2015).
12   For a short, animated preview of *The Honey Hunter* in French, see: https://vimeo.com/76849166

Lions. *The Honey Hunter* comes from a very localized cosmogony, which for me is as important as "majoritarian" Islam or Hinduism; it is a syncretic story, it's about a land (the mangrove forests of the Sundarban) where a Goddess can be Hindu and Muslim at the same time; it's about a land which is extremely fragile, which is between fresh water and sea water, which is both land and water, and which is the first line of defence against external dangers (cyclones, floods) but is also increasingly vulnerable (from oil spills, from new coal plants polluting the river …), and we humans are utter jackasses if we don't recognize that. And if I can say that to a child without at any time "pamphleteering", my job is done.

The story also raises the question that if we need to redeem ourselves as a race, we need to, at least in some ways, undo the damage that we've done to the planet, which is what the child in the story has to do. Of course, solutions have to be found which are not as simple in our lives as in a fable, but the little boy in the story has to undergo a transformation and a great deal of suffering to try and compensate in some ways for the destruction that he's brought. So, you know, how is *The Honey Hunter* not political?

LZ: *I also wanted to evoke the place of pain and damage in your poetry. In our last conversation together, you said that more than anything else, you believed in what Jeannette Winterson said, "which is that poetry can give pain a mouth". And in a section in* Bearings *called "Damaged Goods", you write that it's a relief to see this section as only one among several, because, initially, "poetry threatened to be solely an inventory of damage". One of the poems in that section is called "Pillowtalk"—where the dialogue is not with love or a lover, but with death …*

KN: It's funny you should mention that one poem, because "Pillowtalk" was actually the first poem I ever wrote, as an adult. And it was triggered by that very specific moment and image, when I was really sick one night and a childhood friend came to visit. We met up after 15 years because he was spending a year in Paris. He had known me since the time I was critically ill, in my teens, when I could not swallow and I had what I used to call my "second mouth", a gastrostomy, etc. And he was sitting by my window sill, rolling and smoking a cigarette. And I thought that we keep on picturing death as this ugly, horrible thing (often a crone), but perhaps death could be this really charming young man who knows you so intimately that he is not going to make it tough for you.

LZ: *You've also said: "I may not even be writing if it weren't for dance, and a dysfunctional body" (Naïr 2015b). And if we just focus on that single sentence, it's interesting in itself, because we usually associate dance with a functional, rather than a dysfunctional body ...*

KN: Actually, it's not counter-intuitive. I'd say these words are, in fact, connected. Dance is the thing that allows me to transcend my body. I am not the one dancing but those are the moments when I can sense what the body is capable of. And it is indescribably invigorating to know that the body is something other than the source of incapacity, pain, or dysfunction—the feelings I associate most with my own body. And dancers are also aware of how blessed and transient that sensation is. Dancers have very short lives as dancers. They actually know what it is to have a fragile body. So, oddly enough, I am surrounded by people whose bodies are their art, whose bodies have to perform near-superhuman feats and they are the often the ones most sensitive to my dysfunctionality.

Now, I can't dance, but what I do is facilitate dance, whether as a producer in the early years, or as a writer now. To help make that happen is probably the most empowering thing I can do. And when I write, it is also making that permanent because as I once said, dance is "calligraphy on water". It is the most impermanent of all the arts. It only exists in the moment. And when I write, it is also an attempt at chronicling that moment, or what that moment meant to me.

LZ: *Would you say that perhaps writing is also chronicling a victory over pain ...*

KN: I think it's a constant negotiation, not a victory.

LZ: *But pain is not completely disabling then. For instance, another piece that you say was triggered by pain, by rage and by helplessness, is the dazzling poem "Mohini" (in* Until the Lions*) ...*

KN: Well, it's the only good thing that can come out of it, in my case!

LZ: *That is also what I find extraordinary in your poetry, Karthika, and I have told you that before, but that even when your texts are chronicles of violence, pain, or loss, there is always as well an exultation in movement, in rhythm, in* language. That is perhaps why I was talking about victory (over death, over silence, over immobility), and why I always feel the irrepressible desire to recite your poems out loud, to hear your words sing. There's also a dimension of survival. And you have a whole poem in Over and Underground around the Charlie Hebdo and November 2015 attacks, where your words are woven around the city's motto, "Fluctuat nec mergitur" (Tossed by the waves but never sunk) which was defiantly splashed and proclaimed in the streets of Paris in the aftermaths of terror ...

KN: You know, I think there are two things: there is chronicling, and there is celebrating. Now there is a lot of stuff to celebrate. Even in the *renga* sequence with Marilyn in the midst of the bloody lockdown, there were friends who were coming to see me, and bringing me things to eat, for instance, dishes they had cooked with ingredients they had procured with some difficulty (there was a shortage of many items we'd ordinarily take for granted). The chronicling can be of survival, but the chronicling can also be of wonder, and I think that is one of the things that dance but also all of the last year reminded me of, constantly. And *Over and Underground* is a lot about that, as well: everyday wonder.

LZ: *Yes, of course I wasn't downplaying that dimension of your work when I was talking about survival. There is also so much palpable delight in words, in movement, in stories, in Paris, or in the Metro. And there is so much humour as well, actually, in* Over and Underground.

KN: This is a collection which I am really fond of, because what I've done is document everyday memories, and it's not something I feel we pay enough attention to. And in Paris we encounter more of this everyday wonder in the Metro than anywhere else.

Bibliography

Jussawalla, Adil. [1993] 2014. "Poems after Ayodhya." In *Maps for a Mortal Moon: Essays and Entertainments*, edited by Jerry Pinto, 275–277. New Delhi: Aleph Company.
Naïr, Karthika. 1999. *Bearings*. New Delhi: HarperCollins India.
---. 2013. "Interview: Seeking Movement [with Urvashi Bahuguna]." *Helter Skelter*, Oct. 9. https://helterskelter.in/2013/10/seeking-movement/.
---. 2015a. *Until the Lions: Echoes from the Mahabharata*. New Delhi: Harper Collins India.
---. 2015b. "In Conversation: Tishani Doshi and Karthika Naïr." *Granta*, April 16. https://granta.com/in-conversation-tishani-doshi-and-karthika-nair/.

---. 2017. "Pro Salute Patriae." In "A Border Exists Because It Can Be Crossed", edited by Meena Kandasamy. *Mint*, August 11. https://www.livemint.com/Search/Link/Author/Meena-Kandasamy.

---. 2020. "Tééré, 2017." *Visual Verse: An Anthology of Arts and Words* 7 (Chapter 09). Retrieved July 4, 2020 (https://visualverse.org/images/khadija-saye/).

Naïr, Karthika, and Joëlle Jolivet. 2013. *The Honey Hunter / Le Tigre de Miel*. New Delhi: Zubaan Books.

Naïr, Karthika, and Jai Arjun Singh. 2015. "We Can Often Be Hero to One Person, Villain to Another and Something in Between to Lots of Others." *Scroll.in*, Sept. 6. Retrieved September 26, 2020 (https://scroll.in/article/753741/we-can-often-be-hero-to-one-person-villain-to-another-and-something-in-between-to-lots-of-others).

Naïr, Karthika, Sampurna Chattarji, Joëlle Jolivet, and Roshni Vyam. 2018. *Over and Underground in Mumbai & Paris*. Chennai: Westland Publications.

Naïr, Karthika, and Laetitia Zecchini. 2020. "India's Season of Dissent: An Interview with Poet Karthika Naïr." *South Asia Multidisciplinary Academic Journal* 24/25. http://journals.openedition.org/samaj/6651; DOI: https://doi.org/10.4000/samaj.6651.

Rushdie, Salman. 1990. *Haroun and the Sea of Stories*. London and New York: Granta Books.

Shulman, David. 2020. "The Widows' Laments." *The New York Review of Books*. September 24. Retrieved September 20, 2020, (https://www.nybooks.com/articles/2020/09/24/mahabharata-widows-laments/).

Thayil, Jeet. 2015. "Rules for Citizens." In *Collected Poems*. New Delhi: Aleph Book Company.

Remapping Canada:
Mariam Pirbhai in Conversation with Maryam Mirza

Photograph of Mariam Pirbhai copyright 2021 by Mariam Pirbhai

Mariam Pirbhai was born in Pakistan and spent her childhood in England and the Philippines before her family made their way to Canada. She is the author of a short story collection *Outside People and Other Stories* (Pirbhai 2017), which won the 2018 IPPY (Independent Publisher Book Awards) Gold Medal for Multicultural Fiction, and also the 2019 American BookFest's Award for Short Fiction. The novelist Shani Mootoo commented that "as Diane Arbus is to photography, so is Mariam Pirbhai to literature—bringing forth the margins, but nobly, with understanding and an unusual generosity in her handling of contemporary society's machinations". The "outside people" whose perspectives are evoked skilfully in the stories are usually immigrants to the west or the families that they have left behind. Mariam Pirbhai discusses a number of them in her interview here.

    She is also the author and editor of academic works on the subject of the South Asian diaspora, including *Mythologies of Migration, Vocabularies of Indenture: Novels of the South Asian Diaspora in Africa, the*

Caribbean, and Asia-Pacific (Pirbhai 2009), and a co-edited collection of essays *Critical Perspectives on Indo-Caribbean Women's Literature* (Pirbhai and Mahabir 2013). She has written on a range of diasporic writers, including Salman Rushdie, Shani Mootoo, Rohinton Mistry and Anita Rau Badami. Mariam Pirbhai has served as President of CACLALS (Canadian Association for Commonwealth Literature and Language Studies), Canada's longest-standing association devoted to postcolonial studies. She is Professor of English at Wilfrid Laurier University, where she teaches postcolonial literatures, diaspora studies and creative writing.

Mariam Pirbhai's current projects include a novel, provisionally titled *Isolated Incident*. The novel follows a spate of hate crimes directed at Muslim Canadians settled in and around the cities of Toronto and Montreal. When a rock with a threatening letter and a burning Quran are thrown into a mosque, religious leaders and the police shrug off the attack as an isolated incident, but not everyone is convinced by this tepid response. Among them is Kashif Siddiqui, the son of Pakistani émigrés who agrees to join his "brothers", a group of volunteers at a local Islamic Cultural Centre, on an ill-conceived security watch during the Islamic Festival of Eid-al-Adha, or the Festival of the Sacrifice, which they predict will be the target of a bolder attack. When an unlikely friendship with Frank Snyder, a retired police officer, stokes Kashif's ambitions to enter the police force, he realizes that any form of vigilantism could be a strike against his professional ambitions. But since the Islamic Cultural Centre has become a refuge at a time of personal crisis, Kashif decides to pay it forward and do his part to "serve and protect" the Muslim community. Eid night, a watershed moment, changes everything. For the people in Kashif's orbit, it is a test of friendship, family and faith. For Kashif, it may mean the difference between life and death.

In the following interview with Maryam Mirza, conducted by email during April–June 2018, Mariam Pirbhai reflects on the transformative power of fiction, the trope of social invisibility, and the emergence of South Asian Canadian literature.

For biographical details of the interviewer, Maryam Mirza, see her interview with Rukhsana Ahmad in this volume.

Maryam Mirza (MM)*: Dr Pirbhai, what is it that makes you want to write fiction?*

Mariam Pirbhai (MP): Mohsin Hamid, whose writing I greatly admire, said somewhere that storytelling alters the storyteller. And a story is altered by being told. I think I am drawn to this aspect of fiction—as something that has the potency and power to be transformative. To imagine a world, as Hamid says, against the "tyranny of what was and is" (Hamid 2017).

MM*: Do you see any challenges in being both an academic and a creative writer or do you see the two roles complementing each other?*

MP: I have written a blog post about this subject, titled "My Two Writing Selves: A Heady Affair" (Pirbhai 2018). The long and short of it is that while the two roles complement each other in a variety of ways—such as the love of research or the discipline of revision—finding the time to write is the biggest challenge. Time is always in short supply. But there is also a level of freedom in creative writing that is otherwise harnessed in scholarship and academia.

Having said this, most of the issues and concerns that drive my work as an academic and as a teacher—global migration flows, diasporic identities, citizenship and race, the histories and structures of western imperialism, precarity, labour histories, transnationals—have driven, at least to date, much of my creative writing.

MM*: In your short story "Sunshine Guarantee", the protagonist Lucita, who works as a chambermaid in a tourist resort in Mexico, seems almost startled to realize that "sometimes she couldn't tell the difference between what she called the 'visible staff'—the pool side animators, the fitness club trainers, the life guards, the bartenders—and the guests. They were usually lighter-skinned, spoke English and were generally perceived as untouchable, unlike the invisible army of chambermaids, security guards, busboys, gardeners, dishwashers, and sweepers, who were not meant to be seen". "Sunshine Guarantee" and, indeed, most of the other stories in this collection address various forms of social (in)visibility and are concerned with the tyranny of hierarchies, often in a microsetting (such as a hotel). Could you tell us more about your interest in this trope?*

MP: Yes, invisibility is a major trope throughout this collection. I think I was writing these characters and contexts with the concept of the "visible minority", which is an official state designation for people of colour in Canada, critically in mind.

As I was writing these stories, I felt that those deemed "visible minorities" because of their purported markers of ethno-racial difference, are actually "invisible" people, in many ways—invisible not as a result of some self-induced condition, but because of the hierarchies or roadblocks that deny them a space, as equals, within their own societies—reminding us that citizenship is not "lived equally, freely, or in solidarity".

Even though this story, "Sunshine Guarantee", is set in Mexico, Lucita's invisibility vis à vis her "lighter-skinned" co-workers, the white tourist, or indeed her managerial "superiors", parallels the kind of invisibility experienced by my other characters in Canadian settings, as is typified by the story "Chicken Catchers", narrated from the perspective of Caribbean and Latin American migrant farm labourers holed up in a barracks-style accommodation on a southern Canadian farm. (The majority of seasonal agricultural workers—up to 40,000 per year—come to the province of Ontario. From 2000–2012, Ontario alone received approximately 800,000 temporary migrant workers [or 40 percent of total Temporary Foreign Workers (TFWs) in the country] in this and other sectors.)

MM: Given my own interest as a researcher in the literary depiction of domestic servitude, I was particularly intrigued by the short story "Corazon's Children", featuring a Filipina protagonist who works as a cleaner in Vancouver in order to provide a better life for her children in the Philippines. What drew you to the figure of the transnational domestic servant?

MP: Much of my earlier academic research focused on the history of Indian indentured labour in the former British Empire's overseas colonies. As we continue to rely on transnational or globalized labour, I am struck by the similarity between colonial and contemporary forms of "bonded" or temporary migrant labour. In this story, Corazon is, as you say, part of the transnational domestic labour force.

As a domestic worker employed in Canada, Corazon's story specifically brings to view the gendered dimension of such labour—that is, the so-called "feminized labour sector" that generally includes low-skilled jobs in manufacturing or the global care chain. When one throws motherhood into the mix of gendered transnational labour, a terrible irony of circumstance ensues where a female migrant is helping to care for a family or manage a household at the sacrifice of her own children, family and home.

In this story, Corazon is caught in this paradox, agonizing over the sacrifice she has made in leaving her children behind as she holds on to the dream that her temporary work will eventually facilitate the permanent migration of herself and her children to Canada. (There is a whole history, here, of Filipina migrant workers who have advocated for and won the right to settle in Canada. It is one of many examples of courageous agency on the part of women labourers and migrants that we rarely hear about.)

Suffice it to say, that the stories in this collection focus on individuals in different working conditions: a chambermaid, a domestic worker, farm labourers, a factory worker. Others are nurses, bankers, civil servants, and some are even unemployed or unable to make use of their skills. Neither one is any less or more important than the other; it is the value placed on their labour that I guess I am exploring here—particularly as it is further complicated by migration.

MM: *One cannot help but be struck by the strong multilingualism of your debut collection: the short stories are interspersed with words, and sometimes entire phrases, in Urdu / Hindi, Arabic, French and Spanish but also Jamaican and Haitian Creole as well as Tagalog. It seems to me that your use of multiple languages is not only tied in with your adoption of the realist mode, but is also a way of contesting linguistic hierarchies.*

MP: Thanks for commenting on this aspect of the collection. For me, multilingualism is a natural aspect of our multicultural cities, our hybrid cultures—our world. Monolingualism seems like the enforced and unnatural condition.

I hope the collection's diverse range of languages, like its cast of characters (Caribbean, Maghrebi, South Asian, South-East Asian, etc.), not only contests linguistic hierarchies but also relational hierarchies, in so far as our points of interconnection and interaction are as multifarious as the diasporic groups who populate our cities.

In this regard, I also wanted to break with the implied hegemony of English as our default lingua franca, and focus on inter-ethnic encounters that bring to view other levels of interlingualism and multilingualism. For instance, in "Air Raids", a young Pakistani-Canadian woman living in Montreal has to rely on French (her third language) to communicate with her Moroccan lover; at the same time, both characters are part of a wider Muslim diaspora for whom Arabic is, at least implicitly, another kind of language of mutual recognition.

MM: *Your choice of names for the characters in the collection* Outside People and Other Stories *is also quite striking. I'm thinking, for example, of the Canadian Indian couple Radha and Krishna in the short story "Crossing Over". What's the significance of character names in your fiction?*

MP: Radha and Krishna, like their counterparts Mumtaz and Akbar in the story, are definitely my way of having fun with some of the themes in this story! And of course, names and naming are always markers of identity steeped in our histories, a fact which takes on a particular hue given the ethno-cultural diversity of these characters. So, I guess you caught me out in the act of playing with names here!

Though I will say that over-thinking names can also collapse into a form of overkill. Sometimes a cigar is just a cigar, and all that. On the other hand, the absence of names is also interesting. In the title story, for instance, the male and female protagonists are nameless. But I'll let you be the judge of whether this is something worth reflecting on further!

MM: *As you mentioned earlier, "Air Raids", the opening story of the collection, is set in Montreal, while the action in "Crossing Over" takes place in Halifax and then, of course, there's "Toronto's Dominions", the fourth story of the volume. Was it a conscious decision on your part to give the "Canadian" stories in the collection a varied setting?*

MP: Much of the literature exploring diasporic experience in Canada tends to focus on a single major metropolitan centre like Toronto. I want my reader to see a Canada as it is both lived and witnessed through the eyes of those so-called "outsiders" who are, in their ubiquity and presence across this vast country, an essential feature of its geography. I wanted to shake things up a little bit and create a new kind of mapping of Canada, not only in its cities but also in its suburbs, its rural spaces, and everything in between.

To extend this figurative remapping of Canada, a couple of stories (like "Sunshine Guarantee" and the title story) are set in Latin America or the Caribbean but are implicitly linked, by way of their characters' family histories, to Canada. This is because I also see Canada not just as a part of North America but also as an extension of the rest of the Americas. Canada relies heavily on socioeconomic relations and activities with its Latin American and Caribbean neighbours (not just with the US). There is a trans-hemispheric dimension to the Canadian landscape which has not been adequately explored in Canadian fiction, and one that interests me greatly—including the reasons for its erasure in the Canadian psyche.

MM: *As a teacher of postcolonial literature, do you think South Asian Canadian literature has any distinctive features which set it apart from, say, South Asian British or American literature?*

MP: Most definitely. Without getting into some kind of academic rapture about a subject that I am quite passionate about, I will simply say that South Asian Canadian literature is just coming-of-age (or at least coming into its own in a more fulsome way), while South Asian British literature is its older, more mature cousin. South Asian American literature falls somewhere in between.

In the case of South Asian Canadian literature, I think this is because the second generation—particularly those kids of South Asian émigrés who settled in Canada from the 1960s onward—are only just starting to find a voice and platform in the literary world. Without oversimplifying things, this has created quite a shift in the kinds of stories that are now being told, from an earlier generation who began publishing in the 1980s and 1990s (such as Rohinton Mistry or M.G. Vassanji), and who were largely fixated on the homelands left behind, to a younger generation exploring life in Canada more directly or simply pushing the envelope, stylistically and otherwise.

As far as distinctive features are concerned, it is harder to make such comparisons, but I will hazard a few insights. I would say, given the much older and larger communities of Muslim South Asians in Britain, British literature seems more populated by stories that explore the intersections between Islam and the South Asian diaspora. In Canada, the South Asian population has been represented by a predominantly Hindu and

Indian nationalist perspective, which has obfuscated "South Asianness", if you will, in all its diversity. At least I would argue that Muslim South Asian perspectives have been wholly excluded here—a pretty major absence, if you ask me! In this vein, the kind of emphasis one might see in the US on works that wrestle with "terrorism", the so-called global war on terror or even a post-9/11 era, has been largely absent here as well. Also, at least in fiction, male writers have generally dominated the South Asian Canadian literary landscape. This, too, is changing. I guess I can count myself among those who are swinging the pendulum!

If your readers are interested in learning more about South Asian Canadian literature, permit me this opportunity to direct them to a special commemorative issue of *Studies in Canadian Literature / Études en littérature canadienne*, titled "South Asian Canadian Literature: A Centennial Journey" (Pirbhai 2015).

MM: *I believe you are working on your first novel at the moment. Is it set in Canada?*

MP: My point about the experience of Muslims being largely absent in Canadian fiction has provided much of the impetus for my first novel, *Isolated Incident*, which is very loosely inspired by the recent spate of attacks against Muslim-Canadian communities, including the mass shooting of worshippers at a mosque in Québec City in 2017, which resulted in tragic loss of life. The novel considers anti-Muslim sentiment through the perspective of four very different families. It's not something I intended to write. But there it is. Sometimes the story alters the storyteller.

MM: *Dr. Mariam Pirbhai, thank you very much.*

MP: Thank you for your wonderful questions!

More information on Mariam Pirbhai's work can be found on her official website: www.mariampirbhai.ca.

Acknowledgements

This publication is supported by the Alexander von Humboldt Foundation.

Bibliography

Hamid, Mohsin. 2017. "Mohsin Hamid on the Dangers of Nostalgia: We Need to Imagine a Brighter Future." *The Guardian*, Feb. 25. https://www.theguardian.com/books/2017/feb/25/mohsin-hamid-danger-nostalgia-brighter-future.

Pirbhai, Mariam. 2009. *Mythologies of Migration, Vocabularies of Indenture: Novels of the South Asian Diaspora in Africa, the Caribbean, and Asia-Pacific*. Toronto: University of Toronto Press.

---. 2017. *Outside People and Other Stories*. Toronto: Inanna Publications.

---. 2018. "My Two Writing Selves: A Heady Affair." *Brockton Writers Series*, Jan. 3. https://brocktonwritersseries.wordpress.com/2018/01/03/bws-10-01-18-mariam-pirbhai/

---, ed. 2015. "South Asian Canadian Literature: A Centennial Journey". Special Issue of *Studies in Canadian Literature/Études en littérature canadienne* 42 (1). https://journals.lib.unb.ca/index.php/SCL/article/view/24278.

Pirbhai, Mariam, and Joy Mahabir, eds. 2013. *Critical Perspectives on Indo-Caribbean Women's Literature*. Abingdon: Routledge.

"I Ground Myself in Multiple Spaces": Sehba Sarwar in Conversation with Maryam Mirza

Photograph of Sehba Sarwar by Minal Saldivar

Sehba Sarwar was born and raised in Karachi, Pakistan, and has been based in the United States for more than three decades. An author, activist, visual artist and educator, Sehba Sarwar is the recipient of numerous prestigious grants and awards, including the first prize in the Free Speech Category at the 2011 Houston Art Car Parade, an Artistic Innovations grant (2014–15) awarded by the Mid-America Arts Alliance, and the 2019–20 Individual Artist Grant awarded by the City of Pasadena's Cultural Affairs Division to complete her memoir. She has also served as Artist-in-Residence at the Mitchell Center for the Arts, University of Houston. Moreover, her writings, as well as other material about her life and work, are archived at the University of Houston.

Sehba Sarwar's 2004 novel *Black Wings* was republished in the US in 2019. Its story-within-story format proves ideally suited to the subject matter: Laila and her daughter Yasmeen, reunited in the US along with Laila's grandchildren, renegotiate their relationship and reassess their family history and conflicts. The most difficult of these events to come to terms with is the death of Yasmeen's twin brother, Yasir, at the age of 17. *Black Wings* is very much a "transnational" fiction in the sense that Sehba Sarwar outlines in this interview. The narrative spans Houston and Karachi and has perceptive things to say about both settings and their history. Sarwar herself has suggested that "the heart of the novel [lies in] the healing power of stories and multigenerational exchanges that cross continents". Few have written as searchingly about the meaning of "home": the concept is scrutinized throughout *Black Wings*, as well as in Sarwar's short stories and her highly original performances and installations: *On Belonging*, *What Is Home?* and *Reclaiming Home*.

The Pakistani writer Bina Shah has described Sarwar's voice as "clear and true, breaking boundaries no matter what format she chooses to express herself in". In this interview with Maryam Mirza, conducted by email from May to July 2020, Sehba Sarwar talks about the many creative hats that she dons, and reflects on her abiding exploration of borders, boundaries and identities.

For biographical details of the interviewer, Maryam Mirza, see her interview with Rukhsana Ahmad in this volume.

The poem by Sehba Sarwar, "Rotation", discussed below, has been reproduced at the end of the interview with the kind permission of the author.

Maryam Mirza (MM): *Your novel* Black Wings *(Sarwar [2004] 2019) was first published in 2004 by Alhamra Publishing, a Pakistani publisher; the new US edition with Veliz Books came out in 2019. What was your experience of revisiting a published work? Do you see the latest edition as a palimpsest or do you perceive the two as distinct literary works?*

Sehba Sarwar (SS): That's a great question. I have a personal attachment to both editions. For me each edition is different in many ways, but for the average reader and critic, the two versions of *Black Wings* are largely the same. In 2018 when Minerva Lavage, then editor of Veliz Books, expressed interest in publishing a second edition of the novel, she wanted to make the work available to readers and classrooms in the US and Europe. By then, the Pakistani version had run out of print, and Alhamra Publishing was no longer active. I was excited at the opportunity to have the novel back on bookshelves around the world. I took on the second edition, expecting to make a few edits and return the manuscript to Minerva. But when I opened the file, I found that over the course of 15 years, my writing style had changed. My language is more compressed. I ended up doing a rewrite—I chopped 25,000 words. The content largely stayed the same, though I made a few changes toward the end of the novel. I won't be specific since I don't want to offer any spoilers. I'm attached to both covers because they feature artwork by special people including my daughter, sister, and best friend. But as I said, most readers wouldn't notice the difference between the two versions. So, in that sense the new edition is a palimpsest.

MM: *In* Black Wings, *you are preoccupied with fractured relationships, whether it is the breakdown of Yasmeen's marriage or her strained relationship with her mother Laila. Can you talk about your interest in the intersection of temporal, geographical and emotional distance?*

SS: The personal fractures that Yasmeen experiences—with her mother and her life in Karachi as well as after the collapse of her marriage—are connected to the splintering that occurs after the death of Yasmeen's twin brother Yasir. When Yasmeen begins a new life in the US, she cuts off from Pakistan. In a sense, she's reliving the fracture that her mother's generation experiences after Partition when crossing a new physical border and adjusting to life in Pakistan. Historical events are critical to the narrative since the opening scene in *Black Wings* is set a few months after 9/11 when new borders are drawn within the US, making Yasmeen feel more disconnected from the community around her. On a whim, she invites her mother to visit her in Houston. Yasmeen's personal boundaries begin to collapse when her mother shares stories with her grandchildren, Yasmeen's daughter and son. Through the cycle of storytelling, in which truth and fantasy are intertwined, Yasmeen has to contend with her own past and her family's history.

In some ways, *Black Wings* contains elements of my own life. My family is fragmented because of our history in India, where some family members remained after Partition. After more than 30 years of producing fiction, novels, essays, and artwork, I do recognize that displacement and migration remain central themes in my work.

MM: *How do you conceive of the relationship between activism and literature?*

SS: I was raised in a home where there was no line between activism and literature / art, and I was politicized during my teenage years in the late 70s and early 80s when I marched on the streets with Women's Action Forum (WAF)[1] alongside my mother, sister, and family friends. Also, before flying to the US to attend college, I worked at the *Star* evening newspaper, which was a hub of dissent where many women activists and journalists were trained.

My parents were passionate supporters of the arts. They hosted poetry, music and dance recitals in our living room, sofas pushed back and white sheets spread on the carpets for guests at these interactive gatherings. Their network included poets such as Faiz Ahmed Faiz, Ahmed Faraz, Habib Jalib, whose voices are symbolic of the protest movements during the Zia and Ayub dictatorships. In our home, there was no line between activism and art—art *was* activism and activism *was* art. The term "social justice" has become popular over the last decade. My parents were part of Pakistan's social justice movement from the 1950s onward when they arrived in Pakistan after leaving their home cities in Uttar Pradesh (UP), India. While my father was in medical college, he led Pakistan's first nationwide student movement, the Democratic Students Federation (DSF), and was jailed for a year in the 1950s along with hundreds of other progressive activists. My mother Zakia Sarwar, an educator, participated in hunger strikes for teachers' rights during the 1960s. My parents continued their support of the arts through the 1970s and 1980s during Pakistan's darkest history. Also, my sister Beena Sarwar is a journalist involved in peace and democracy movements and has connected me to resources including *Himal SouthAsian* (published originally in Nepal, now in Sri Lanka

---

1   The Women's Action Forum (WAF) was formed by a group of 15 women in Karachi in September 1981. It was initially established to respond to the Hudood Ordinances (part of military ruler Zia-ul-Haq's "Islamization" process), and to promote women's interests in Pakistan.

[himalmag.com]), and to writers such as Arundhati Roy (India) and Salman Rashid (Pakistan).

When I write or create art, I don't have a message in mind; I allow the work to unravel. Since being published, *Black Wings* has been tagged as a feminist text, which makes sense since the protagonists are women. In the novel, Yasmeen resists being defined in the stereotypical image of "immigrant"; she has a career path and views herself as transnational. Through stories that Yasmeen and her mother share with Yasmeen's children and each other, the border between India and Pakistan is erased, and the Pakistani army's violence in Bangladesh is revisited.

MM: *You founded Voices Breaking Boundaries 20 years ago; can you tell our readers about the kinds of voices that the organization has sought to foreground, as well as the kinds of boundaries that it has worked to contest since its inception?*

SS: I initiated Voices Breaking Boundaries (VBB) as a women's literary collective in fall 1999. At the time in Houston, there were few opportunities for emerging writers to share their work. Within a year, I received grants to support the project. In 2001, after a successful screening of South Asian films, I could no longer manage the collective through my personal bank account. I formed a board and filed for non-profit status. A local non-profit organization offered me office space and the organization took off. After 9/11, VBB's work became even more urgent. In 2002, I collaborated with several Houston writers to create a series called "Words for Peace". At the first event (that was pre-Skype), we created a production in which Arundhati Roy, Salman Rashid, Irena Klepfisz, and Naomi Shihab Nye read work over a speaker telephone while we projected images on a screen. Bapsi Sidhwa, who lives in Houston and served on VBB's first board, also participated in the event. Over the years, we received grants through local and national arts foundations including the National Endowment for the Arts (NEA). Currently, the organization is dormant, though our website is still active (vbbarts.org) and we still have publications to sell. Ultimately, my goal was to create connections across borders and feature alternative perspectives about the world.

For the first two years, since I was teaching full-time, I only paid myself when I ran workshops, but in 2004, after my daughter was born, I could no longer dedicate time to the organization without pay. The board and I raised funds for a part-time position that went on to be a full-time salaried position with health benefits and competitive salary. At the time, I didn't realize how radical it was for a transnational person of colour to create a professional non-profit arts organization that offered salaried positions, paid artists, and wasn't operating on a "volunteer" model.

After I began working full-time, the organization's most popular series was our "living room art" productions through which I collaborated with artists to transform residential homes into art spaces. When my father passed away in Karachi in 2009, I created a production, *Honoring Dissent / Descent* in the house that my husband and I had purchased in Houston. I wanted people to know about my father's work in Pakistan. After the night ended and more than 400 people passed through our home to witness videos, performance, visual art, and music, I realized that I was replicating gatherings that my parents had hosted in our Karachi house. *Honoring Dissent / Descent* kicked off a new series for VBB through which I co-curated *living room art* productions each year. The productions tackled issues including race, women's rights, immigration. The last of the series, *Borderlines*, was a 5-year project (2014–17) through which we explored connections between border regions in South Asia and North America. I was lucky to be able spend time in Karachi, Delhi, Dhaka, and Toronto to conduct research for the project, while other members of the organization visited Mexico CDMX.

MM: *Since 2013 you have created several variations of a multidisciplinary initiative focusing on notions of home and belonging. It encompasses a number of exciting projects, such as* On Belonging, What Is Home? *and* Reclaiming Home. *Has your understanding of "home" shifted as a result of this project?*

SS: All of the projects that you list in your question—*On Belonging, What Is Home?* and *Reclaiming Home*—are connected to my memoir, which I started in 2013 while undertaking a two-year artist residency at the Mitchell Center for the Arts at the University of Houston. As I worked on text, I had opportunities to exhibit, perform, and offer workshops around the theme of displacement and memory, and my memoir evolved into a multidisciplinary project and took on different names. For my site-specific installation *Reclaiming Home*, I was inspired by spice bead necklaces that are sold in old Karachi at a market called Khujoor bazaar (a market where dates can be purchased in bulk). And my production, *What Is Home?*, had many elements including a storytelling workshop for undocumented and documented South Asian women, a performance, and a site-specific installation.[2] Most recently, I created *On Belonging* when I was invited by a Houston museum, the Menil Collection, to create art in response to Palestinian artist Mona Hatoum's exhibition.[3] For each performance, I extracted content from my memoir and converted the work to performative text. This year, 2020, I am finally back to working on my memoir.

Your question, whether my understanding of home has shifted as I've worked on the project, is interesting. I'm not sure if my "understanding of home" has shifted. Rather, over the past seven years as I've worked on the project through visual art, performances, workshops, and writing, I've become more conscious of how the issue of "home"—in a literal and temporal sense—is connected to my exploration of displacement and the urgency of memory. My 27-year partnership with my husband also factors into my consciousness. He is Chicano with roots in the US–Mexico border that has shifted many times. Together, we're raising a mixed-race daughter, whose family history connects her to two continents and forced borders.

MM: *Please tell us what inspired your short story "Railway Track", which can perhaps be referred to as political detective fiction, set against the backdrop of the rise of racism following the 2016 US presidential election.*

SS: In January 2017, former Houston Poet Laureate Gwendolyn Zepeda invited me to submit a crime story for Akashic Books' new publication, *Houston Noir*. I've always been intrigued by crime stories, and my fiction—including *Black Wings*—contains mystery (though not murder). Akashic Books has a template for its Noir series: writers have to pre-select neighbourhoods where they will set their stories. I decided to write the story from the perspective of a social worker who lives in the Houston house

---

2   Images from *What Is Home?* can be found at https://www.flickr.com/photos/133215264@N08/albums/72157650333659513.
3   Images from *On Belonging* can be found at https://www.flickr.com/photos/133215264@N08/albums/72157663489854847.

that my husband and I had owned for ten years in a neighbourhood that was on the east side of Houston and was home to a majority Latinx community. While living in that corner of the city, we had learned about the political leanings of many of our neighbours. Many were progressive while others were more conservative.

Gwen contacted me literally one day before Donald Trump's inauguration. By then, anti-immigration and racist sentiments were on the rise all around the US—and the globe—and the issues emerged as the story's backdrop. The story, as it unfolded, was an organic process, but the content makes sense given the dark time in which we live—on a global and local level.

MM: *In your short story "Soot", you present us with an unusual example of border crossing, with its protagonist, a young Pakistani woman, working for an NGO in Calcutta. In "Railway Track", we have another Pakistani student living in the US and dating a young man of Indian origin. Your work displays an enduring interest in Indo-Pakistan relations both "back home" and in the diaspora.*

SS: "Soot" is based on a true experience. While in graduate school during the late 1980s, I had the opportunity to intern at a Calcutta newspaper and spend three months in the city without a police reporting visa. At the time, my mother's uncle was serving as the Governor of West Bengal, and during my teens, I had visited UP several times along with my mother and siblings. I was always struck by the similarity in landscapes, language, culture, and food. And of course, because we had such close family ties across the border, we never felt as if we were "other".

Certainly, though Calcutta was different from UP in that Bengali culture is so rich, and the language is different from the colloquial Hindi / Urdu spoken around Pakistan and North India, I still felt welcome in the city. Since I'd spent time in Calcutta, I wanted to write the story from the perspective of a Pakistani living in a land that wasn't so foreign after all. And in "Railway Track", Mona Naeem—the Pakistani protagonist—is in a relationship with Sanjay, whose family is from India. The story is based on my experience of Houston's community, where I have friends who hail from different backgrounds and countries. "Sandstone Past" (Sarwar 2007) is another short story that I wrote in which the protagonist is a teenager in Karachi. Her best friend is Hindu, and her family has to make difficult decisions about migration. In some ways, the fact that cross-cultural relationships wind their way into my work is a conscious choice—relationships don't need to be limited by national borders that are, in the end, temporary. That's why the word "diaspora" feels remote to me. Most people I meet and work with have a history of displacement. Ultimately, I prefer the term "transnational"—because I ground myself in multiple spaces, and I don't feel the need to select only one as my "home."

MM: *With poignant humour, your piece in* The New York Times *entitled "A Delicate Matter in the Examination Room" (Sarwar 2016) charts the challenges of translation, interpretation and, more broadly, cross-cultural communication faced by immigrants in the US. How did this collaborative piece come about?*

SS: Azeb Yusuf, whose story I recounted in *The New York Times'* "Lives" column, participated in a 2015 women's storytelling workshop that I offered at the Somali Bantu Community of Greater Houston. I had taught the first version of the workshop for South Asian women earlier that year, but the community centre where I ran sessions didn't have any space that fall. They connected me with the Somali Bantu Community Centre, where Azeb served as a social worker. She joined my workshop and was a great storyteller. When *The New York Times* "Lives" column editor—I had written for them before—invited me to submit another Lives story for their new series, I knew that Azeb would be a great match. The narrative that she shared is sad and humorous at the same time, serving as a reminder of the challenges in translation—especially in medicine.

Azeb's story underscores the dilemma faced by translators, as well as by immigrants and refugees, who are well-educated in their own languages but are often judged for not having fluency in the languages used in their adopted lands. Language is so political. Ethiopia is one of the few nations in the developing world that was not colonized by the Europeans, but Ethiopians still have to deal with racism and bias when visiting or living in countries away from their home—if they lack fluency in the language spoken in the nation(s) they adopt.

MM: *You have successfully worked in multiple literary genres (much like Rukhsana Ahmad, another Pakistani diasporic writer interviewed in this*

Creative Lives *volume*). *Additionally, you are a visual artist. Do you see an affinity between specific themes or stories and particular literary genres / artistic media?*

SS: Thank you. While I was studying for my Cambridge examination in Karachi—before I flew to the US to acquire my bachelor's degree—I was a visual artist. I loved working with charcoal and oil painting, and I didn't think of myself as a writer because I hadn't read many South Asian writers, who were producing work in English. Bapsi Sidhwa and Salman Rushdie were only just becoming known names. Back then, the syllabus for my Cambridge English literature exams included work by Shakespeare, Jane Austen and the British Romantic Poets, but when I was an undergraduate at Mount Holyoke College, I began to read English texts by writers of colour and took creative writing classes. I also studied at Hampshire College with scholar Eqbal Ahmed, who exposed me and my friends to global issues, which later informed my artistic practice. In those days, I was most drawn to producing fiction—in English unfortunately—because my "English-medium school" in Karachi had not offered quality Urdu education. I have written essays about language, so I won't get on to the subject here.

Through the career path that I chose—first by teaching writing workshops in Houston followed by initiating my own non-profit arts organization—I expanded my writing to produce not just fiction but also nonfiction and poetry, and I experimented with art and generated video collages, site-specific installations, and performances. I've had wonderful teachers along the way whose work has influenced what I produce. I'm part of a writers' network called the Macondo Writers Workshop[4] and I've been fortunate to take a few writing workshops with Sandra Cisneros and learn from her. I also follow the work of visual artists and projects including Britto Arts Trust (Bangladesh), Mel Chin (USA), Shirin Neshat (Iran / USA) and many more. My bookshelf right now is stacked with nonfiction books since I'm teaching two online nonfiction courses and the texts include: *Borderlands: La*

---

4   The Macondo Arts Workshop was founded in 1995 by writer Sandra Cisneros and is described by her as a collaboration between writers "who view their work and talents as part of a larger task of community-building and non-violent social change". It has more than 200 lifetime members.

Frontera by Gloria Anzaldúa (1987), *Just Kids* by Patti Smith (2010), *Running in the Family* by Michael Ondaatje (1982)—and more.

MM: *Your poem "Rotation" is a powerful meditation upon the precarious forms of immigration and the surge in anti-immigrant sentiment in the Global North. Could you expand on your use of culinary imagery in the poem?*

SS: In 2018, author Sorayya Khan invited me to submit for Desi Writers' Lounge's "Nomad" edition, which she was co-editing alongside Torsa Ghosal. I hadn't written poetry for a while, but Sorayya's invitation came at the perfect time. I had just finished my *On Belonging* performance and installation, so I submitted three poems, one of which was "Rotation"; since the first release, I've performed the poem many times, and it has been republished. I dedicated the text to my mother, whom I pictured when I wrote the poem. The lesson I learned from my mother was that I don't have to assimilate—I can wear what I want, cook as I please, and be the person I am. The dish that I describe in the poem is one that my mother learned from my grandmother. The smell and sound of coriander seeds popping lingers long after the potatoes have been eaten, and the metaphor of the dish underscores that fact that immigrants, refugees, transnationals do not have to hide. The poem is included at the end of this interview—I wish I had been able to include a recording of the popping sound of the seeds!

MM: *From one interviewer to another, how would you describe your experience of interviewing the legendary American singer Patti Smith?*

SS: I interviewed Patti Smith twice—both times were wonderful. I first met Patti at LaGuardia Airport. My husband, René, who knows everything about alternative music, recognized her and nudged me to talk to her—we were getting ready to board the same flight to Houston. René and I were returning to Houston after a vacation in New York where we had participated in a protest against the US invasion of Iraq and we had witnessed police on horses and cars breaking up a peaceful rally in Chelsea, Manhattan. Patti Smith had also attended the rally. She was flying to Houston with her band to perform and to launch her exhibition, *Strange Messenger*, at Houston's Contemporary Museum of Art. I was already scheduled to interview her because I was co-hosting a radio show, *Living Art*, in Houston's Pacifica station, 90.1 FM.

I prepared for the first interview by visiting her exhibition, seeing her performance, and reading about her. Afterwards, I kept in touch with Patti. Once her memoir *Just Kids* was released, I invited her to Houston to read. She took me up on the offer and flew to Houston to perform and read from *Just Kids* and also participate in a second interview. By then, I had read her memoir and other works, and have deep respect for her commitment to dissent. Spending time with her was profound.

MM: *As we speak, the world finds itself in the midst of the coronavirus crisis. In what ways has your creative process been affected by the pandemic? Are there any art forms that you find especially appropriate when grappling with the current crisis?*

SS: As with everyone around us, COVID-19 has impacted me, professionally and personally. Los Angeles, California, where I'm based right now, was one of the first corners of the US to enforce "stay-at-home" orders. All readings and workshops for my spring semester were wiped out. But that reality was faced by most artists and independent workers. The more difficult adjustment has been the impact on travel. I was supposed to be in Karachi this summer with my mother and daughter. Now, I'm staying connected to my mother by calling her regularly. She's in Karachi and has not been able to travel either. And the stay-at-home has been tough. I've attended a couple of Black Lives Matter protest marches in Los Angeles along with thousands of others, but of course, even with masks, we are at risk. Given the restrictions that we face today, the art form that I can focus on is writing. I've been able to reserve mornings for working on my memoir, and I'm hoping to finish this round of revision by the end of summer. I've also formed a couple of writing groups, so I'm participating in regular video meetings. I'm enjoying the process—feedback is such a necessary part of writing. Also, there's an eruption of accessible readings and talks around the world. I've attended quite a few and also offered readings online. In some ways, the virus has flattened distances between people even while the pandemic prevents us from physically connecting.

MM: *I am really looking forward to the publication of your memoir, which promises to be a fascinating read!*

Sehba Sarwar's website can be accessed at: https://sehbasarwar.com.

Rotation

She heats oil
Rolls puri
Drops flat flour into bubbling oil

> *You conquer*
> *enforce rules*
> *ban travel*

In another pan
She pops coriander seeds
Tosses sliced potatoes

> *You build walls*
> *deport passengers*
> *obstruct asylum-seekers*

She serves flaky puri
With crisp potatoes
—we devour together

> *You demand documents*
> *collect fingerprints*
> *require face-identification*

Our choice: eat, speak, wear
Practice as we please
Where we wish

> *You cannot hinder climbs*
> *prevent tide*
> *stop earth rotation*

Like waves we cross
We fly
We roar
We stay or leave
—our movement permanent.

Bibliography

Anzaldúa, Gloria. 1987. *Borderlands: La Frontera*. San Francisco, CA: Aunt Lute Books.
Ondaatje, Michael. 1982. *Running in the Family*. New York: Random House / Vintage.
Sarwar, Sehba. [2004] 2019. *Black Wings*. El Paso, TX: Veliz Books.
---. 2007. "Sandstone Past." In *Neither Night nor Day: 13 Stories by Pakistani Women*, edited by Rakshanda Jalil, 119–132. New Delhi: Harper Collins India.
---. 2008. "Soot." In *And the World Changed: Contemporary Stories by Pakistani Women*, edited by Muneeza Shamsie, 252–65. New York: The Feminist Press.
---. 2012. "Reclaiming Home." Site-specific installation, *Coming Through the Gap in the Mountain on an Elephant*. Houston, TX: Texas Southern University.
---. 2015. "What Is Home?" Performance and Site-specific Installation, Baker Ripley Neighborhood Center, Houston, Texas, funded by Mid-America Arts Alliance's Artistic Innovations Grant.
---. 2016. "A Delicate Matter in the Examination Room." *The New York Times*, July 12. https://www.nytimes.com/2016/06/12/magazine/a-delicate-matter-in-the-examination-room.html
---. 2018a. "Rotation." In "Nomad" issue, ed. Sorayya Khan, of *Papercuts* 20 (Fall). http://desiwriterslounge.net/articles/papercuts-nomad-sehba-sarwar/
---. 2018b. "On Belonging." Performance and site-specific installation, commissioned by Menil Collection, Houston, Texas.
---. 2019. "Railway Track." In *Houston Noir*, edited by Gwendolyn Zepeda, 219–38. New York: Akashic Press.
Smith, Patti. 2010. *Just Kids*. New York: Bloomsbury.

The Processes of Fiction, Theatre and Life: Rajith Savanadasa in Conversation with Alexandra Watkins

Photograph of Rajith Savanadasa copyright 2021 by Rajith Savanadasa

Rajith Savanadasa was born in Sri Lanka and now lives in Melbourne. He was named a Best Young Australian Novelist by the *Sydney Morning Herald* in 2017 for *Ruins* (Savanadasa 2016), his first novel. It was shortlisted for both the Readings Prize for New Australian Fiction and the ALS Gold Medal.

Ruins is an ambitious novel, with elements of a family saga but embodying a searching exploration of relationships, ambitions and compromises, in the context of the aftermath of Sri Lankas's civil war. Rajith Savanadasa speaks in this interview of his decision to "step back [...] and let the characters speak for themselves". The narrative is structured to allow them to do just that, as four family members plus their "servant" take turns to step forward and narrate their sections of the story. The father of the household is Mano Herath—a newspaper editor possessed by unease about different aspects of his life, including his relationship with his wife Lakshmi ("There was nothing I could tell her to win back her trust"). Lakshmi herself is of Tamil heritage; "but she's just like a Sinhala person" (5) says the servant Latha to her inquisitive brother. Some of the novel's trajectory will put that simple judgement to the test. Lakshmi herself remembers how "most of [Mano's] family didn't come to our wedding" (291), and the depiction of their "mixed marriage" brings in issues of inclusion and exclusion. Their son, Niranjan, has studied in Australia and has ambitions; his tone is initially rebarbative. Anoushka is their troubled sixteen-year-old daughter, while the reflections of Latha, the orphaned servant who has known Anoushka all the teenager's life, underpin the novel from its very first words: "This family is good. That's why I work for them" (1).

Rajith's work offers significant additions to the fields of Sri Lankan diaspora fiction and refugee life writing in Australia and internationally. In this interview, which took place in central Melbourne, he reveals the progress of his literary career, from its local beginning at RMIT University, to his current projects triggered by the success of *Ruins* and *Open City Stories*, an oral history project on the lives of asylum-seekers in Melbourne. These include a creative non-fiction project, *Exposure*, and a pair of linked plays, *Another Name for Gold* and *Ordainment*, that are informed by the Sri Lankan theatrical tradition, Kolam. In this conversation with Alexandra Watkins, Rajith reflects on the literary influences that have inspired his cultural commentaries. He explores the processes of writing fiction and theatre and the frustrations that emerge when working with "big ideas". This lively discourse unearths Rajith's continued concerns about ethnic conflict in Sri Lanka, the challenges of capitalism, and the ongoing struggle for refugees in Australia, which he believes is intensified by Australia's lack of progress on asylum-seeker issues.

The interviewer, Alexandra Watkins (PhD, MEd) is a literary studies scholar and teacher who has worked at Deakin and Monash Universities in Melbourne Australia. She has published *Problematic Identities in Women's Fiction of the Sri Lankan Diaspora* (Brill, 2015). This illuminates the significance of Sri Lankan diaspora fiction by women as "political, critical and subversive [. . .] collectively concerned with the problematic of identity, especially with regard to the production of gendered identities, mourning, and psychic disturbances". Her work has also appeared in *Mediating Literary Borders: Asian Australian Writing* (Routledge, 2018), *Post-*

colonial Text, Journal of Postcolonial Writing, and *Mascara Literary Review,* and she has been a guest panellist on the Radio National "Subcontinental Bookclub Show". Alix was the first Project Manager of *Creative Lives: the Interview Series* (2017-19) in connection with her roles as the South Asian Diaspora International Researchers' Network (SADIRN) Project Assistant and Adjunct Research Fellow for the School of Languages, Literatures, Cultures and Linguistics at Monash University.

Alexandra Watkins (AW): *I am interested in your progress from the nascence of your writing career until now. Of course, I already know a bit about this, because we discussed it last year in an interview for the journal* Postcolonial Text. *At that time, you explained your writing career as "unexpected". You were close to completing a Bachelor of Engineering at RMIT and as part of this you took up a single "elective" subject in creative writing, which was allowed as part of your course. This "dalliance" was supposed to be a one-off. Then, to the shock of your parents who were expecting you to become an engineer, you made a radical shift by instead completing another RMIT course, but this time in Creative Writing. Was it really in that writing unit, when studying engineering, that you first attempted creative writing?*

Rajith Savanadasa (RS): Well, perhaps not the first attempt. I think there were little essays and things like that. My mum still pulls out things from when I was in school. There was, for instance, a letter that I had written about seeing a UFO. But still, that was about it. I never wrote a proper story, or even a short story, before starting that course.

AW: *Your first novel,* Ruins, *tells the story of a family and their servant. It explores media censorship in Sri Lanka and the persistence of class prejudice in Colombo. Was it around that time—during your creative writing course—that you first started thinking critically about the big issues that it deals with? Or was it prior to that?*

RS: I think I would have started thinking about those issues before that. The issues were already kind of there—I knew about them, but I think there was some sort of wilful blindness, a denial of the issues that were really present in that country. So, it really took getting away from Colombo and from that culture, and not being part of that culture anymore, to see it clearly. Reading has been important too. Reading Arundhati Roy (1997), for example. *The God of Small Things* caused me to reflect a bit more about my privilege and where I came from, and how that affects other people in the world.

AW: *There is an inter-racial marriage in* Ruins. *Mixed marriages are a key focus in various Sri Lankan diasporic novels. Examples include Yasmine Gooneratne's (1991)* A Change of Skies, *Karen Roberts's (2001)* July *and V.V. Ganeshananthan's (2008)* Love Marriage. *Was it a conscious decision to continue this?*

RS: I didn't think about it so much as continuing a tradition, but it was a way for me to explore the fault lines, the divides in class, generation, ethnicity, religion, gender and sexual orientation, and the tensions caused by those divides. Having the novel narrated from five first-person perspectives, with a Sinhala-Tamil marriage at the centre of it, allowed me to do that. I wanted to ask the question of who we consider family, who we choose to include and exclude, whether that definition was a narrow and harmful one.

AW: *In that sense the "servant" Latha is a key figure, isn't she?*

RS: Yes. The servant is the only narrator in the book who isn't related by blood, but also such an important part of this family. She essentially keeps the family together. She does all the work and carries a lot of emotional weight for the family, and yet she's forever marginalized. She's also the person who comes to the realization, when she visits her childhood home in the middle chapter of the book, that family is a construct. It's a thing we create; we imagine it into being, much like a country, or an ethnicity or an economy. I wanted to ask why that imagining of it needs to be so limited?

AW: *Was there a tipping point that made you think you had to write about those issues?*

RS: Not necessarily. There were points at which I wanted to write about them, but I think wanting to write about issues is counterproductive to writing a novel. I wrote two drafts of a novel before *Ruins*. They were very political, in terms of wanting to communicate a message or wanting to prove a point, and I think those drafts didn't work for that reason—because they felt overly contrived. The plot was contrived, and the characters felt contrived too.

So, I had to step back from that and let the characters speak for themselves. And it felt dangerous in a way, because there are these people who aren't me [in the novel *Ruins*] and aren't like me at all, who might be saying things or doing things that are politically inconvenient. They might falsely represent me. But I think that's something we need to be open to, to allow the complexity of life to play out because life doesn't play out in convenient ways.

AW: *Are you suggesting that people have read your characters autobiographically?*

RS: They have read characters' opinions as being mine. That's how my mother read it. Certain people read *Ruins* and commented "So you think this about us? About our country? Our people?"

AW: *That must be frustrating ... But it does raise a question about your works. Where did they begin? Was it with a character, or an idea?*

RS: I would like to say a character. Because I know that's the best place to start. But at this point I haven't been able to do that. It's one of my great failings. I start with ideas. I have all these ideas about what I want a story to be, so it's been a difficult process—stripping it back and trying to work out who it's about. And maybe, in a way, this leads me to the characters. Upon finding them, though, I always have to remind myself to set those ideas aside and let the characters lead.

AW: *So, do you experiment with many characters before you find the right ones?*

RS: Sometimes. With *Ruins*, for instance, I experimented with the character Anoushka. I tried to write the whole book from her point of view, and then had to kind of abandon the whole thing, and start again. Instead, she became part of this larger cast, which worked.

With this, similarly, I wanted to write from one person's perspective, and to keep it really contained. But once again, I feel like it might not be sustainable, so I'm looking at different ways of telling these stories. And that's part of the difficulty of it: experimenting with the form.

AW: *Do you think that the complexity of the ideas that you're dealing with demands multiple characters?*

RS: Maybe, but then at the same time, it complicates the original idea. The point of it becomes less clear. So, I start wondering, what does it mean, and does it have to mean anything? I don't think there should be a message, necessarily. But then, equally, I feel like there should be some rigor to the process; what I'm exploring has to lead me somewhere—somewhere useful.

AW: Interesting ... Would you mind outlining the concept of the plays?

RS: They're two two-handers. Each performed by the same actors. The first plays a character called Sash, a marketing executive in New York who finds out she's pregnant. She begins to imagine what the father of the child—a young man called Run, who used to be her neighbour but who she doesn't know all that well—might be like. So, in the first play the other actor plays Sash's imaginary version of Run. And the second play is from Run's perspective, with the first actor playing Run's imagination of Sash.

I sort of came to it by thinking about archetypes, and what they are to us. I mean, often we look at South Asians from a western sort of perspective, so much so it's been hard for us to imagine ourselves as anything different. I began to think of the earliest Sri Lankan archetypes and began researching the ancient form of theatre called Kolam. It's a bit like Kabuki, heavily stylized with masks and dance and music, and ends in an exorcism. I've tried to locate the Kolam archetypes in these characters, and also structured it within that tradition.

AW: I recall your saying that when writing Ruins *you followed the three-act play model. Do you think that that supported your transition into playwriting?*

RS: Yes and no. I'm discovering that playwriting's really different ... It's defined by its limitations. I didn't realize how much freedom I had as a novelist. Because you can pretty much dream up anything and write it, whereas with playwriting, you've got to be very careful about what can and can't be done. So, I'll often pitch ideas to a dramaturg and they'll just be like, "No, that's not going to work as a play. That'll make a great film or maybe a novel, but not a play".

AW: So, when did this start? This writing for theatre?

RS: It started with an email from someone at Malthouse Theatre who said, "We have this program called LIVING NOW, would you like to be a part of it?" I was always interested in visual storytelling, and I put in an application and went through the interview process. After being accepted, I got to sit in at the Malthouse and look at how plays are made. I got to see a lot of theatre, which was pretty cool.

Most of the work I did with the Malthouse was in verbatim theatre, or documentary theatre. I thought of building on the Oral History work that I did [*Open City Stories*] into a play. I tried to organize some of the asylum-seekers but none of them showed up. Instead there was a man who came to that event from Sri Lanka who used to be a photographer. I kind of became obsessed with that story and decided to turn that into the next book.

AW: *Can you tell me more about that?*

RS: During the 1970s and 1980s [1971 and 1983], there was an attempted revolution in Sri Lanka, an insurgency which was quashed by the government, and he was accused of being Janatha Vimukthi Peramuna (JVP)—part of the Marxist movement that led the insurgency. This man was thrown into a camp, where horrible things happened to him. He spent ten months in there. When he came out, he didn't want to live in Sri Lanka anymore.

He came to Australia in 2000, and spent 13 years trying to get a visa. He went through so many hearings and appeals and was denied at every turn, until finally, someone he knew made a personal appeal to a minister in government, and he got a visa.

He then managed to bring his family over whilst working at a factory making photo albums. He asks his employer, "Can I do some more work because I need money?" And they say, "Sure. You can do overtime". He does, and they start paying him overtime. But they also exploit him by having him do other things—like the boss's brother getting him to wash his car, and clean the bathrooms. And then we also found out recently that he was being paid the lowest possible rate: a probationary level rate, for about eight years. Eventually, he joined the union. He retired last year, but decided to pursue the money he was owed as back pay. The story sort of comes full circle, starting and ending with leftist movements.

AW: *It seems like you're still, with this new project, very focused on Sri Lankan politics, even though you're saying that you can't necessarily embed all of the elements that you might like to explore?*

RS: Well ... One of the big obstacles is that this man doesn't want to talk about a particular incident at all. It means we have to exclude all of his working life in Sri Lanka, which was all very interesting.

AW: *Which is not necessarily uncommon. I mean, I have met people like that, Sri Lankan immigrants who were my neighbours and whom I knew fairly well. I asked them what it was like to live through the Sri Lankan Civil War. "Oh, we don't talk about that", they said. End of conversation. So, I guess it's a coping mechanism. But still, it's fascinating with regard to your photographer who knows that you're writing about him.*

RS: I think he's really interested in the process, and he wants to be a part of it. At first, he was like, "Okay", and then the next time I met him, he said, "My wife doesn't want me to talk about this at all". Which is fair. He says, "I've got kids". So, I don't know what the repercussions might be for him.

AW: *Do you think that this is a product of what's happened in the past? I mean, you've spoken about censorship in Sri Lanka, do you think more generally that Sri Lankan refugees in Australia still sense that need to protect themselves?*

RS: Absolutely. This guy also points out how the people who were in power back then are still in power, in Sri Lanka. When I asked him about the government, suggesting that things may have changed, and that it's possibly safer now, he disagrees. He names names, saying, "This person's still a minister. This person's still around. And these are the guys who did X, Y, and Z". And although the things that he mentions are kind of contested now, and not considered facts by the general public, they are facts to him. For instance, there are rumours that certain individuals ordered the torture of various people. He was exposed to torture, and the effects of torture, in that camp so that's worrying for him.

AW: *When we last spoke, you were saying that there is less media censorship in Sri Lanka now than is depicted in* Ruins. *Are you still of this opinion?*

RS: It's less of an issue than in wartime, but the current government is the same one that was there during the war. They've returned to power and I have no faith in our media institutions' ability to stand up to them. That's exacerbated by the fact most Sri Lankans don't like to talk about the things that make them uncomfortable, the root causes of the war, of what transpired between the Sinhalese and the Tamil people. I suppose it's like most people—like Americans don't like to talk about slavery and its continued effects on African Americans today, or like Australians don't want to talk about the Stolen Generations or how Indigenous people were, and still are, worse off than everyone else in this country.

AW: *Do you think that there's a sense that people want to move on?*

RS: Yes. People think that all of that is in the past, and that we don't really need to dig that all up because we're fine now, we're all happy. Even my parents are like that. "Why do you want to talk about this?" they say.

AW: *But you think there is still a strong need to talk about it?*

RS: Absolutely. Yes, because there are still things going on now that are reminiscent of horrible things that happened in the past, days when you kind of go, "Oh, this sounds like what happened 20 years ago, or 30 years ago". And if we haven't learned from it, maybe we should talk about it some more.

AW: *Yes. And of course, these problems, these injustices, they're bigger than Sri Lanka. Look at the ongoing refugee crisis, it's a global problem, and western nations, including Australia, really need to care. Last time we spoke, you mentioned your work with the Darebin Council. They were representing local refugees and in doing so contesting the Australian Government's refugee policy.*

RS: I was working with the Darebin Council. In fact, it was through the Darebin Council that I met this guy who I'm writing about, so I'm still sort of connected to it through the people that I used to work with. But apart from meeting refugees and talking to them, I don't think I did much for the Council. They're still working to help refugees, of course. But with the way the government's handling immigration, I don't think there's been much progress on asylum-seeker issues.

AW: *Are there any ongoing issues for Sri Lankan asylum-seekers that you know of?*

RS: Well. To be honest, I don't think the Australian government sees nuance, in terms of Sri Lankan asylum-seekers or other asylum-seekers. They just see the asylum-seekers as a kind of ...

AW: *Homogeneous whole?*

RS: Yes, which is the crux of the problem. And I think that's partly why I'm talking about the specificity of a Sri Lankan. I think every case has to be handled on its own terms. And that we need to take a long-term view of the immigration / asylum experience.

What's interesting about this particular guy [the one the book's about] is that he's been in Australia for a long time now, since 2000. That is almost 18 years, and yet he still doesn't feel entirely accepted and that's reflected in his workplace. This really makes me wonder what it takes for someone to feel at home, or to feel accepted, and to become part of a community.

AW: *And what do you think? What does it take to be accepted? From a personal point of view?*

RS: Well, the more I see, the more I think the idea of assimilation is a myth. I don't think you can really assimilate, especially when considering a person like the man I'm writing about. He's at an age where he can't really change too much anymore.

I think it's easier for people who travel at a younger age and who have more time, more energy to learn a language, to speak a certain way, to dress a certain way. I've been here 20 years; I have friends who've been here all their lives but don't look "Australian". We still get asked "Where are you from", or "How come you speak such good English?" This particular guy was in his 40s or 50s, and he had to work for his family, and, in that context, there isn't really any time to develop any other sort of cultural capital that kind of brings you a bit more acceptance.

AW: *Could it be dependent on attitude? I ask this because of my personal family experience. My dad's family were migrants. They arrived in 1958 and my granddad was really excited to have an adventure and come to Australia. But my nanna was different. She mourned England for 30 years until she went back there and realized that that wasn't home either.*

I've noticed this dyad in diaspora fiction from a variety of origins. So, I think it's fairly universal. Certain characters flourish regardless, while others really struggle to get through. Could it be that some people are more adaptable than others, and as such that this is reflected in the genre?

RS: Perhaps. That might be true. But then, I think it begs the question, does one have to have a good attitude to find acceptance? And, also, what's the process of acceptance? In the play, I explore this from a cultural perspective. *Ordainment* starts with when a character realizes the T-shirt he's wearing, while it was OK over in Sri Lanka, is not cool over here. So, he buys new shoes in an attempt to change. And that's partly a critique of capitalism—how as a consumer, you're told to have certain things to be happy, or to be part of something. But it doesn't actually buy you happiness or acceptance.

AW: *Of course, you have mentioned in the past that this is an issue for certain groups in Sri Lanka. In fact, it is something that you critiqued throughout* Ruins: *commodity fetishism as iconized by the iPod. Do you think that this kind of pressure is as pronounced in Australia?*

RS: I think so. It might not be as marked, and it might not be as overt, but I think the pressure is still there. It's a bit like how we divide people in Melbourne as north of the river, or south of the river types. We pretend it's about an aesthetic or about a sub-culture, but there's a class consciousness in the mix too. It might be subtler than in Sri Lanka, where someone might say "That guy doesn't drive a Benz", or something like that. But I think it's still there. It's present.

AW: *And in your own world, do you find that personal pressure to, I suppose, "keep up with the Joneses"?*

RS: In some respects. Like recently, I've felt the pressure to buy a house. And not just a house but in the right suburb, a certain kind of house. I have to stop myself and go, is that what I really want? I find myself pushed in a certain direction. And it's hard to articulate because, once again, it's not an overt pressure, it's subtle. The subtle little nudges coming at you from different directions, from advertising, from people, the idea slowly pushed at you that you should be owning a house at your age, and that you need stability. The guilt that you're throwing your money on a rental property that you're not going to own in the end. It's no less powerful than your mother telling you to buy a house.

AW: *And, in the face of this, are you comfortable with where you are as a writer?*

RS: Probably not. I mean, I'm pretty comfortable with where I am in life, but I also always feel I haven't done enough or am not good enough to do what I want to do. I'm still uncomfortable in my art, and I think that's fine. I'm OK with that discomfort.

AW: *Absolutely. It also seems exciting, and the fact that you've got two projects on the go is very impressive.*

RS: Thank you. It's a bit crazy, too, with the limited time that I have, but I think they complement each other. I feel like one informs the other. So, it might take longer to complete them. But that's okay.

AW: *I wish you the very best with them both. Thank you so much for meeting me today. I look forward to the new work!*

RS: Thank you.

Bibliography

Gooneratne, Yasmine. 1991. *A Change of Skies*. Sydney: Picador Australia.
Roberts. Karen. 2001. *July*. London: Weidenfeld and Nicholson.
Ganeshananthan, V.V. 2008. *Love Marriage*. New York: Random House.
Roy, Arundhati. 1997. *The God of Small Things*. New York: Random House.
Savanadasa, Rajith. 2016. *Ruins*. Sydney: Hachette Australia.

Where Politics and Climate Meet:
Sungchuk Kyi in Conversation with Ruth Gamble

Photograph of Sungchuck Kyi by Yankho Gyal

I had been hearing about Sungchuk Kyi and her poetry for nearly two decades before I finally met her. As I moved through the spaces of the exile Tibetan community in South Asia, Europe, and Australia, I heard snippets of her poems in cafes and caught glimpses of her image on books and blogs. People read her poems quietly, often to each other, with breaking voices. The raw emotions the poems elicited were breathtaking and heartbreaking. I heard them again in her homeland, near the vast Blue Lake, Tso Ngön (Qinghai), in Amdo, Eastern Tibet, within the People's Republic of China (PRC). People whispered lines to me and talked about her absence, how she and her poems had disappeared, gone into exile. She had been a rising star as a poet, and it means a lot to be a poet in Amdo, but she fled into exile after her husband got into political trouble. The people in Amdo said that they had heard she was selling bread on the street in India. They did not know any bread sellers in India, but I did. On my next trip to Tibetan settlements in India, I scanned the bread sellers, looking for Sungchuk Kyi.

As the people in Amdo spoke of Sungchuk Kyi, their sadness at the loss of their poet merged with the overwhelming loss her poems describe. They would also talk of old threats like occupation, dispossession, religious restrictions, disappearing languages, jailed friends, malfunctioning communities, and newer threats like intensive resource extraction, surveillance, and climate change. Without self-determination, the Tibetan people are continually negotiating an onslaught of modernity planned for them elsewhere, without much allowance for input from them. Bureaucrats in Beijing and local capitals decided the Tibetans' traditional lives as herders and farmers were no longer viable, and forced them into government-built settlements. These are often isolated suburbs built in the middle of grass plains. They are highly surveilled and, according to most reports, their inhabitants are struggling with increased social disfunction (Ptackova 2011). This social change is happening at the same time that the Tibetan Plateau—with average altitudes more than 3000 meters above sea level—experiences some of the earliest and worst impacts of climate change. Global warming is occurring there at over twice the average global rate, and as the snow melts and the flow of the rivers changes, the Tibetans' home is transforming around them (Ji and Yuan 2020). Instead of listening to and being directed by the herders' knowledge of these places, the Chinese government has opted for technocratic planning. This approach prioritizes hydropower dams and fortress conservation, transforming the Tibetans' waterways and locking them out of their land to preserve its biodiversity for tourists to see (Nyima 2014).

While reflecting on this loss, Sungchuk Kyi's poems are also acts of resistance against it. They evoke the sights, sounds, smells, and sensations of long-remembered families and lost lands: the grasslands' smell in summer, and of yak-dung stoves in winter. For those in Amdo, they speak of other times and increasingly rare family gatherings, evoking different ways of seeing outside the state's pervasive influence. In exile from Tibet, people immerse themselves in her poems. As their bodies sit in cafes on busy Indian and Nepali streets, their minds travel with the poems to far-away grasslands.

Perhaps because of the joy they were bringing people, Sungchuk Kyi's poems kept appearing despite her journey into exile. News and pain flow in waves from Tibet into exile and back onto the Plateau again. In Tibetan settlements in exile, the pain sometimes becomes quiet, humming along under the surface, marked by the Dalai Lama's ubiquitous image, anniversaries, Tibetan religious and resistance songs, and the Tibetan national flags draped out of windows. At other times, when there is news of a fresh tragedy, people weep in the streets and scream with protest, assimilating the latest horror.

In the early 2010s, when Tibetans inside Tibet began their most desperate act of protest against Chinese rule, self-immolation, there was a dense mood of sadness and solidarity in these exile settlements. Sungchuk Kyi, reacting to this sadness, wrote a poem that caught this mood. Its title was "I Will Burn Myself Again and Again". Even more so than her other poems, it was passed around the community, handed out in local newspapers, sent from phone to phone. Once translated into English by another exiled Tibetan poet, Om Gangthik, it even garnered her an international audience. Those writing about the immolations quoted it (Norbu 2012; Vajpeyi et al. 2013; Sarin and Sonam 2016), hoping to understand the levels of devastation and community that would encourage such acts.

All through this time, I would ask people if they knew Sungchuk Kyi and what they thought of her poems. I heard that she had won a grant to study Tibetan folklore and no longer needed to sell bread. I then heard that she had moved to the west as a refugee. I imagined her on the streets of a large American or European city, where an established Tibetan community would gather to hear recitations of her poems. I translated some of her poems and gave a talk on them, undoing my professional veneer by crying as I read them. I asked people if they knew where she had gone. Eventually, I told my friend Chung Tsering that I had translated some more of her poems and needed to get in touch with her. "Why don't you drop over for tea?" he said. "She lives in Melbourne, in a suburb called Narre Warren". "Wait, what?" I replied, confused. My decade-long search for Sungchuk Kyi was going to end in the outer-Melbourne suburb of Narre Warren? How did that happen?

In 2020, Sungchuk Kyi and I had two conversations about her life—one over Skype (it was 2020 in Melbourne, after all) and another in person. She and her daughter Nyenngak Tso made my daughter and me momo dumplings. She talked about her unlikely journey from the grasslands of Tibet through India to Melbourne's suburbs, the continuing political struggles of her people for self-determination, the threat of cultural extinction and climate change, and how she is adjusting to life in her new home.¹ What follows here are extracts from these interviews, interspersed with translations of two of her best-known poems, "I Will Burn Myself Again and Again", and the poem about environmental destruction, "Lament for a Great Earth". The poems reflect the experiences she talks about in the interview.

Ruth Gamble

The interviewer, Ruth Gamble (PhD) is a lecturer in history and the environmental humanities at La Trobe University, Melbourne, Australia. She is the author of two books on Tibetan history, *Reincarnation in Tibetan Buddhism: The Invention of a Tradition* (Oxford University Press, 2018) and *The Third Karmapa, Master of Mahamudra* (Shambhala, 2020). Her forthcoming third book, *Tears of the Gods, Life, Death and Rebirth on the Banks of the Yarlung Tsangpo River*, is an environmental and cultural history of Tibet's longest river. She has also co-written a Tibetan language textbook series, *An Introduction to the Tibetan Language: An ETextbook Part 1, 2 and 3* (Canberra: ANU EPress, 2018), and articles on Himalayan environmental history, religion and ecology, and political ecology that have appeared in *Bulletin of the School of African and Oriental Studies, GeoHumanities, Australian Journal of International Affairs* and *Cahiers d'Exteme Asie*. Her overview of Tibetan water politics was recently included by Gallimard (Paris) as part of the *Penser en Chine* series. She has written for several international media outlets, including *The Quint* and *The Press*, appeared on Radio National's *Breakfast, Future Tense* and *Big Ideas* programs in Australia, and has been a fellow of Yale University's Forestry and Environment School, and the Numata Program at the University of Toronto.

From the Grasslands to Melbourne

Ruth Gamble (RG): *Sungchuk, can you introduce yourself and tell us where you were born?*

Sungchuk Kyi (SK): My name is Sungchuk Kyi. That is what people call me. The place I was born is called Tso Ngön, Qinghai in Chinese. The name means Blue Lake.² I was born in an area called Mangdzong to a nomadic family. That's near the town called Chabcha. We lived in tents until I was

---

1 The interview was conducted in Tibetan and translated by the author.
2 The contemporary Chinese province Qinghai covers about three-quarters of the land that the Tibetans know as Amdo.

about ten years old. When I was born, I was called Wangmo Drölma, but I became ill when I was young, so I was given a new name. This is a Tibetan tradition. If a child gets sick when they are young, we change their name. So, my name was changed to Sungchuk Kyi, and I stopped getting sick.

RG: What was home like?

SK: There were large grass plains everywhere. Most of the people there were herders, nomads. There were a few farmers, but most of our community were herders. We lived in tents. We had herds of yak, sheep, goats. I remember it very vividly. We had to look after the yak; we call them "wealth" or "jewel" in Tibetan (*nor*). They gave us so much. They gave us milk, meat, butter, and cheese. We also got the material for our tents and clothes from the yak and goats and sheep. Everything we had, we got from the animals. They were critical.

I was born in a tent, and my whole family lived in a tent. They were black tents made out of yak wool. Nomads don't use those tents anymore when they go herding. They use white canvas tents. But those older ones were amazing. It didn't matter how much rain we had or how hard the storms blew; the tent would keep us warm and dry.

We had to move pastures between winter and summer because the yak don't like the heat. We had to take them up to higher pastures in summer. We would pack up our tent and move to the summer or winter pastures.

I lived in our tent until I was about 14 or 15. Then we had to move into a house. We weren't forced to move into a house, but we were given a parcel of land, and we weren't allowed to follow the herd anymore. Instead of sharing the land, we had to live on a little bit of land. So, there was no point staying in a tent.

RG: Was it at this time that you went to school?

SK: Yes. Before that, I had not been to school, but I had studied Tibetan and Tibetan literature at home. My family told stories. They loved stories. My uncle was a wonderful storyteller. In Tibet, we have an epic, many volumes long, called *The Epic of Gesar*. When I was young, my uncle taught me that story. He and his friend taught me the entire Gesar story. When they first came, the Chinese government banned the telling of the Gesar epic. They got rid of it. They said that it was religion. They said we could not recite it.

But then, when I was young, they decided that we were allowed to tell the story and read about it again. They even allowed it to be re-published in a series of books. My uncle bought it and read us the entire thing. Young people and elders, we all gathered around to listen to the adventures of Gesar. I was so happy. The elders loved it.

RG: *What was so appealing about the Gesar epic?*

SK: Gesar is amazing because it has both stories and culture in it. It transmits our culture to us through the stories. It is right there in the story. People talk, they exchange ideas as the story progresses, and you learn with them. Reading Gesar made me love the Tibetan language. And that made me want to study Tibetan. My grandad told me that he thought it was a good idea to study reading and writing. He did not know how to read and write. My uncle did, and my brother was literate. I used to pick up books and try to read them even though I didn't know how to read.

There were Chinese schools for young children, and people sometimes went to study at them, but I didn't go to one of the schools for very young children. I was a small girl from a nomad family, so there was no discussion about my attending school. When I got older, then they sent me to school. There, I learnt mainly Chinese. By that stage, the others who went to school had already taught me how to read and write Tibetan. After Gesar, I started reading love stories. I liked those stories. My grandmother liked them too. There are heaps of love stories in Amdo's literary traditions. Oh, and I read histories. So, I didn't learn from school. I learnt a lot more from reading those books and even more from my elders.

RG: *Did you have ambitions to be a writer at this stage?*

SK: People said that I liked books and stories so much that I would be a writer. I started writing poems. People liked them. I was a bit surprised. But it also made me happy. I wrote my first book of poetry before I left Amdo. It was called *Churu's Destiny* (Gzungs phyug skyid 1999). I also published my poems in magazines and poetry anthologies. I had a friend who taught at the university in Xining (Qinghai's capital city). She liked my poems and other writing and used to talk about them to people. Then other influential people started reciting my poems.

RG: *And what were your poems about at that stage?*

SK: Lots of things. One of them was praise to a goddess, Yangchen, the goddess of poetry. Others were about the environment and how our culture intertwines with it.

RG: Why did you leave home for exile in India?

SK: Everyone was going. It was hard being in Tibet. The Dalai Lama was in India. My husband wanted to go. He had been a political prisoner for a while. We did not want to live under Chinese government rule anymore. It was 2002. My husband, my young daughter and I left home and started travelling toward India. We had another friend come with us as well. All four of us travelled to India. It is a very long way. My husband was still a teacher despite being in trouble, and that meant that we could get permission to travel to Lhasa (the capital of the Tibetan Autonomous Region) by train. From Lhasa, we travelled down to Drum, a town on the Nepali border. Decades ago, when Tibetans crossed into exile, they could walk across the border at Drum. But by the time we got there, it was closed off. We needed help sneaking across the border. We had to give money to the people who guided us across the border. We had to give quite a few people money in order to leave Tibet. We had to give people money to look the other way and show us where to go. The Nepali people from the border region knew how to get across the border. When we gave them money, they guided us across. We had to walk through the mountains to get there, through the Nepali forests. There were so many bugs! So many bugs! Some of them were so big they were the size of my finger! I was terrified.

When we got to India, it was good. I travelled to Dharamsala, where the Dalai Lama lives. There is a large Tibetan community there. We got to meet the Dalai Lama when we arrived in India. The Tibetans in India helped us. It was difficult at the start, but it got better. We lived in India for 13 years. My son was born there. We were there for a long time, but it was never home.

RG: And you continued to write in India?

SK: When I arrived in Dharamsala, I wrote the story of my journey from home to India in a memoir interspersed with poems. This book was called *Lament for a Great Land* (Gzungs phyug skyid 2006). I was in India for quite a while and published another book of poetry and writing called *The*

Grave (Gzungs phyug skyid 2007). I also had a blog for a while that I would publish on.[3]

RG: *Then you travelled to Australia ...*

SK: While we were in India, we heard about a program through which the Australian government and the Tibetan Government in Exile brought Tibetan ex-political prisoners to Australia to live. If you had been a political prisoner like my husband, you could apply for the lottery to come. They have a lottery (in the refugee community in India) each year, in which they pick people's names out of a hat. If your name comes out of the hat, you get to go and live in Australia. In 2014, they picked out our names. And we could come to Australia.

It wasn't harder coming to Australia than travelling to India. We had already left home. It is hard getting around, but it is OK. I have been writing since I arrived in Australia, but I haven't been published that much in books since I arrived. It seems as though using social media means that my poems get out to a broader audience than through conventional publishing. They get shared from one person to the next across the internet. It's very efficient.

****

When Politics Isn't a Choice: Being Tibetan

RG: *After an unsuccessful uprising in 2008 (see Barnett 2009), simmering tensions among Tibetans within the PRC, combined with harsh restrictions against protest and dissent, led to a series of self-immolations. By July 2020, at least 156 people had self-immolated as a form of protest in Tibet. The majority of these self-immolations were performed in your home region, Amdo. They were seen as desperate acts of protest by people who were still committed to the principles of non-violence. There was a heated debate among Tibetans, between Tibetans and representatives of the PRC state, and more broadly, about the ethics and efficacy of these actions.*

---

3   http://sungchuk-kyi.blogspot.com/

It is clear that, among the Tibetan community in exile, news of the self-immolations was met with waves of sorrow and support. This combination of emotions was the primary subject of your best-known poem, "I Will Burn Myself Again and Again", which you wrote in early 2011 as the number of self-immolations increased. After Om Gangthik translated the poem, I gather that members of the Tibetan community began using it as an explanation for the immolations when they talked to international supporters. If you want to understand how we feel, they would say, read Sungchuk Kyi's poem.

I did not find reading your poem easy. It is visceral. It layers the pain of mourning onto the pain of dispossession and cultural, environmental, political and social loss. But, as suggested by the Tibetans who used your poem to explain their feelings, reading it also provides a window into the community's reasons for immolating and its support of the immolators.

Yet your poems are not directly about politics. They don't discuss political theory or anything. But they are political. You talk about people self-immolating. You talk about the situation in Tibet. Do you write about politics or feelings or to inspire others?

SK: I write about my feelings, experiences. But my feelings reflect what is happening in Tibet. We are made political by the events that occur there. So, for example, when I wrote about self-immolations, I wrote what I felt. I was in Dharamsala at that time. There are many Tibetans there. When we began to get word of the immolations, we were all distraught. I cried and cried. Others cried and cried. One of the people that immolated herself was a mother with kids. I'm a mother. The thought was horrifying. Other people were crying. People saw the photos of them and cried. They just cried. Others were praying. Both the immolations and the outpouring of grief seemed to last a long time. My poem "I Will Burn Myself Again and Again" was a response to that pain. It was my experience. It was not particularly political in intent, but it became so when it was written.

I Will Burn Myself Again and Again

Is my grassland still green? Are my blue lakes still crystal clear? Do my mountain rivers still sing their songs?
Eyes of the great gods, do you see them?

Can all the bloody crimes of the world be burned and transformed by
the heat of a fire?
Who is sucking the blood and marrow from my body?
Who is erasing the bloody images on my chest?
Who dug up and desecrated my father's grave right before my eyes?
Who cut the life force from my mother tongue?
While I am still listening?
How can I bear this? My mind cannot lift this body.
My heart can no longer endure the pain from this wound.
Why am I tortured like this?

Yesterday, I was amidst dreams the bandits destroyed my ancestral home.
Today, in front of me, my mother is stripped naked.
Tomorrow, my children's brains and bones will be scattered in the sky.
I cannot take this anymore.

I think, I feel, and then this becomes the path of my dreams.

Today, just like that, I will burn without regret.
My mind ignites (my body) like a magnificent butter lamp.
It is like an offering bowl, one I want to sacrifice.
Brothers and sisters, you will live in my heart forever.
Gods and goddesses light up my conviction, my faith.
Mountains and rivers, your splendour is in my heart.
As my consciousness rises higher, I leave you all behind.
As I leave, my aspirations nurture everything.

From now on,
Let me, alone, take a thousand guns' bullets.
Let me, alone, bear the endless tortures and beatings.
Let me, alone, take all your accusations and orders.

Previously, I gave you a responsibility that I should have taken.
From now on, I offer you my precious life continuously.
From now on, take care of my lineage's traditions and heritage
Take care of my homeland and its environment.
Respect the life in my mother tongue.
And, above all, give my beloved brothers and sisters freedom!

This is my last message, written in blood.
These are my reasons, my wishes. They are why I burn myself,
again and again.
They must happen!

The power of the gods who dwell in love and faith,
And the thoughts of all the world's living humans,
Are in solidarity with what I did yesterday.
Bear witness to what is happening now.
Show support for my family tomorrow.
This is the way I travel the path of light.
This is the way I burn in the sad face of my reality.

For my brothers and sisters who live in sorrow and misery,
For the people of the world who live in peace and freedom,
For the tyrannical authorities who prefer torture and suppression,
All I want is lasting peace and freedom.
I search for a life of equity and fairness.
Until I get it, I will burn myself again and again.[4]

****

Climate Change: Losing Home Again

RG: *In your poetry, you frequently talk about the environment in Tibet. What changes have occurred in your homeland that made you focus on the environment in this way?*

SK: There have been so many changes, so many. When I was a kid, it was one way, and now it has changed completely. In our culture—when I say culture, I mean the way that people think—we are close to the environment. In our songs, in our stories, in our traditions, there are mountains, there is water. And all the gods and spirits that live in these places all come into the stories. Through all of these songs and stories, we are told how to relate to the environment. Don't throw things in the water. Don't use fire indiscriminately. Don't throw things into the air indiscriminately. It is not OK.

Our understanding of the water, for example, is that there are spirits in the water. We call them *lu*.[5] You do not throw anything into springs or damp places because you do not want to upset the *lu*. And the

---

4   This translation is adapted from the work of Om Gangthik, another outstanding Tibetan poet, whose work is available at https://gangthik.wordpress.com/.
5   Tib. *glu*. *Glu* are often linked to *nāga*, which are prominent in South Asian traditions.

mountains are the homes of deities, so we don't dig into the mountains. We treat the mountains with respect. There is a real connection between the environment and the culture, that brings us relaxation and comfort.

But in the last few decades, there have been a lot of changes. The government made it so that everyone had to move onto smaller blocks of land. In the past, we used to share all the land. We all used the same land and rotated our animals across large areas. And then, after the Chinese government came, they took charge. They began separating us into little sections of land. We had to lease our land (from the government) from that point onwards. We had to put up fences between us, and we were only allowed to run our animals on our own land. Each family was given a plot of land. This was your land, and that was their land. Some people were lucky. They were given land that had minerals beneath it. They got more money for that. But others did not even have access to water. Then they went even further and tried to get all the Tibetans to move into houses.

RG: *Were people also worried about the climate changing?*

SK: When I was young, it had already started changing slightly. Now it is much worse. I have not seen the worst of it recently because I have been here, but everyone tells me how bad it is getting. I used to get messages about family and government issues. Now everyone at home sends me messages about the changing climate. They say that the earth and the water are different from what they used to be.

The thing that started going first was the water. When I was a kid, we noticed that the water was decreasing—that there was less and less water. Everything was drying out. I saw it, and the old people would say, "It used to be that the water came up through a spring here and there". And you know how Tibetans are. We said that it was something to do with the gods. That the gods and the spirits had been offended, so they had stopped producing the water. When I was young, there was one very wet place, but it just disappeared by the time I was 15. The water went black, and the frogs that lived there all died. Hundreds of frogs just floated to the top of the water. The elders said that the *lu* were upset. They said that the government had made all the springs and waterways dirty, so the *lu* had retaliated.

RG: *Is this what you mean when you say your culture and nature are blended?*

SK: They are the same thing. One doesn't exist without the other.

RG: So, would you say that your poetry has a specific environmental focus? Or was your experience just environmental, so that is what you write about?

SK: That's it. It was my experience. I experienced nature. When you live in a house, it's a bit different. Nature is outside the window. You are at a remove from it. But I grew up in tents and spent my time outside, most of my time out there. I lived in nature. Everything was there, the sun, the rain, the snow, the sun, the moon. Everything seems massive out there. The sky is enormous. The mountains are massive. There are always birds. I lived with birds. I miss home. I miss the place in which I grew up. I miss the place, and I miss the elders. I don't miss the young people that much, to be honest. I miss the elders. We used to have such a good relationship. I loved their stories. We used to do so much together. I loved them. Their way of thinking was sound. And if you think about it, the environment was "front of mind" for them. Their relationship to the earth was something special. They were something special. They had a lightness of spirit. They didn't have all of those tensions in their mind. They were just hanging out.

I miss the environment. I mean, it is nice here, but it is not like home. But then, if I went home, home would not be the same. It's changed.

****

Poem Two: The Earth's Lament

RG: As for many Indigenous people, the Tibetans' connection to their land is a distinct part of their identity. Their disconnection from this land shows through in your poetry. In your more recent poems, however, written since you came to Australia, you have begun to link your homeland's destruction to larger environmental issues that are unfolding worldwide. In these songs, you combine your experience as an Indigenous person with that of a refugee. In one of the most powerful of these songs, "A Great Earth's Lament", you speak from the earth's perspective, scared about how it is being perceived. The perspective is, in some ways, quite gendered. In some of your other works, you address the difficulties of being a woman within an already marginalized group and the labour required.[6] Here, however, you

---

6   For an insightful study of gender relations in Amdo, see Makley (2007).

represent the earth as an objectified and overworked mother, begging those draining her life force to understand what they are doing. Should we end with this poem?

A Great Earth's Lament

Wayé! You! What are you doing? Do you need to disembowel me?
Do you want to cast my insides to the wind?
You are not swords or arrows, but you split apart my body.
You are not bandits or thieves, but you steal my body's vitality.

Really! What evil have I done?
It was my youthful fertility that produced civilisations,
Provided a future for human nations.
Why then do you humans neglect me?

My lifeblood nurtured countless plants and beings,
My dear children,
And you have smashed them.
In anger, you even pluck out (my grass, my trees) my body hairs. Why?

Is living like this my karma, or is it just a trick of the times? I am afraid.
Everyone stares at me with their eyes and mouths open.
They want to consume my abundance, my vitality.
My flesh is on fire. Can you smell it burning? Can you smell the fat sizzling?

You! You turn my precious guts inside out.
You take out the parts of me prized for their gold and silver
and scatter them.
You have inflicted such pain on my body, and yet it still heaves
with more treasures.
How do I cope with what's to come?

Heavens look at me!
My lifeblood moves through each one of my golden sand grains.
I'm here for the happiness, sadness, the lives of all wanderers,
everyone under the sky.
How did I provoke such hostility?

My outer husk, my green, grassy plains, have become deserts.
My moist insides are brimming with toxins.
Kye Hu! What is this unbearable torture?
How do I bear your unbearable beatings?

It shouldn't be like this!
When my life supports collapse, they block my blood flow.
I am this world, this vessel. I hold many beings within me.
How will I nurture them all now?

I'm begging you.
Right now, I cannot maintain my life supports. I cannot sustain my breath.
If you want your expected long lives, then let me rest and recuperate.
Please, let me sing my lament.

And you, earth's evil vandals, will you hear it?[7]

Bibliography

Barnett, Robert. 2009. "The Tibet Protests of Spring, 2008: Conflict Between the Nation and the State." *China Perspectives* 3: 6–23.

Gzungs phyug skyid. 1999. *Pyu ru'i las dbang* [Churu's Destiny]. Chabcha: Zhang kang then ma'i dpe skrun kung.

---. 2006. *Sa chen gyi smre ngag* [Lament for a Great Land]. Dharamsala: Shes bya kun 'dus rtsom sgris lhe gnas.

---. 2007. *Bang so* [The Grave]. Dharamsala: Shes bya kun 'dus rtsom sgris lhe gnas.

Ji, P. and X. Yuan. 2020. "Underestimation of the Warming Trend over the Tibetan Plateau during 1998–2013 by Global Land Data Assimilation Systems and Atmospheric Reanalyses." *Journal of Meteorological Research* 34 (1): 88–100.

Makley, Charlene. 2007. *The Violence of Liberation: Gender and Tibetan Buddhist Revival in Post-Mao China*. Berkeley, CA: University of California Press.

Norbu, Jamyang. 2012. "I Will Burn Myself Again and Again." *Shadow Tibet*, March 27.

Nyima, Tashi. 2014. "In the Name of Conservation and Harmonious Development: The Separation of Pastoralists from Pastures in Tibet." In *On the Fringes of the Harmonious Society: Tibetans and Uyghurs in Socialist China*, edited by Trine Brox and Ildikó Bellér-Hann, 127–158. Copenhagen: Nias Press.

Ptackova, J. 2011. "Sedentarisation of Tibetan Nomads in China: Implementation of the Nomadic Settlement Project in the Tibetan Amdo Area: Qinghai and Sichuan Provinces." *Pastoralism: Research, Policy and Practice* 1 (1): 1–11.

Sarin, Ritu, and Tenzing Sonam. 2016. "I Will Burn Myself Again and Again: Notes on the Self-immolations in Tibet." *Hearings: The Online Journal of Contour Biennale*, Nov. 30. http://hearings.contour8.be/2016/11/30/i-will-burn-myself-again-and-again-notes-on-the-self-immolations-in-tibet/.

Vajpeyi, Ananya, et al., eds. 2013. "Special Issue: Tibet Burning." *Seminar* 664 (April). New Delhi.

---

7   Translated by Ruth Gamble with assistance from Chung Tsering.

Places and Proximities:
Samrat Upadhyay in Conversation with Prakash Subedi

Photograph of Samrat Upadhyay by permission of Samrat Upadhyay

Samrat Upadhyay's (2001) first book, the collection of nine stories *Arresting God in Kathmandu*, which was also the first work of fiction by a Nepali writer to be published in the west, garnered praise for a fresh and promising new voice as well as criticism, especially from some Nepali readers, for its not-so-glorious portrayal of the country.

The majority of the stories in this collection are set in Kathmandu, and while the Pashupatinath Hindu Temple complex, the Royal Palace, Asan market and Gokarna Forest Resort are referenced, it eschews exoticism, focusing instead on matters of desire, love, family, marriage, class and modernization. Richard Bernstein (2001), in his favourable *New York Times* review of stories that he found "subtle and spiritually complex", seemed almost surprised to discover that:

> Katmandu [sic] seems almost local in Mr. Upadhyay's stories,
> full of middle-class people worried about what their neighbors
> will think, dreaming about sex, getting tired of their wives or

husbands, struggling against illicit desire. This book reminds us that there is truly no place to hide from the temptations of cosmopolitanism, from globalized culture or from the universal human condition. (37)

Arresting God in Kathmandu attracted considerable attention in Nepal and internationally—so much so that Upadhyay remarks in this interview that "many of my readers identify me with that book only". Since then, however, he has published three novels, *The Guru of Love* (Upadhyay 2003), *Buddha's Orphans* (Upadhyay 2010), and *The City Son* (Upadhyay 2014), two collections of stories, *The Royal Ghosts* (Upadhyay 2006), and *Mad Country* (Upadhyay 2017), and a number of essays. His early works such as *Arresting* and *The Guru of Love*, as Upadhyay comments in the course of this interview, follow the "conventional story structure of conflict-crisis-resolution", and can be broadly categorized as being closer to social realism. In his later works, starting with *The City Son* (with its startling portrayal of the abusive and quasi-incestuous revenge wrought by the character Didi) and even more boldly with his latest collection of short stories, *Mad Country*, he experiments extensively with elements of magic realism, dark humour, and tragic irony. He also draws on bleaker political themes. *Mad Country* explores the themes of identity and nationality in a number of original and disturbing ways. In the title story, Nepali businesswoman Anamika finds herself held in detention after approaching the police to enquire about her son, while well-to-do, youthful Ramesh in "Beggar Boy" assumes the identity and clothes of a poor beggar to satisfy his fascination with the lives of the underprivileged.

Upadhyay's works tell the stories of common people caught up in the mesh of personal and social convolutions of a country that has seen a series of social and political upheavals during the last three decades. He is adept at digging out extraordinary moments from otherwise ordinary lives, and recounting them to his readers in a lucid and playful prose.

Samrat Upadhyay is a professor of creative writing at Indiana University, and lives in Bloomington, Indiana. In this interview carried out by email in October–December 2020, he shares with Prakash Subedi his work habits, publishing experience, literary influences, and future plans.

The interviewer, Prakash Subedi, is a Nepali academic, writer, and translator. He has published two volumes of poetry, two co-edited collection of essays on Ibsen in performance, and a number of essays, and works of translation. He has served as an editor to the journals *Of Nepalese Clay*,

Literary Studies, and *Devkota Studies*. He is currently working on a PhD in Literary and Cultural Studies at Monash University, Melbourne, with a focus on the narrative of nation / nationalism in Nepali literature.

Prakash Subedi [PS]: It's been almost two decades since the publication of your first book, Arresting God in Kathmandu, in 2001. Reflecting on your writing over the years, how has your work evolved in terms of subject and style? Are there any highlights from this journey that you would like to share with us?

Samrat Upadhyay [SU]: Well, I'm always moving on, always writing, and always completely engrossed with the project I'm working on at the moment, so *Arresting God in Kathmandu* does seem very far away. It should—it has been nearly 20 years since that book was published. I find it interesting that many of my readers identify me with that book only, even though I have published five more since then. Well, now I know what it means to be typecast! It's been a deeply satisfying writing journey. I feel like I have not conformed to anyone else's notion of what I ought to be writing, so each book has been an experiment and discovery. I have paid homage to my imagination, and my imagination has rewarded me with an occupation that has been a deep source of joy and fulfilment, which I hope I've been able to transmit to my readers. Over the years I think I have become bolder, madder (thus the title of my 2017 collection of eight stories *Mad Country*), and even more irreverent. Many Nepalis thought that I was irreverent ("too sexy") in *Arresting*; they should read what I'm writing right now. *Mad Country*, it seems, is a glimpse into the kind of territories I'm moving into: magical, dystopian, comical—crazy stories, really. And I'm having a lot of fun with it.

On the other hand, while my work has changed substantially over the years, how much can one change, really? Readers who've read my previous work will probably find echoes of familiar sentences and images. Yet there's a type of mania, an undercurrent of the wild and the improbable, running through my work now. I do see *Mad Country* as a pivotal moment in this transition, although my novel *The City Son*, which I published before *Mad Country*, was like an appetizer of things to come.

Some of my most interesting moments are when I'm interacting with my Nepali readers in Kathmandu. About a decade ago, I gave a talk, in Nepali, to a bunch of well-known *sahityakars* [*littérateurs*] in Pokhara in a very crowded room. I sweated profusely in Pokhara's humidity as I desperately attempted to recall high literary terms in Nepali that I have lost over the years once my literary and professional language switched to English. In another incident, during a book signing in Kathmandu that was also attended by my parents, an elderly gentleman scold-lectured me—finger pointing and all—about the sexual content in my work, then gleefully took a selfie with me.

PS: *Please shed some more light on "experiments and discoveries" in your writing over the years, from, let's say, the localized stories told in a more traditional narrative in* Arresting *to more cosmopolitan tales like "Dreaming of Ghana" or "America the Great Equalizer" in* Mad Country, *where you take more liberties with both your subjects and your narrative techniques. Are these mostly spontaneous discoveries, or have you deliberately experimented with certain forms (and contents)?*

SU: I would say that they are both—spontaneous and deliberate. Sometimes the more deliberate experimentations result in failed stories that never make it to print. At other times a story that starts out with a deliberate intention turns into something else that is unanticipated, so it appears as though it's spontaneous but much of the "planning" has already happened in its initial phases.

The experimentation and discoveries have happened mostly with the form, both in the novel and the short story. As you mention above, my early stories are fairly conventional, but over the years I've realized that the conventional story structure of conflict-crisis-resolution can be played with in a number of ways. As for the novel, it's been a delight to discover how playful it can be too! For example, I have been experimenting quite a bit with dark comedy, especially in the novel, so I think my readers can expect more humor (I hope) in the future.

PS: *Arresting God in Kathmandu met with some harsh criticism in the Nepali media, especially from Nepali academics, who accused you of portraying the dark side of Nepal in your stories. What impact did this have, if any, on your subsequent works?*

SU: The response to *Arresting* made me realize that once a book is published, then readers can claim it in their own subjective ways that might sharply differ from your own motivations for, and interpretations of, your work. I also understood that there's a lot of subjectivity baked into the whole thing: people read my work according to their own readings of Nepal. I had readers who recognized themselves in my characters and their situations, and I had readers who felt very alienated from them. My work was being scrutinized in a way I hadn't even thought possible. Initially, I might have been a bit defensive but I quickly understood that all this attention was partly because Indian writers had dominated the scene and here was a Nepali kid who, for many (especially the older academics), literally "came out of nowhere". Some people thought that I had written the book on the fly with the express purpose of selling Nepali sex to westerners, who, presumably, wanted to read about Nepalis having sex under the mountains. Some were outright dismissive of any attempt at depicting Nepali culture and peoples in a language that is largely foreign to Nepali culture and peoples. Some applauded me for my boldness, and for writing about things that they felt always existed in our society but no one had written about before, which is not true, as sexual content by a Nepali writer didn't start with *Arresting* (but there might have been some truth that it was the first time when mild—and quotidian by my standards—eroticism involving Nepali characters was being consumed by western readers, in English).

In the end, it dawned on me that the most sensible course for writers is to follow their truths to the best of their abilities. I think it made me bolder in a way, and my most recent work reflects that. Some of my readers who loved *Arresting God in Kathmandu* want me to write the same thing over and over, *Arresting God in Kathmandu* Part II, Part III, Part IV, if you will. But I'm not the same writer who was writing 20 years ago. Can we say a writer can't step into the same river twice?

PS: *Can you tell us about your writing process? For instance, how do you choose your subject matter and develop your characters? What is your editing process? Are there any parts to this process that you especially enjoy or find challenging? Do you ever find yourself thinking about your readers while you are writing? Or targetting a particular audience?*

SU: I am a fairly imagistic writer, so I move through my fiction with images, letting one image dictate the next. Often I have a vision of a character in a pickle, and I move with it and see where it goes. My first draft is always language-oriented (each sentence triggers the next) and an exploration of character. I don't know what is going to happen next, and that's important to me because it keeps me interested in the work. I hope that this sense of suspense will also transfer itself onto the reader. I don't "choose" my subject matter. Nobel prize-winner Nadine Gordimer said that the subject chooses you, and I have found that to be true. The first draft is the most enjoyable—I write my first drafts by hand, and I find it quite freeing in allowing me to go where I want to go, do what I want to do. I often don't know what's going to happen to my characters, and that in itself is very exciting, even though at times it can also create anxiety. I have written long novels in this way. Subsequent revisions are progressively more difficult. In the end, the story or the novel has to arrive at the reader's hands with a kind of a logical cohesiveness, which needs rethinking, reimagining, reorienting, and refining on the writer's part. But increasingly I'm also interested in the illogicality of it all, and I suppose that's where my writing of late has drifted to. Not everything has to make sense, because not everything in life makes sense—at least not in the way we define "sense".

I'm not sure, either, that I am consciously thinking about specific readers when I'm writing. There might be particular moments in the story or novel when I imagine how someone—a teacher from my past, a family member, a friend, a reader—might react to something I've written, but I don't pause to change my course because of that. I feel that I'm critical enough of my own work that I don't need extraneous critical voices inside me. I do want my work to be read and enjoyed by everyone: Nepalis, Americans, and everyone in between.

PS: *The notion of starting with "a character in a pickle" is both interesting and intriguing. Could you give us an example or two of such "pickles" that you started with, and how and where they ultimately arrived?*

SU: One of my better-known stories, "The Good Shopkeeper", for example, started out with the idea of a young householder, Pramod, who loses his job once computers become prevalent in Nepal. The idea for the story came after one of my visits to Kathmandu, when I saw offices starting to use computers and heard some acquaintances complaining that they didn't know how to use them at all. I wondered what would happen if an office worker was let go because he didn't know how to use computers in an increasingly competitive workplace. But the story takes an unexpected turn when Pramod meets a woman in a park who works as a domestic servant. In his anxiety and depression, he starts having an illicit affair with her and his rigid notions about class and status begin to crumble.

PS: *You mentioned earlier that* The City Son, *published before* Mad Country, *was like an "appetizer of things to come". Didi in* The City Son *is definitely one of the most haunting characters you have created. Could you tell us about the genesis and development of the story, and its poignant characters?*

SU: *The City Son* in its finished form was not the novel that I started writing, and Didi was only a peripheral character in the beginning. But she increasingly came to dominate the narrative in ways that I hadn't anticipated. I also hadn't anticipated writing the deeply disturbing story of sexual abuse that became the most pressing—and unrelenting—theme in the novel. But as a writer I always find it helpful not to plan and to allow the story to take its course. A large part of writing that novel was permitting the characters to be who they were, and letting the subjectivity of the characters dictate the story.

PS: *All of your six books so far have been works of fiction: three collections of short stories and three novels. How did you arrive at fiction? Was it a conscious choice? Why do you think this genre works best for you?*

SU: I think I need some room to move; that's why I have gravitated toward fiction. I used to write poetry when I was young and in graduate school, and I still admire poets, but for me fiction provides the necessary space where I can explore and probe and put characters in bind for longer periods. My short stories tend to be quite long, too, and lately I have been fascinated by the novel and its possibilities. I like stories, in the broadest sense of the term, and fiction allows me to tell stories better than poems do (while recognizing that good poets tell damn good stories as well).

PS: *You have been alternating between writing short stories and novels (except perhaps for the novel* The City Son, *which followed* Buddha's Orphans*). Is this deliberate, or a coincidence?*

SU: Novels can be quite taxing. You can spend years on one and still not know if it works until you've finished a draft or two and see how it all fits together. Once I have completed a novel and sent it off to an agent, then I find working on short stories a welcome relief. Given my academic responsibilities, I have found a nice rhythm alternating between a story collection and a novel, although all three books that I'm currently working on are novels. I'm increasingly fascinated by the novel form and am delighting in its possibilities.

PS: *When you say you are fascinated by the potential of the novel form, are there any specific methods or styles you have been intrigued by? Is there anything new in terms of form, or even content, that you are thinking about or exploring in your upcoming works?*

SU: I am experimenting with dystopian and absurd forms, so my readers can expect a leaning towards them in the coming years. Even in my realistic novels, I am stretching the boundaries of the possible. To me, this seems perfectly in alignment with global political changes—the rise of authoritarian regimes, for example, including Trump and his presidency, which has truly extended our sense of the absurd.

PS: *How do you balance your academic responsibilities and your writing both in terms of time spent and processing ideas?*

SU: My writing life and my academic life are different, yet they also feed into each other. My teaching and my students stimulate me, give me ideas, point out new paths. I don't think I could ever be a full-time writer. Even when I'm on leave or on sabbatical, I tend to write for only four or five hours a day, then I need another activity. I have been a full-time professor for nearly 20 years now (from about the time when *Arresting* came out), and I have trained myself over the years to shift quickly between my academic mind and my writer mind. For example, these days it's not unusual for me to dash off an email to a student, write the next paragraph of my novel, participate in a Zoom meeting with colleagues, write another page of the novel, then help my daughter edit her paper for a class, etc. I have learned how to shift gears quickly. If I waited for that perfect moment in order to write, it probably would never arrive. In the busiest of days during the semester, I have found that it is helpful to stay connected to whatever I'm writing, even if it means working on a few sentences, or clarifying some plot points, or even reviewing what I've written thus far. I also advise my students to write whenever they can (morning, afternoon, night), wherever they can (coffee shop, bus station, airport), with whatever they have available (a pencil and a sheet of paper, laptop, voice recorder on your phone), for however long they can, even if that is just a few minutes. I also advise them not to get tied up in their self-image as an artist but devote themselves to the art. So, fewer accoutrements, less ceremony, more discipline and more work produced.

PS: *What is your view on the positionality of a creative writer? What does it mean to be a Nepali / South Asian writer in the western world? Do you feel these national / regional categories are as relevant to you as a creative writer as they seem to be in academic discussions? Do you think these labels might actually be deleterious to writers coming from relatively small-scale national or linguistic backgrounds? For instance, is it important to differentiate between Indian and Nepali writers within the "South Asian" category in the west?*

SU: I don't pay attention to positionalities when I'm writing. I don't want these identities influencing what I write, at least not consciously. I'm not sure it's helpful to the writer to be thinking about these labels during the writing process itself, although there's no doubt that we are all shaped by the city, region, country, language that is part and parcel of who we are. Since I am one of the few Nepali writers writing in English and publishing in the west, there is, I know, a certain expectation of what I ought to be writing, both from my South Asian readers as well as readers and publishers here in the US. At times the publishing world wants to pigeonhole writers into certain categories, but I hope that my work itself defies categories. I think being typecast is not good for a writer.

PS: *As a writer who writes primarily about Nepal while living abroad, what does "place" mean to you? Where do you find yourself in the insider-outsider equation? There is a big Nepali community in the US and in the "western" world in general, yet not much has been written about the Nepali diasporic experience. Can we be hopeful that* Mad Country *signals a step in this direction for future work?*

SU: I don't feel like I have left Nepal behind, even though I live and work in a place halfway around the world. I am a Nepali through and through (and to this day the term Nepali American, as it might apply to me, creates a kind of cognitive dissonance in me, as though it's not really me)—whatever that means. Is it not possible for us to have two homes, especially in these globally fluid times? For example, right now I am typing these answers on an airplane on the way to Nepal, midair somewhere above the Bafra district of Turkey. For the next few weeks I will be teaching my American students from my room in Kathmandu, where my parents live. Next week, as I sit in the sun in Toukhel eating some *bhogatey sandeko*, I will most likely be giving feedback on a student story about a criminal transferring illegal drugs between Chicago and Atlanta. I am not an outsider to Nepal. I was born there, spent my formative years there, return at least once or twice a year. The insider-outsider equation is too black and white and sees "Nepal" as an ossified place, frozen in place, time, and culture.

My material is beginning to incorporate more of the west but I'm still invested in exploring Nepal. Perhaps some other writers, if it interests them, can write about the Nepali communities in the diaspora? Obviously, there is plenty of room here for everyone.

PS: *How was the title* Mad Country *received in Nepal? Have you come across any comments from your Nepali readers that remind you of your* Arresting *days?*

SU: I saw some comments about how some of my fans of *Arresting* didn't recognize me in *Mad Country* and were disappointed. It certainly didn't receive as much attention as my first book. For some Nepali readers I'm identified solely as the guy who wrote *Arresting*. Earlier this month an immigration officer recognized me at Kathmandu airport (I seem to be popular with immigration officers as this happens in almost every visit) and appeared surprised to learn that I had penned five more books since *Arresting*.

PS: *How do you feel about the role of "cultural translator" often assigned to diasporic writers? How do you deal with the challenges of translating cultural innuendos, idiomatic expressions, and native content to your audience in the Anglophone world? What role does cultural / geographical distance play in your writing? What bearing does your life in the US have on the way you view Nepal and people from Nepal?*

SU: I don't see myself primarily as a cultural translator, although I do understand that it can be a byproduct of my writing and I accept it. As with positionalities and insider-outsider, taking on the role of a cultural translator could easily lead you to compromise your art. Clarity in my writing is important to me, and if I can guide my reader into a clearer understanding of contexts, political history, culture etc. regarding my work, then I'm happy to do so as long as I don't feel like I'm sacrificing something important. I really do think that sometimes too much noise is made about this "translating" business. I admire South Asian writers across the spectrum, from Rohinton Mistry who is careful about providing contextual clues, to Vikram Chandra who, at least in his more recent work, doesn't seem to give a damn. I think the totality of the work is important. And I think if you look at it that way, then all writers are translating in some ways. For example, wouldn't you say that African American writers are also always attempting to translate their world (with its history and experience of racism and oppression) for their readers?

PS*: When it comes to giving a socio-cultural, political, and historical background and context to your stories, do you ever find yourself caught up in the dilemma of "over-explaining" versus "under-explaining" for your Nepali / South Asian versus western readers? How do you strike a balance in such instances?*

SU: Sure, there is some balancing that needs to be done, for I am keenly aware that my readership is diverse and global, but I hope that I have developed a good strategy over the years. I don't want my work to read like a *Lonely Planet* guide, so I certainly don't want to over-explain, and certainly not in a language that "pauses" to explain. Whatever explaining needs to be done has to be successfully incorporated within the narrative, without interrupting its momentum. The story is always paramount, and the character's thoughts, emotions, and actions themselves can do a lot of the explaining. But it's useful to remember, too, that even in Nepal there are many readers who might not know the details that I'm writing about. For example, in *Buddha's Orphans* I give specifics about the 1934 earthquake that even I had to research; I'm sure many Nepali readers, especially those of my generation and younger, wouldn't be aware of those specifics.

PS: *There is so much happening with Nepali literature in recent years, especially after the country transitioned from the Hindu Kingdom to a secular republic in 2008. Writers from ethnic, linguistic, religious, and regional margins are making their mark in the mainstream literary scene with exciting works of fiction and poetry. Do you read contemporary Nepali literature? Has it influenced your writing in any way?*

SU: I do read Nepali literature occasionally, but my professional life is mostly devoted to works written in English. Many of my waking hours are spent on work by my students—either current students or past students or friends who want me to read their manuscripts, whether for feedback or for blurbs. Sometimes I read Nepali books that are gifted to me by authors I meet during my talks in Nepal. And I have read some of the books that have received attention in recent years: Sanjeev Upreti's *Ghanachakkar*, Amar Neupane's work, and of course Narayan Wagle's ([2005] 2018) *Palpasa Café* which has found its way into a novel I'm currently working on.

PS: *I am not aware of many intertextual imbrications between your works and the works of mainstream literature in Nepali. Could you tell us a little more about how the popular Nepali novel,* Palpasa Café, *has found its way into your new novel?*

SU: I've used Wagle's novel and celebrity status as a way to poke fun at the idiosyncracies of literary culture in Nepal. The intertextuality is less about that novel's content than about, in this specific context, attempts at censorship from an authoritarian regime. In another work in progress, a character who is based on a well-known Nepali celebrity journalist takes center stage.

PS: *What genre(s) do you enjoy reading? Do you have any favourite books or authors? Has your writing been influenced by any of them?*

SU: I'm quite a news addict, although I mostly read fiction. Some of my favorite authors are old timers, such as Franz Kafka and Fyodor Dosteyevsky. Among more recent writers, I was a voracious reader of William Trevor and Nadine Gordimer, both of whom have had a great impact on my career. Contemporary writers who have taught me the art of fiction have been Kazuo Ishiguro and J.M. Coetzee. And of course, there is an entire slew of Indian-origin writers who kind of paved the way when I first began to write: Anita Desai, Salman Rushdie, Vikram Seth, and Rohinton Mistry. These are some of the writers who regularly feature in my orbit, who have shaped the writer that I am today. And each of them has taught me different things: Trevor has taught me to maintain my objectivity about all of my characters, Mistry has taught me the nuts and bolts of cultural translation, Desai has taught me how to delve deep into my protagonist's psyche, etc. There are many new writers I admire as well: Tayari Jones, Sally Rooney, and so many others. I encourage younger writers to maintain a sense of awe about the literary works they encounter and be less cynical and critical—it will help to foster their own creativity. Admire everyone's imagination, its awe-inspiring potential.

PS: *What are you currently working on? Is there anything you wanted to write about, but have not been able to tackle yet?*

SU: I am trying to finish a long dystopian novel that I have been working on for the past six years. It's nearly complete, and I hope to get it out in the market in the next couple of years or so. It's been an enormously challenging work, but one that I have enjoyed enormously as well. I've found that the two go hand-in-hand: the challenge is what brings me pleasure as a writer. Because this project is so big, I took a break last year and wrote a novella that also feels like a departure for my fiction. I feel quite lucky in that way: the material keeps coming and I'm able to shape it into the kind of fiction that I want to write. I'm quite happy that I'm experimenting with every project. Each of my works feels new and different to me, and that keeps me young and fresh and in awe of the power of the mind.

What more could a writer want?

Bibliography

Bernstein, Richard. 2001. "In Nepal, Too, Desire Defies Modern Times." *The New York Times*, August 24, Section E: 37. https://www.nytimes.com/2001/08/24/books/books-of-the-times-in-nepal-too-desire-defies-modern-times.html

Upadhyay, Samrat. 2001. *Arresting God in Kathmandu*. New York: Houghton Mifflin.

---. 2003. *The Guru of Love*. New York: Houghton Mifflin.

---. 2006. *The Royal Ghosts*. New Delhi: Rupa Publications.

---. 2010. *Buddha's Orphans*. New York: Houghton Mifflin.

---. 2014. *The City Son*. New York: Soho Press.

---. 2017. *Mad Country*. New Delhi: Rupa Publications.

Wagle, Narayan. [2005] 2018. *Palpasa Café*. Kathmandu, Nepal: Nepa-Laya.

About the Editors

A former Australian Commonwealth Scholar from Sri Lanka, **Chandani Lokuge** is currently Honorary Associate Professor in Literary Studies at Australian National University, Canberra, Australia. She was formerly Associate Professor in Creative Writing at Monash University, Melbourne, Australia. She has also held guest professorships in Germany, France, and the USA. She has published 16 books, including her novels *My Van Gogh* (2019), *Softly as I Leave You* (Winner of Sri Lanka's Godage National Literary Award for Best Novel 2013), and *If the Moon Smiled* (Shortlisted for New South Wales Premier's Prize 2001) and a recent book of essays edited with Janet Wilson, *Mediating Literary Borders: Asian Australian Writing* (2018). As Editor of the Oxford Classics Reissues series, she has published six critical editions of pioneering Indian women's writing in English.

Chris Ringrose was educated at Cambridge University and the University of Alberta, and has held posts at Dalhousie University, the University of North Carolina, and the University of Northampton. He is currently Adjunct Associate Professor of English at Monash University, Melbourne, Australia. His poetry and short fiction have won awards in England, Canada, and Australia, and he has published critical work on modern fiction, literary theory, and children's literature. He co-edits with Janet Wilson the *Journal of Postcolonial Writing* and ibidem's book series, Studies in World Literature. His most recent book of poetry is *Palmistry* (2019).

ibidem.eu